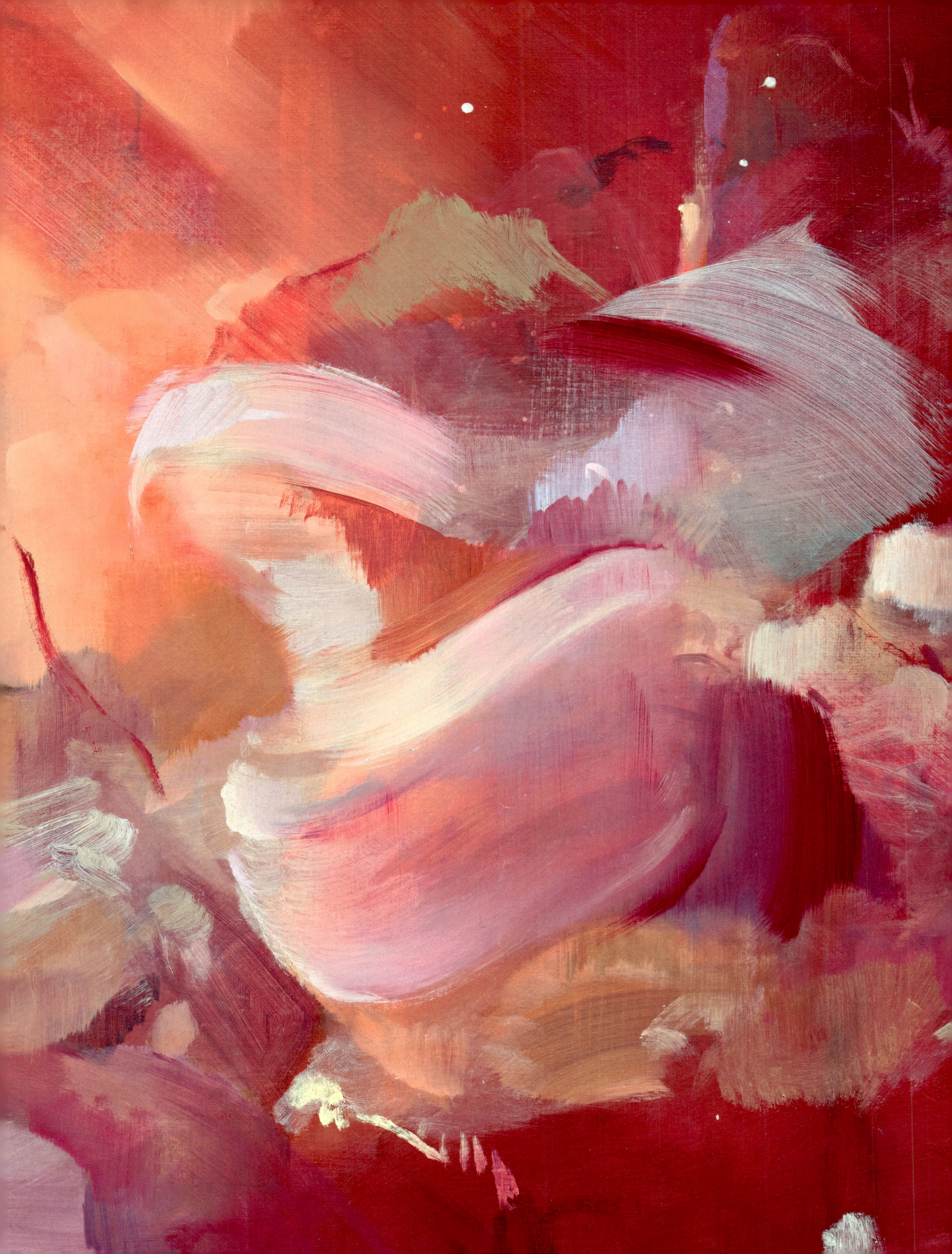

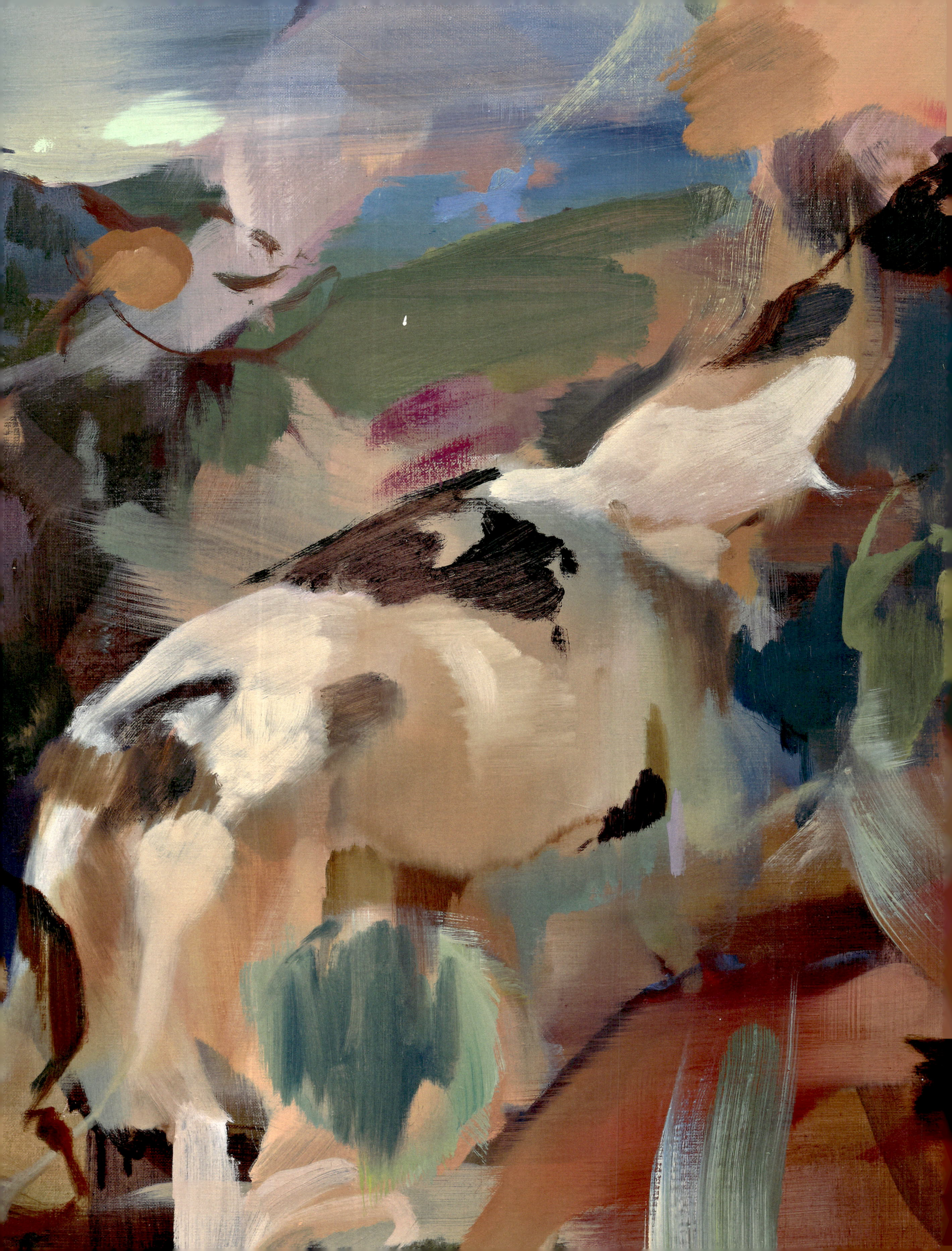

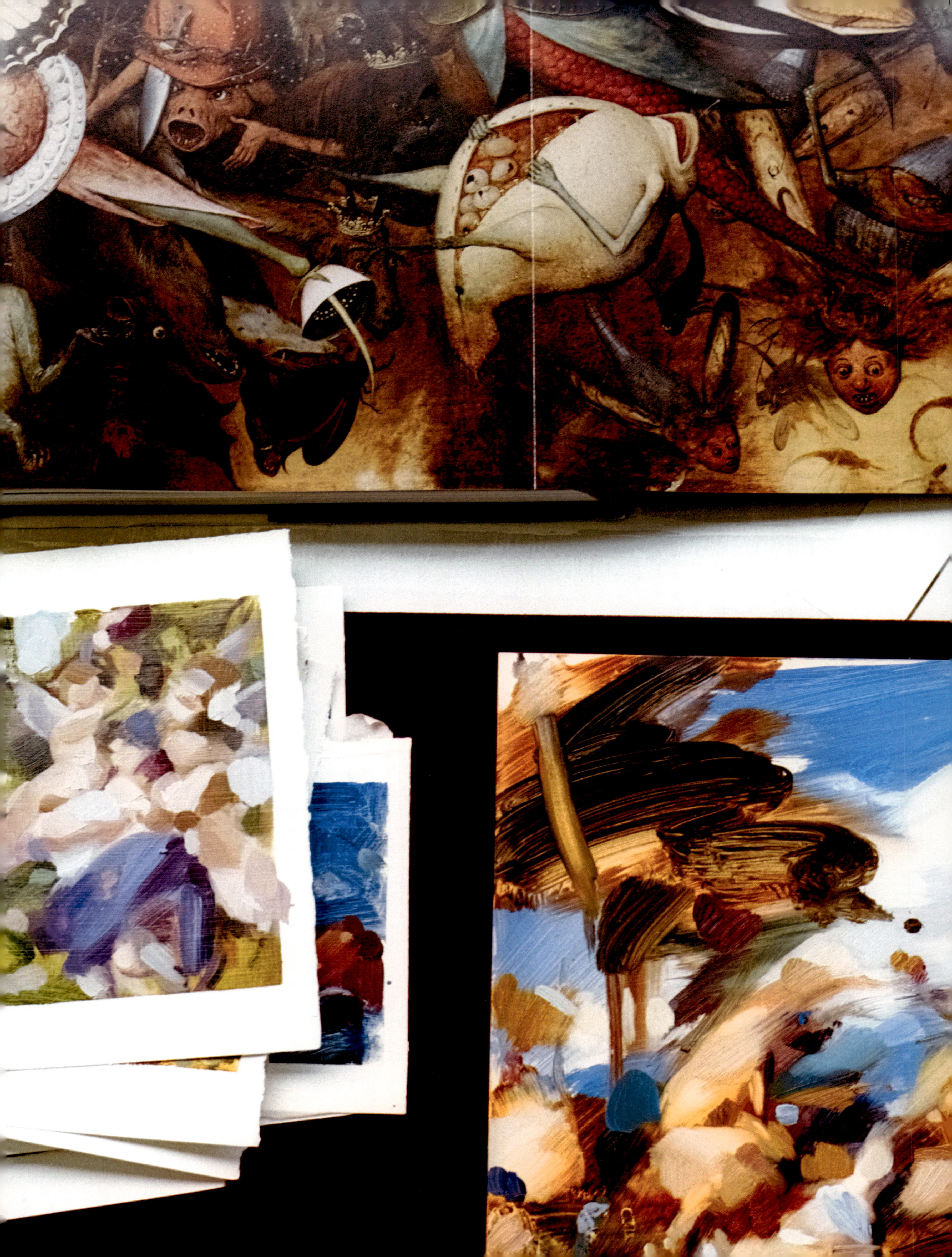

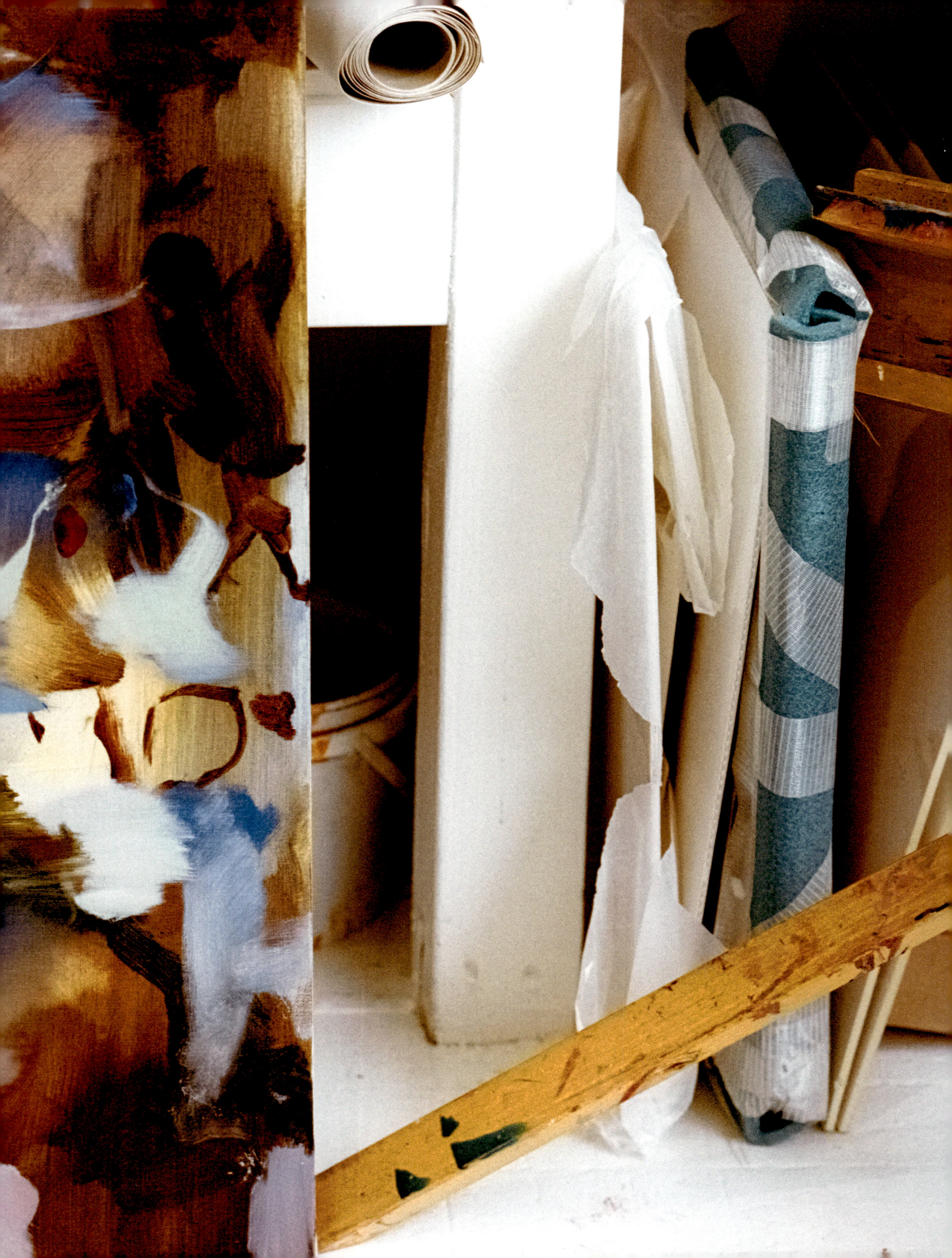

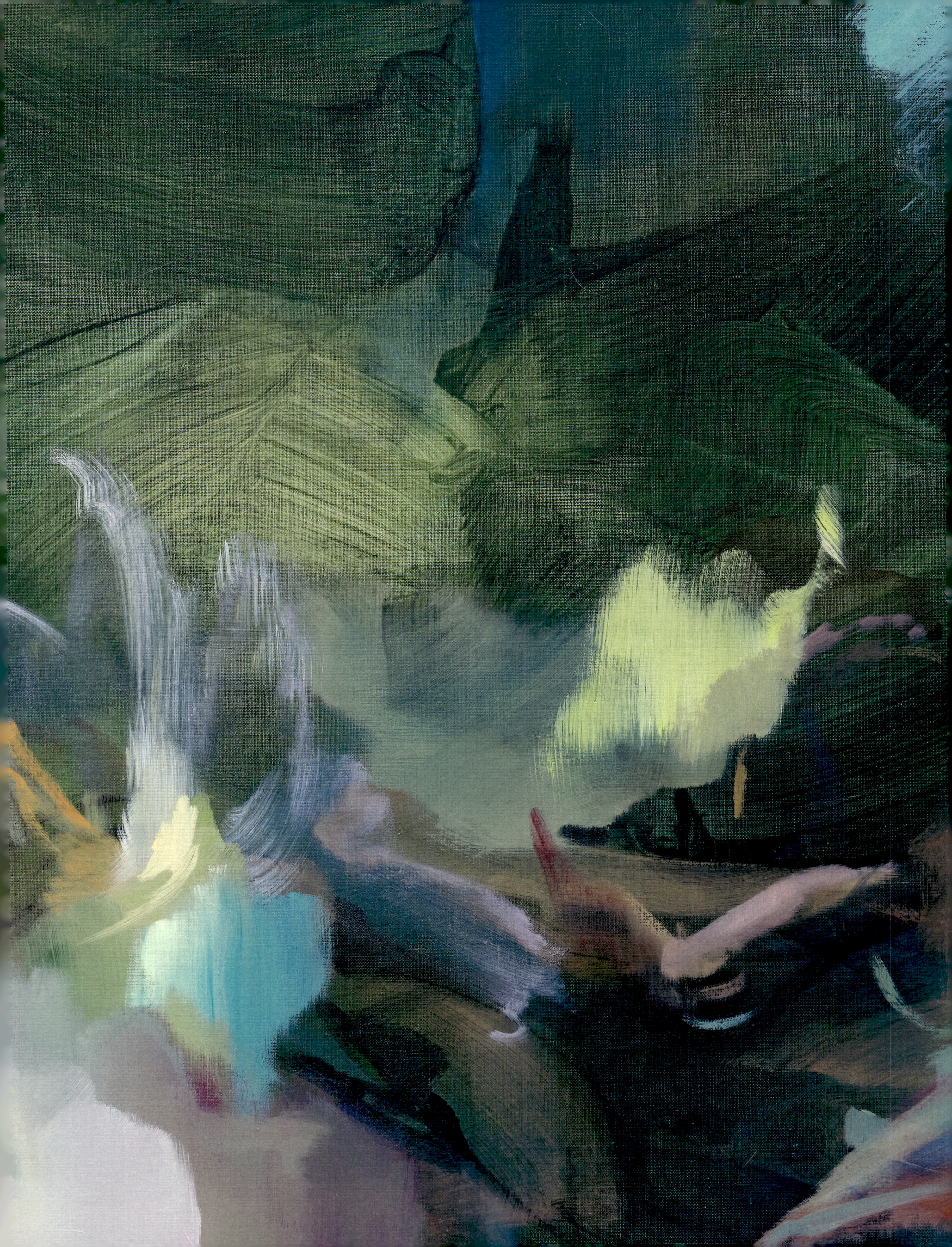

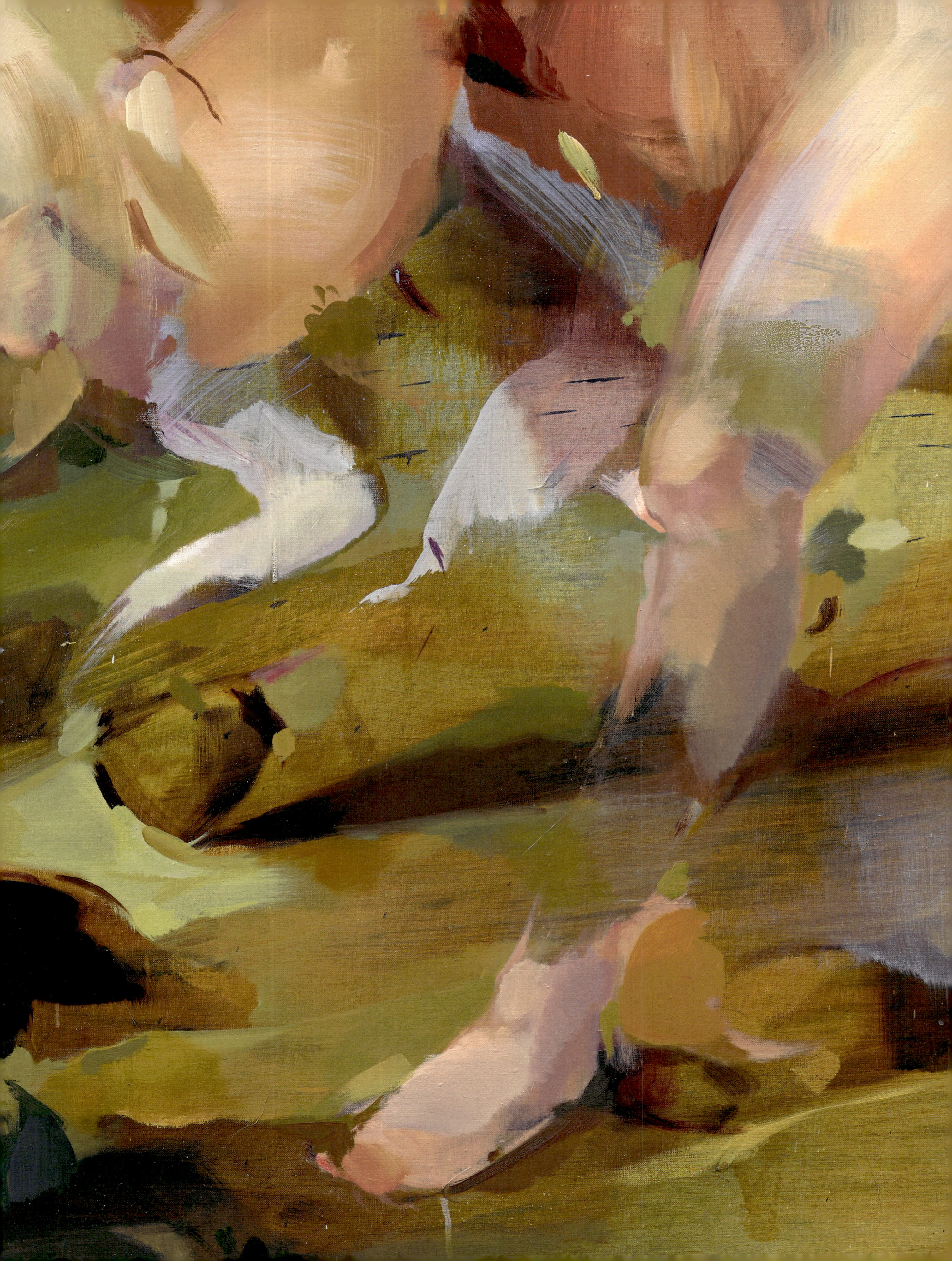

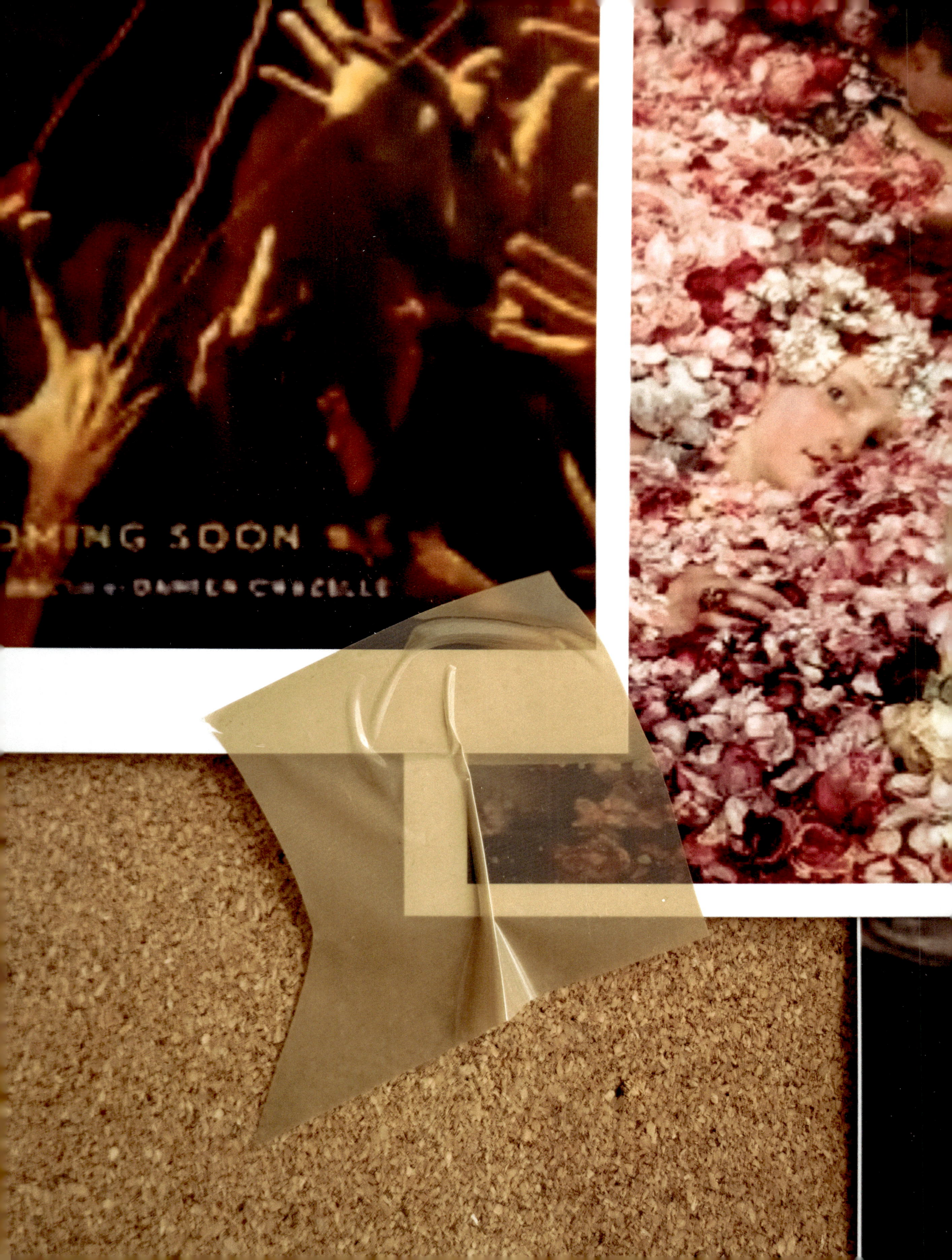
OMING SOON

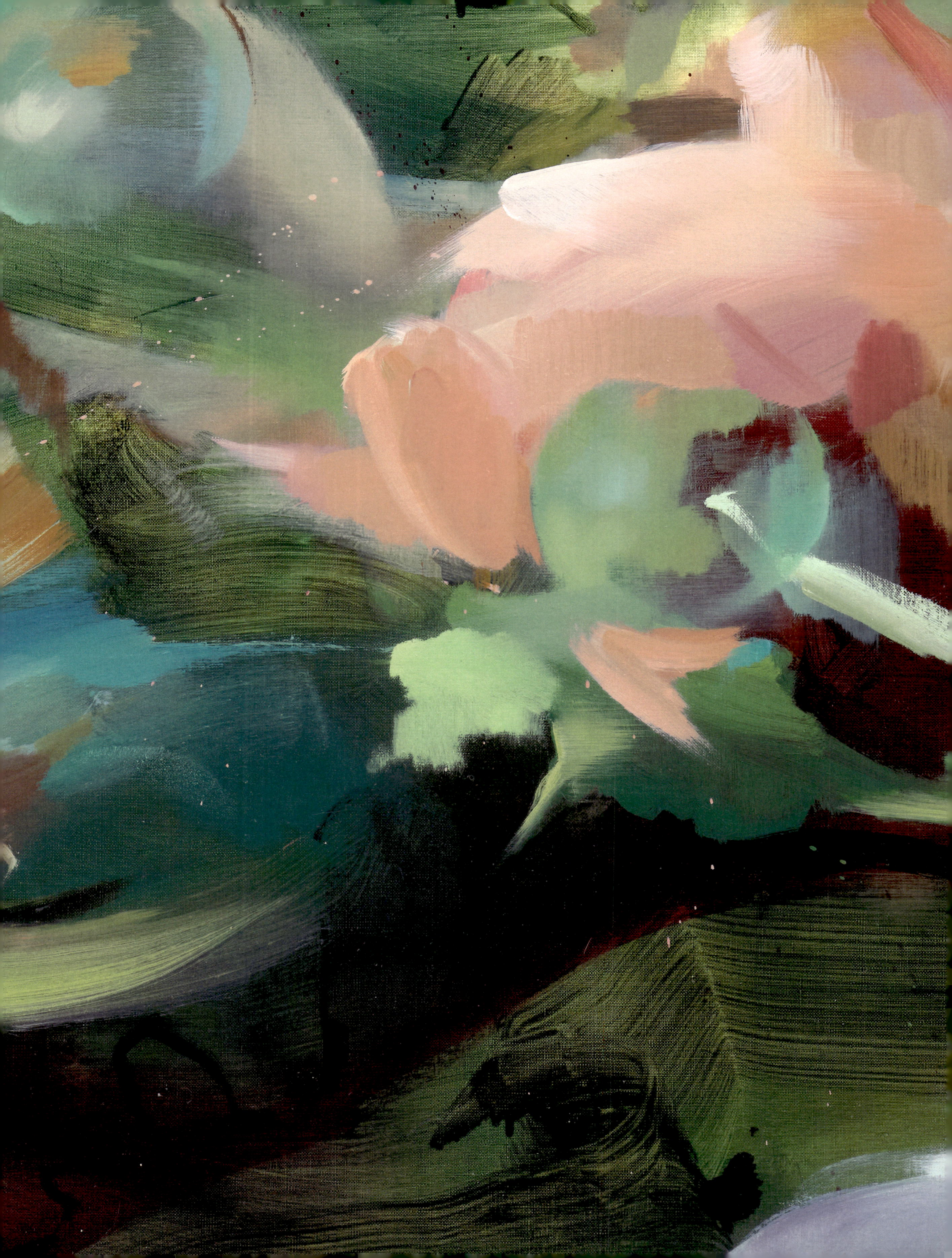

Flora Yukhnovich

Flora Yukhnovich Bacchanalia

With text by Eleanor Nairne and Flora Yukhnovich

HAUSER & WIRTH PUBLISHERS

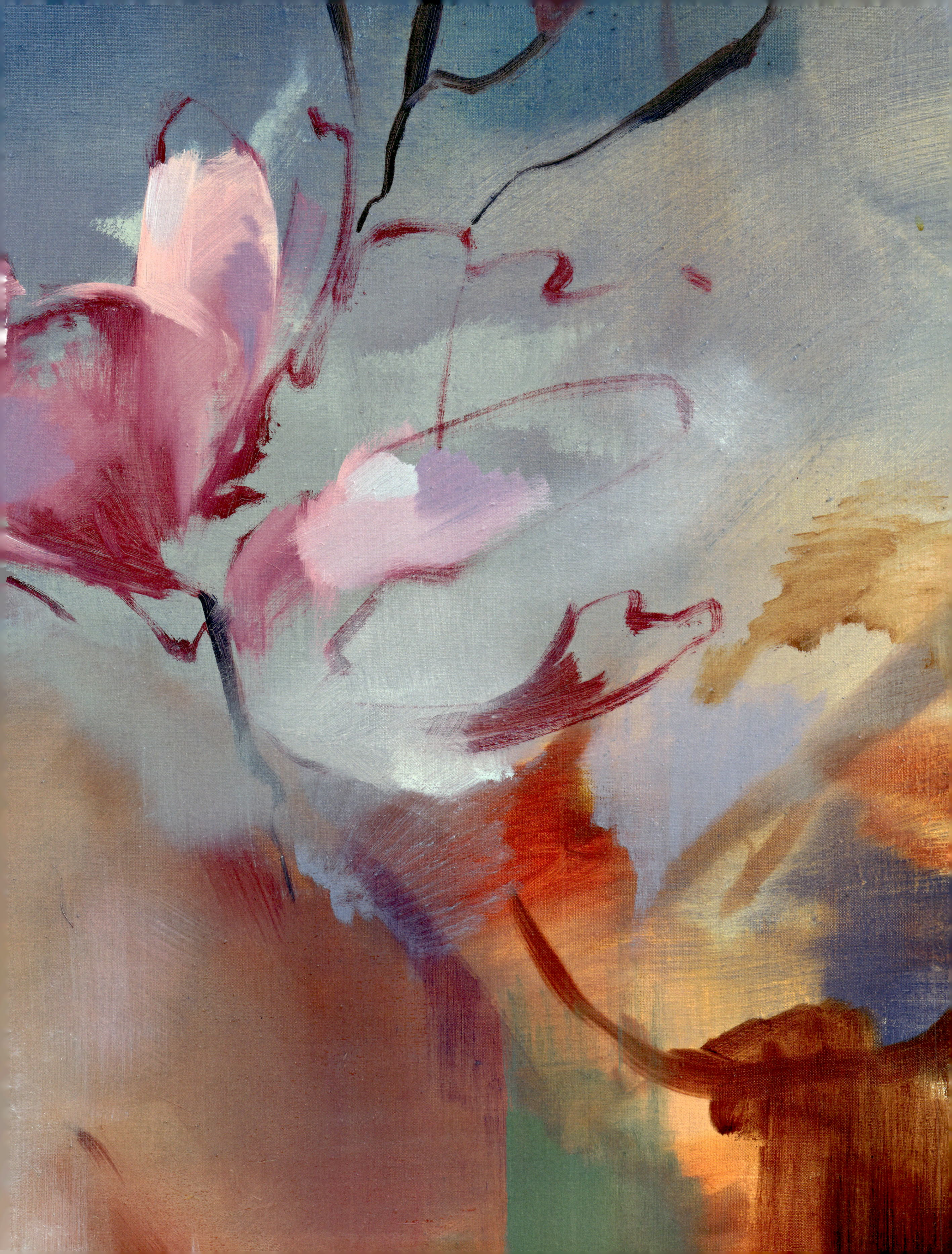

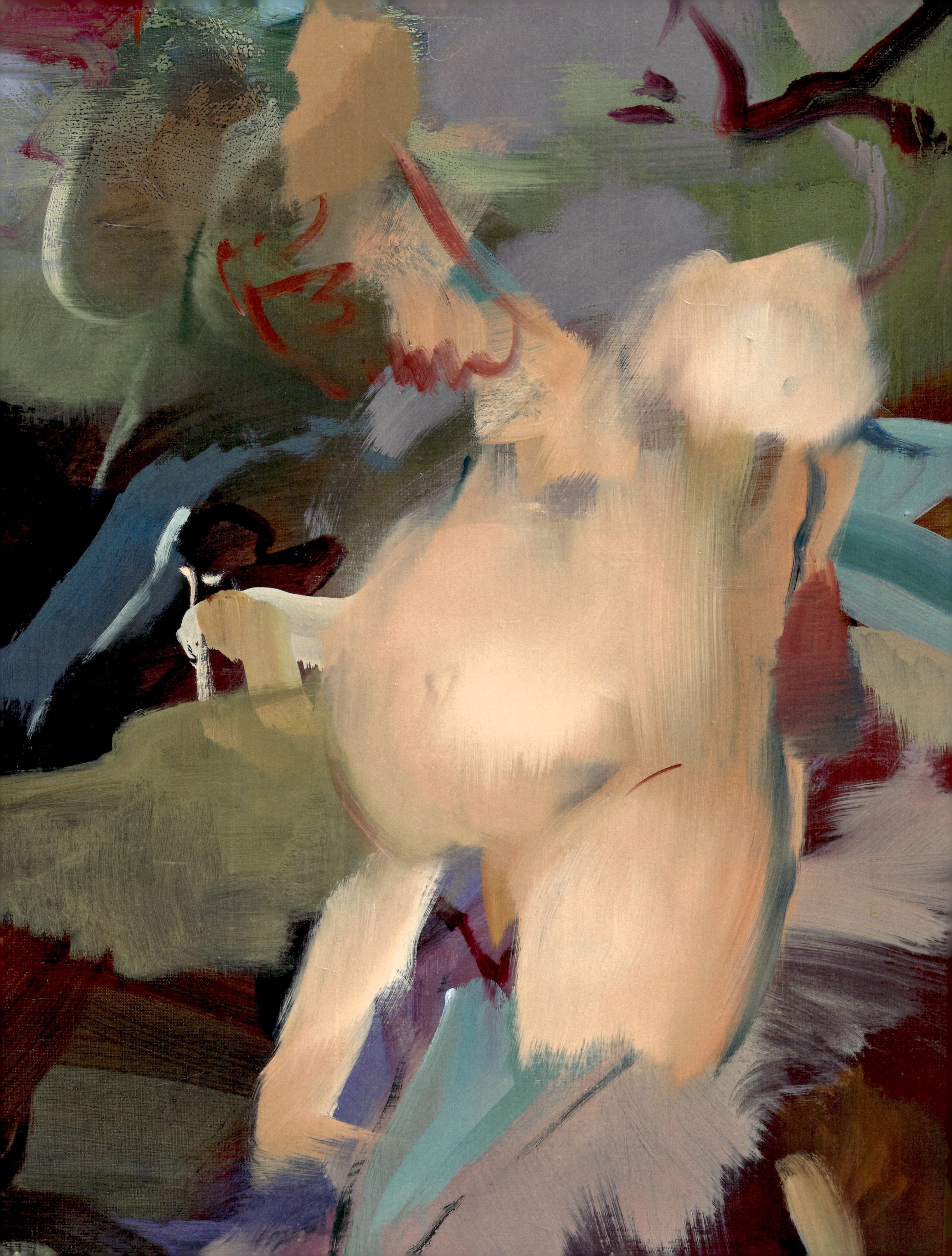

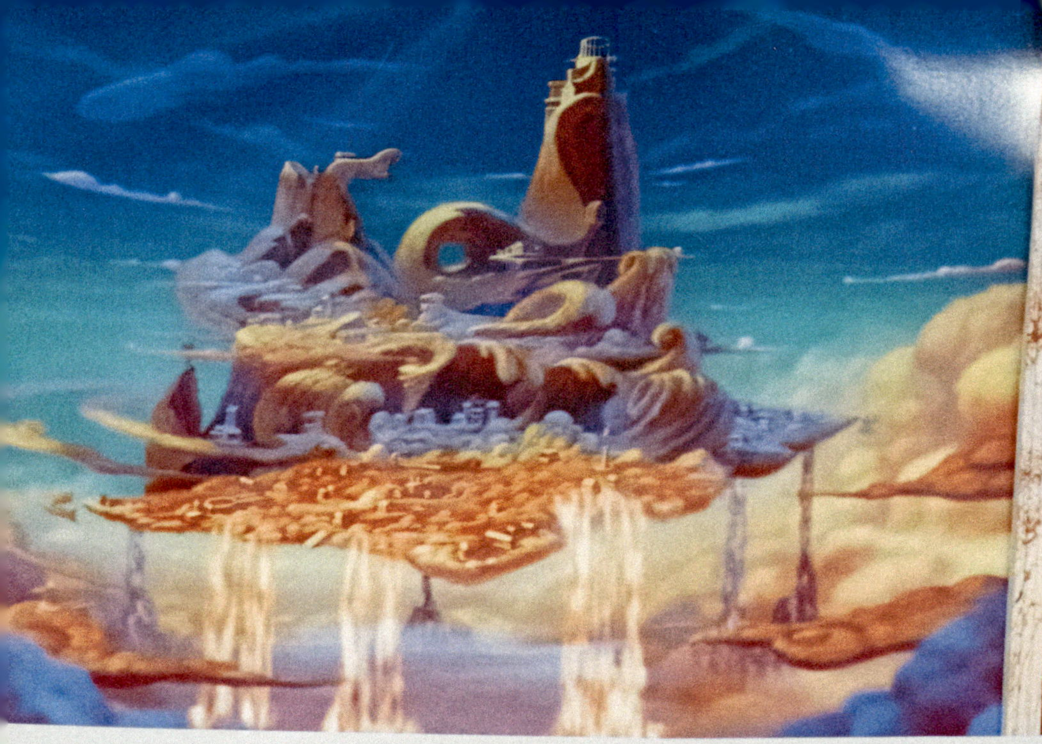
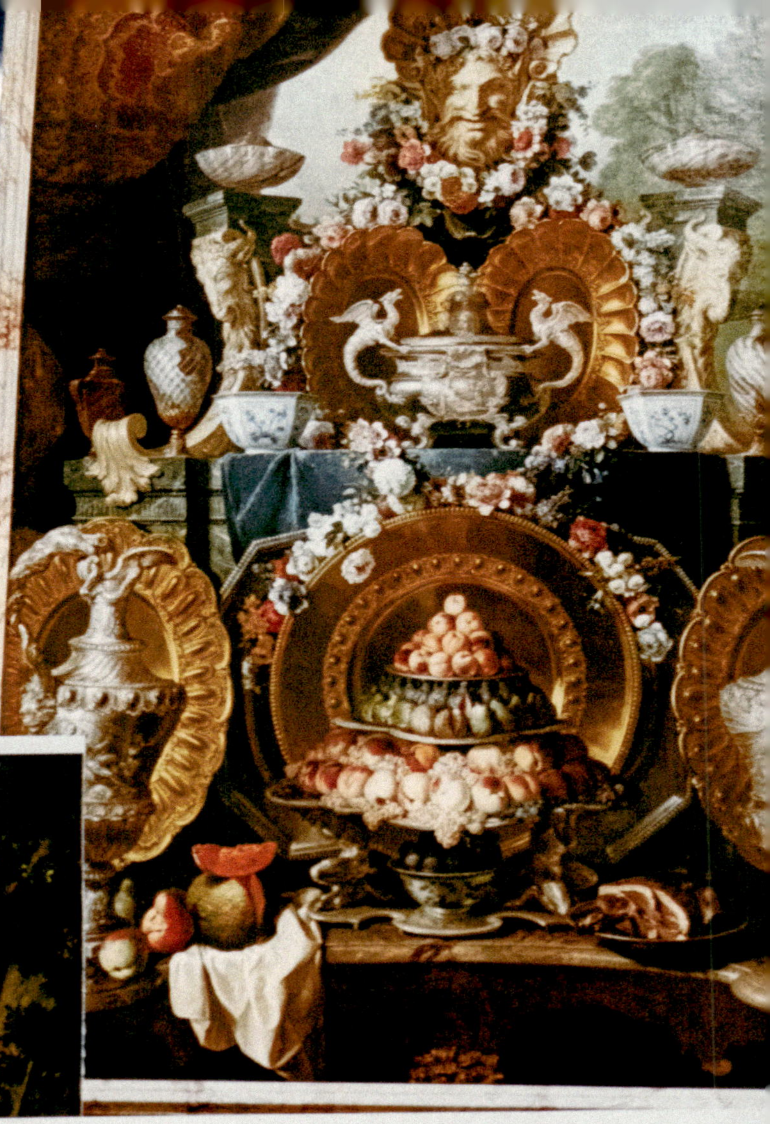
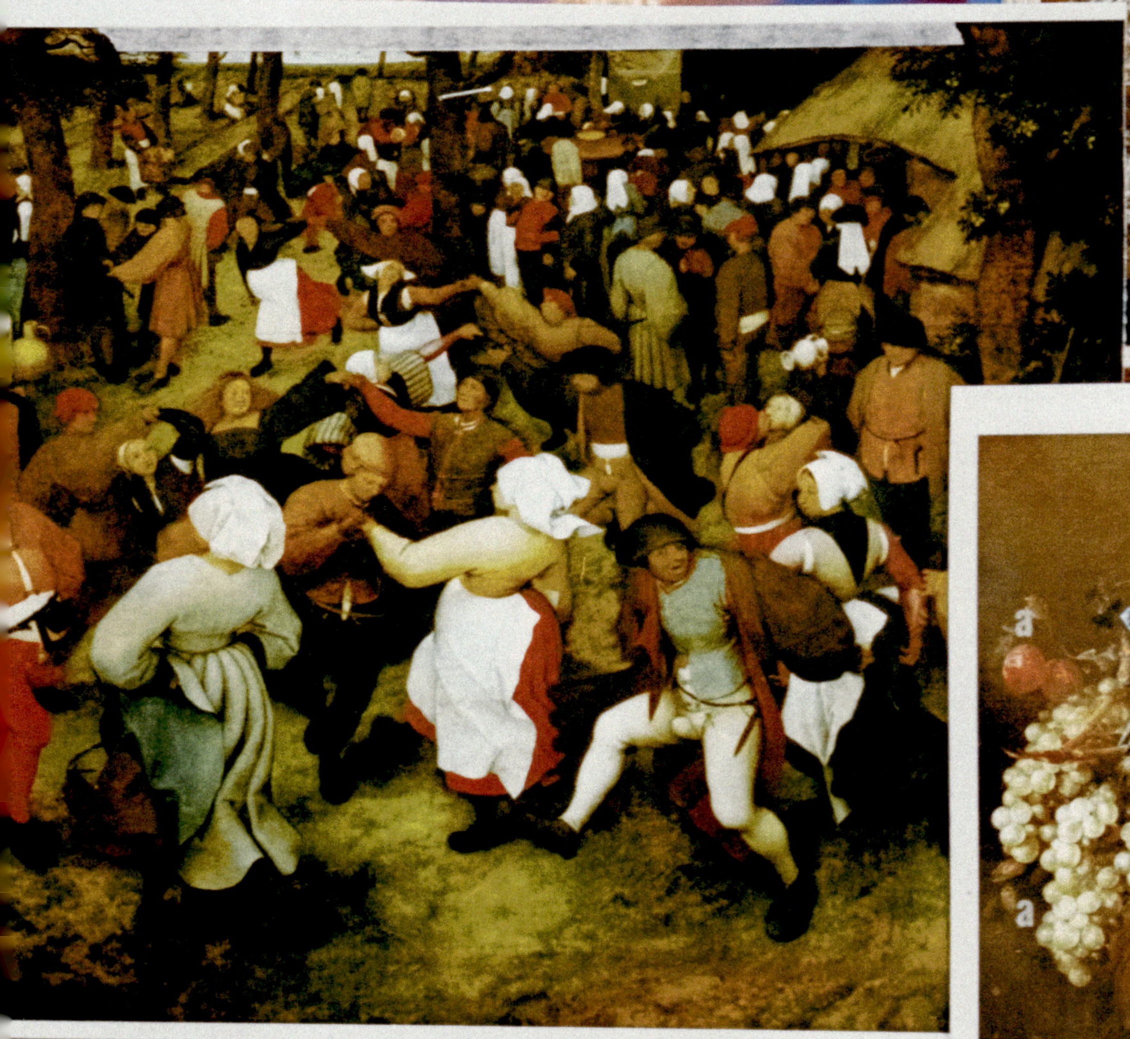
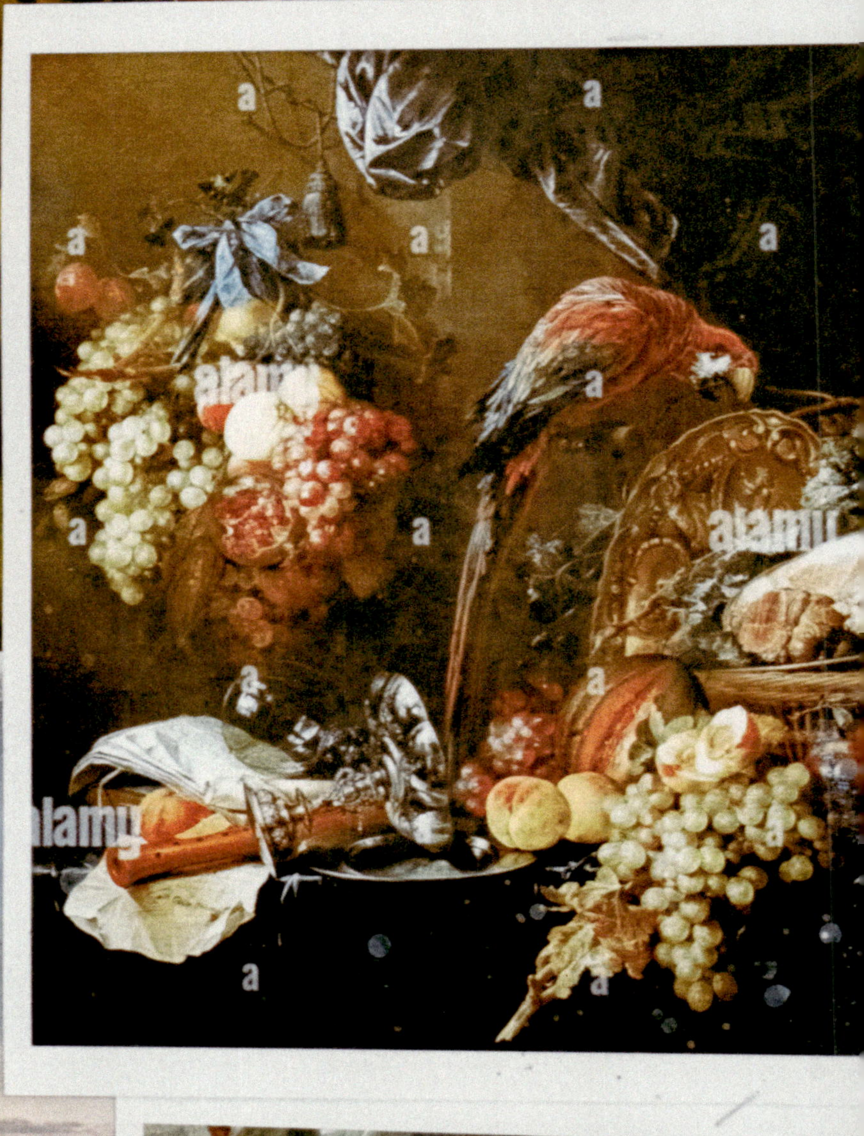
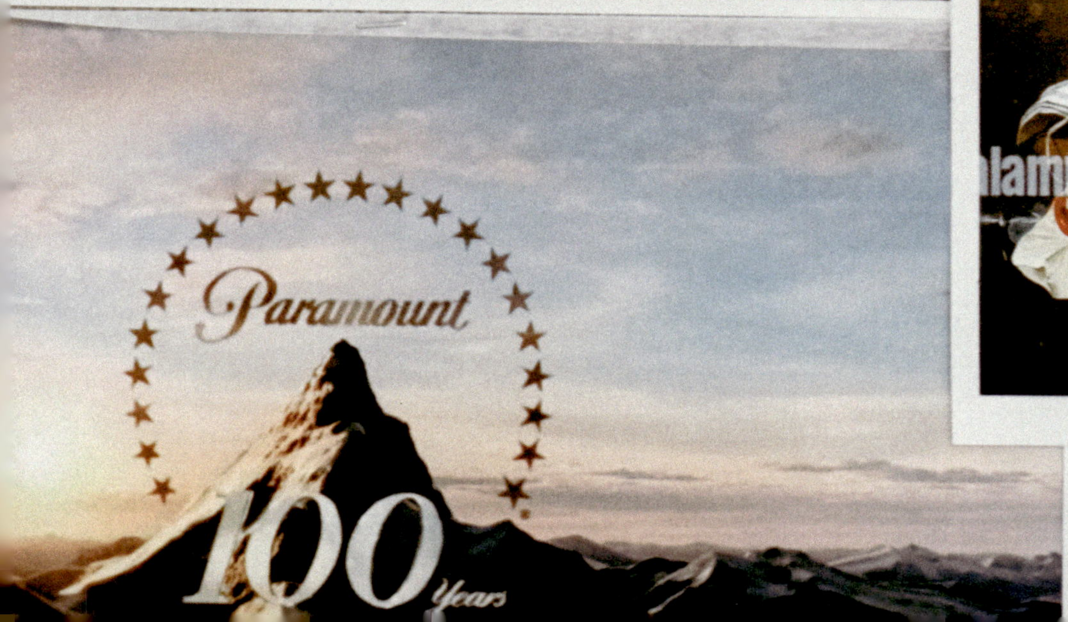
Paramount
100
Years
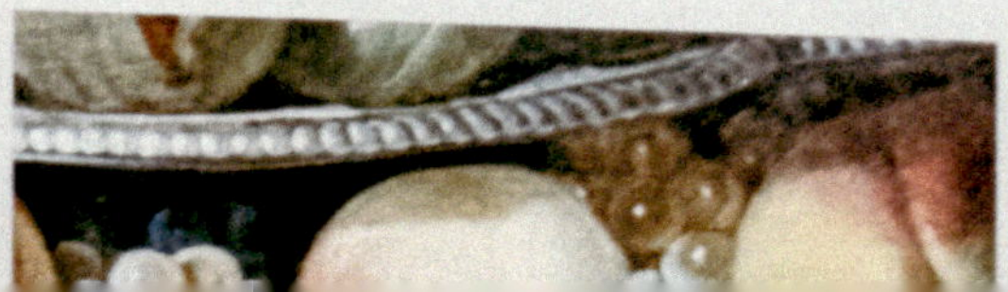
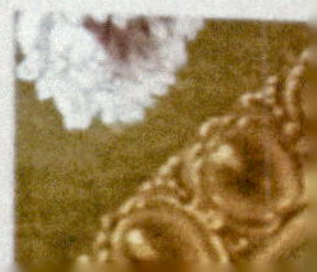

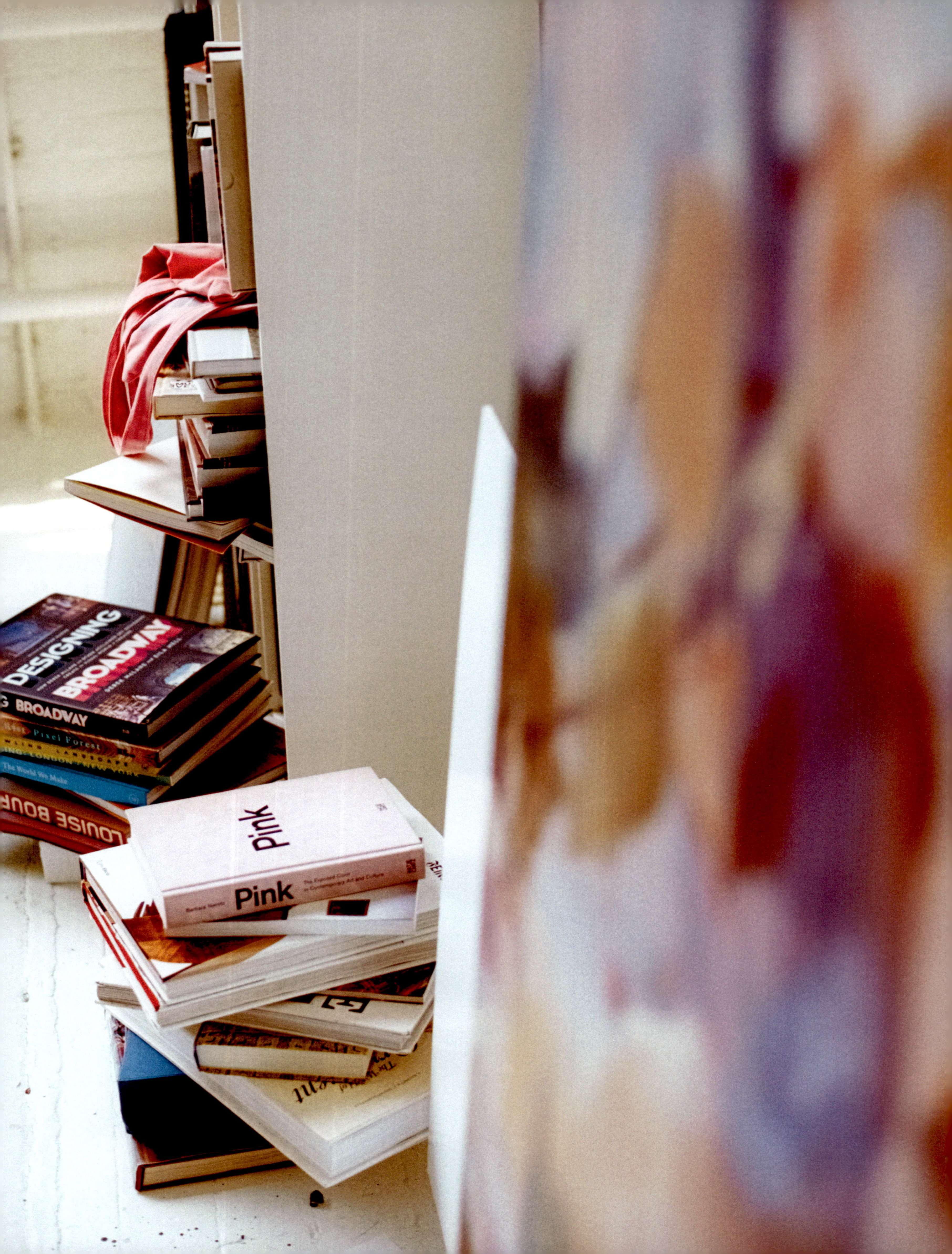
DESIGNING
BROADWAY
BROADWAY
Pixel Forest
The World We Make
Pink
Pink

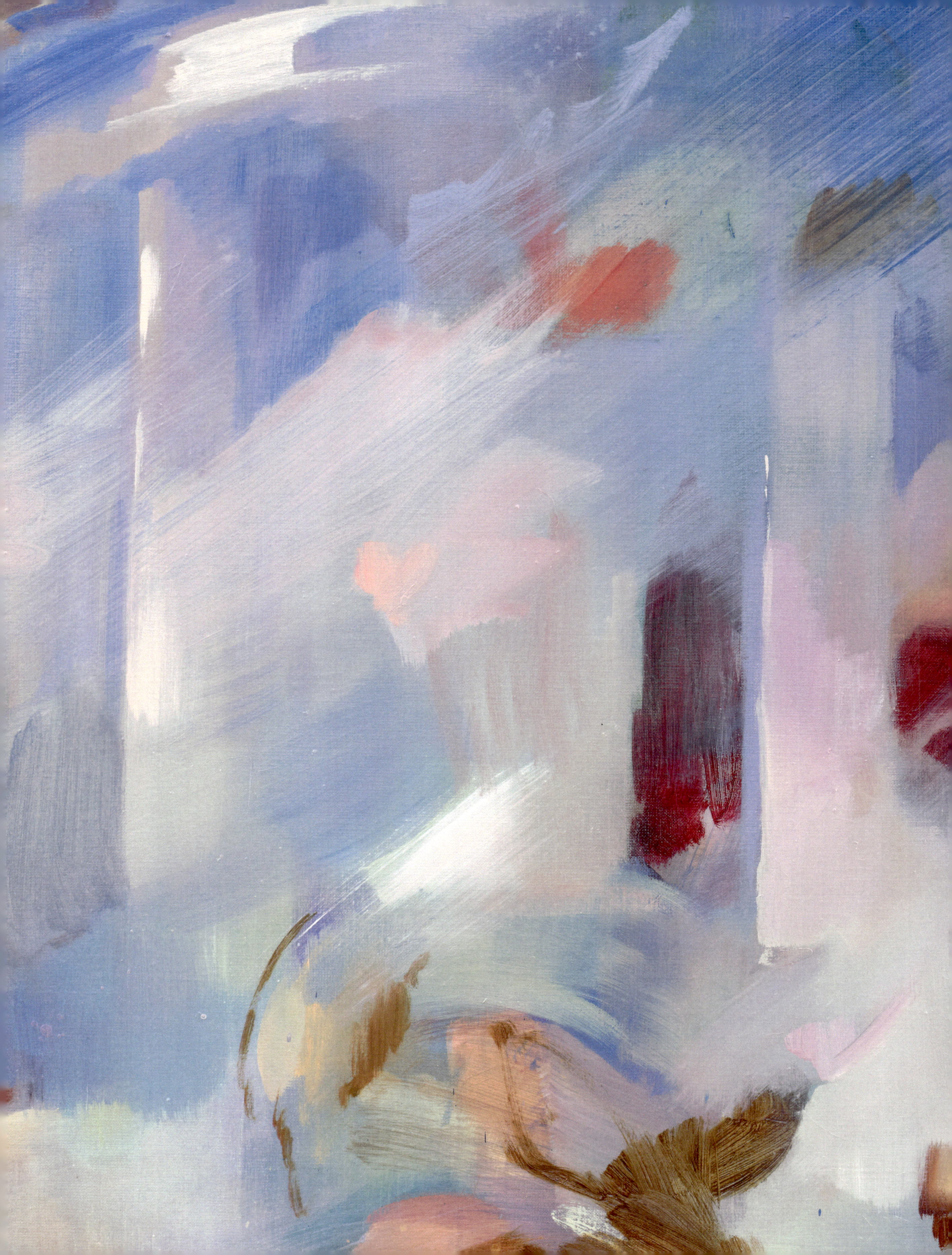

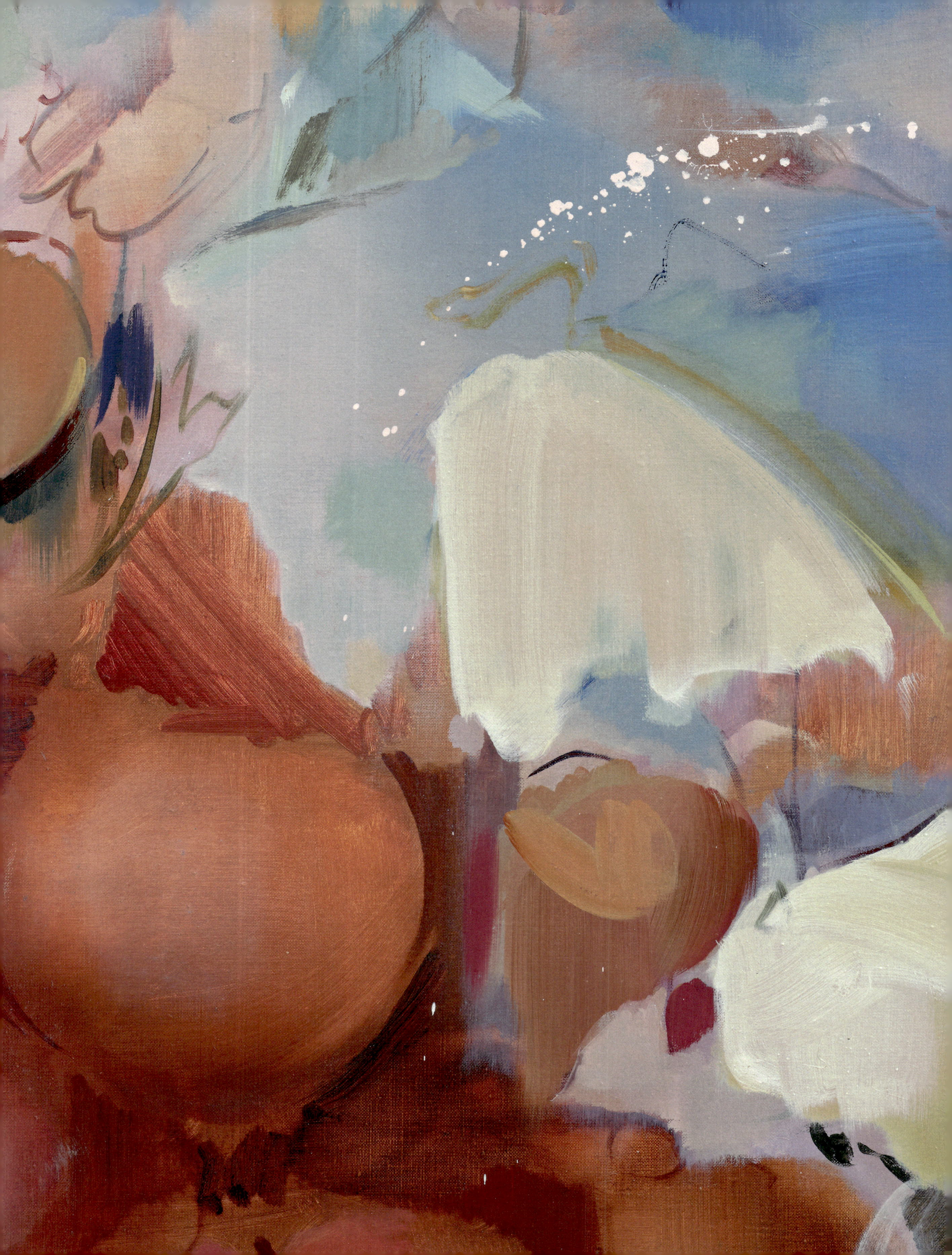

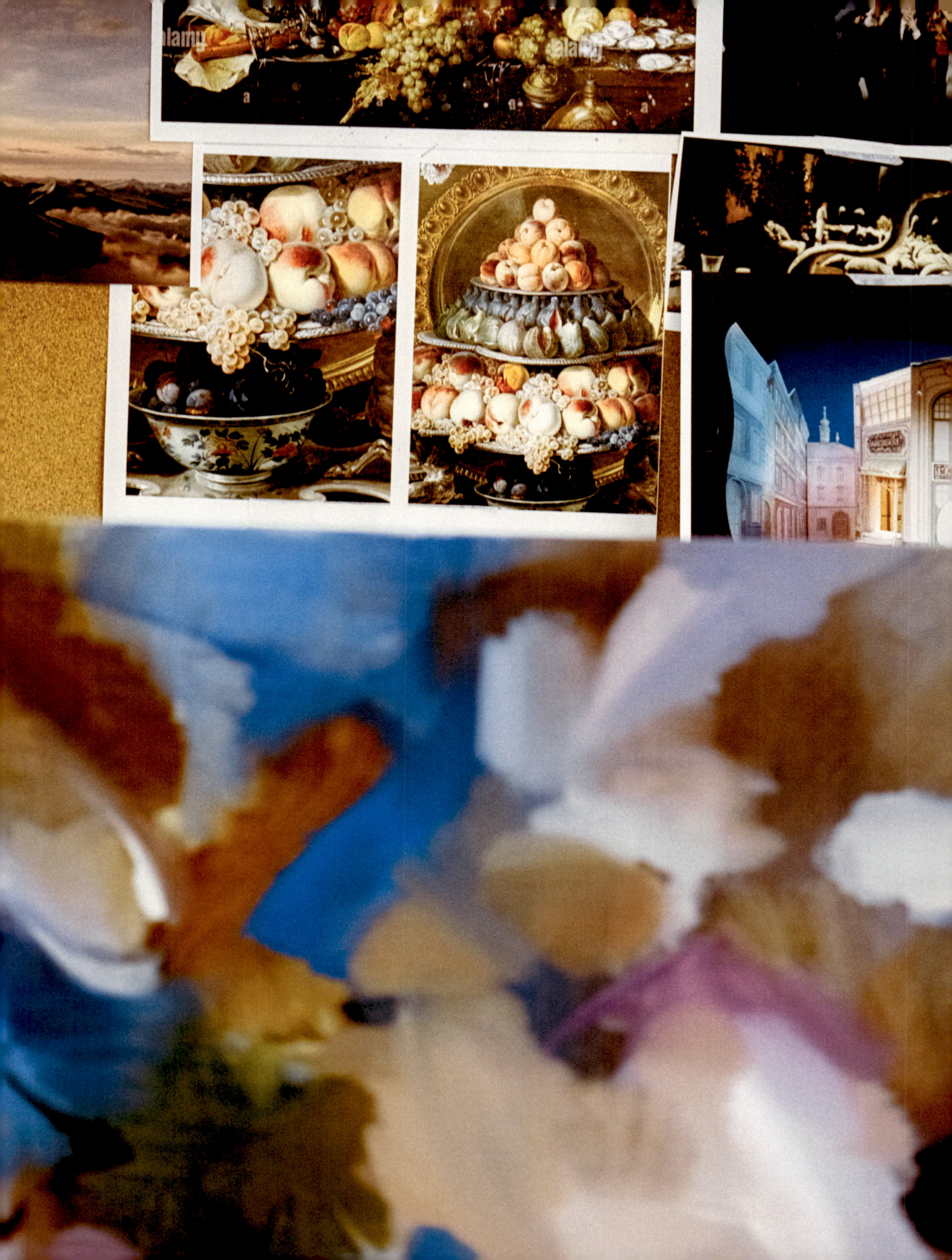

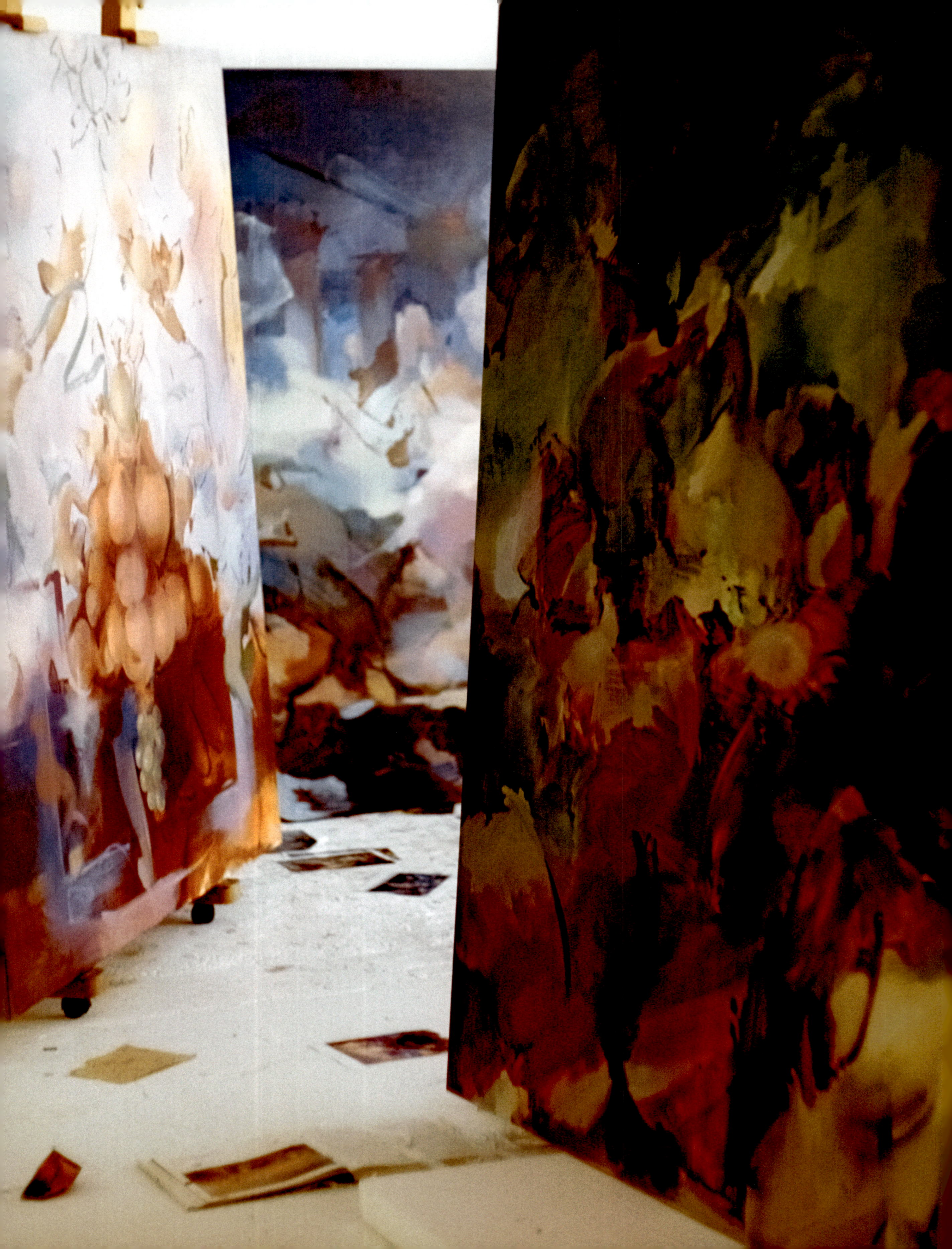

FLORA BY GUCCI

ELEANOR NAIRNE

And on the first day He said: let there be Me, maximum Me, and there He was, in all his apricot splendor, signing executive orders like He needed to keep His wrist moving to keep warm. He called the light night and the darkness day and this was all on the first day of the second term.

It was the 20th of January 2025 and the wind chill temperature in Washington D.C. was 14° Fahrenheit, or -10° Celsius for those of us who made the leap into the metric age. Amid the fleet of paper airplanes He sent flying about Foreign Aid and Tik Tok and DEIA and Alaska's resources it was all too easy to miss His memorandum calling for the amelioration of Federal Civic Architecture. Make them "respect regional, traditional and classical heritage in order to uplift and beautify public spaces and ennoble the United States," He said, and make them tell Me how they plan to do it in sixty days.

What is the classical heritage of the United States I wonder? That brief spell that Caligula spent down in Monticello? Perhaps we need Lin-Manuel Miranda to help us tell that little-known chapter of the tale. Of course, inauguration has its own roots in the Republic, when the soothsayers would look to the flight patterns of birds to determine if the Gods deemed a public official worthy of assuming office. A post on His Truth Social platform bemoaned that there had been an "Artic Blast" and so the ceremony would be held indoors. Alas, this year there would be no skies to tell.

And while He claimed to be ushering in "the golden age of America," the English artist Flora Yukhnovich was at work on a new body of paintings in the former factory of Pierce Arrow in Long Island City. How fitting to be in the husk of the American automobile industry as you reckon with the obscene decadence of our times: boom born of bust. There is a certain morning-after-the-night-before spirit in the studio, too: stretched canvases stand propped up on foam blocks amid the wreckage of a party of painterly references strewn every which way about the floor.

The most important of these are gathered on a pin board that is overwhelming in its merry glut of images. Here is the poster for the 2022 film <u>Babylon</u> with Margot Robbie in a Marilyn moment, as outstretched hands reach up to touch her backlit glamor. And here is Lawrence Alma-Tadema's painting of <u>The Roses of Heliogabalus</u> from 1888, for which he had flowers shipped from the French Riviera so that he could faithfully depict the episode from the <u>Augustan History</u> in which the teenage emperor Elagabalus, adorned in silk robe and tiara, watched as his guests were smothered in a carpet of pink petals.

Then there is Claudia Schiffer and Nadja Auermann, photographed naked and tousled by Richard Avedon behind a cascade of cushions embroidered with classical iconography in a Versace ad from 1995. And a photo of a besmirched five-dollar bill depicting the neoclassical grandeur of the Lincoln Memorial. And two details of the electric-pink elephants from the scene in Dumbo (1941), in which Timothy Q. Mouse and Dumbo accidentally drink water spiked with champagne and find themselves in a drunken reverie with bubbly elephants parading before their eyes.

At times these kinds of free associations provide specific points of departure for Yukhnovich's paintings, and at others they establish an atmosphere in which the work bathes. Glancing back and forth between the new paintings and these bedecked, bedrowned, bedancing bodies I feel a deep sympathy for what a strange time it has been to wash up on American shores (I arrived some six months earlier): the year of the clamorous election, of course—only the second time in history that a president has been elected for a nonconsecutive second term—but also the year that bridges collapsed and planes undressed themselves in the air and Luigi Mangione became a kind of folk hero for assassinating the United-Healthcare CEO Brian Thompson.

What times are these? Nerves hypersensitive to ever-breaking news, especially if your native time zone sleeps while you are kept wired by the internet. These paintings take months and months to make, as layers of washy underpainting are built up into vibrant swathes of color, glitching in and out of recognizable forms, and so their surfaces are porous to life beyond the walls of the studio. Slickness and vanity have always been in the swill of Yukhnovich's work, but these themes feel especially pronounced now, made as they have been amid the decadent decline of 2024 and 2025, and in the knowledge that they were destined for Los Angeles, playground to the stars. How brazen and bewildering and hollow it all seems at this precise moment in the land of plenty.

You could say that the still life is the poster child for superabundance, a traditional means for a patron to peacock their wealth, while an artist might slip in their sense of the perilous brevity of carnal pleasures. On the pinboard there's a reproduction and two details of Alexandre François Desportes's painting Still Life with Silver from the 1720s. Desportes was a favorite of Louis XIV and Louis XV, and so it figures that his still lifes would be almost comedically opulent: heavily gilded trays laden with fruit are set alongside ewers and Japanese porcelain all wreathed in blossoms, quite possibly modelled on an actual banquet, the painting in turn intended to adorn the same walls.

The two details pinned beneath the still life are from the lower section of Desportes' painting in which furry skinned peaches are nestled amid trailing green grapes—a fruit closely associated with Bacchus, who was the Roman god of wine, as well as of fertility and revelry. These appear in Yukhnovich's Trifle (all paintings 2025), the fruit piled high like a tray of profiteroles awaiting their chocolate sauce. The brushwork is loose and luscious and, if you think I am salivating needlessly, look at Apple threatening in 2016 to give their peach emoji a less pronounced suture in order to dampen its sexual connotations. Which is before we consider what an artist saturated in contemporary culture might mean by this croquembouche after that scene in Call Me by Your Name (2017). Contrails of paint dance mid-air and cherubim hover above the fruit, as if to coyly reassert the innocence of the scene, while amping up its seedy underside.

The Bacchanal is a familiar topic in art history, beloved by Titian and Poussin and Velazquez. Depicting the disinhibited capers of revelers was the perfect device for animating a grand painterly space and captivating a crowd. And the classical origins of these tales were the perfect foil for escaping into the lascivious realm of bacchantes, fauns, and satyrs, whose festivities in ancient Rome were said to encourage a good harvest (any excuse). Yukhnovich's two larger paintings, Fever Pitch and Seeing Pink Elephants, are made on a scale to rival her forbears, but the definition of individual forms melts into liquid lust. There remains the distinctive sense of a retinue of lolling celebrants, but the picture becomes all gesture over body. If you smeared Vaseline over a camera lens and made a timelapse of an orgy in the wilderness of Central Park you might end up with something in this visual domain.

The sense of movement in these paintings is remarkable. Looking at Seeing Pink Elephants feels like sitting in a static carriage while your neighboring train gets going. There is all the verdancy of a pastoral bacchanal, but the intermingling passages of fleshy pink paint feel like they are dissolving into the ground and doing so at rapid speed. I think of T. J. Clark's reading of the impossibly conjoined figures in Cezanne's The Large Bathers (1900-1906). Yukhnovich similarly makes restless forms that ridicule our futile attempts to render them into a simple vocabulary of distinguishable body parts: hand, ear, nipple, bum. Beckett looked at Cezanne and understood immediately how he "seems to have been the first to see landscape and state it as material of a strictly peculiar order";[1] Yukhnovich takes that peculiarity and draws out its erotic pulse.

Such pursuits take on a greasy edge when they collide with the language of advertising. Luncheon is one of her first paintings to smuggle lettering into its pastel background. Squint and you can see the faint trace of reversed stenciled letters in the periwinkle blue, partially obscured by ribbony forms that suggests a cursive script—that queasy fake personality of a hand-written scrawl on a mass-produced printed label. A woman is gestured towards in the upper right, her face demurely turned away, her cropped, dark hair tucked under a wide-brimmed hat and a string of pearls gracing her neck. Apparently she orignates from a search for vintage porn, a fact I enjoy immensely. Alighting her shoulder are what looks like the petals of a cotton-candy pink magnolia bloom, while several peaches have exploded to Roald Dahl proportions in the foreground.

The outline of a bottle can be made out on the lower left—the common spot for parading one's latest product on a billboard. In Gucci's ad for their perfume Flora, Miley Cyrus holds her bottle up, lounging like a latter-day odalisque below the lettering of the Hollywood sign, which has somehow shrunk to the perfect proportions to fit in shot, while the hills have miraculously sprouted roses and clematis in the wild grass of that sun-baked spot. I wonder what Cyrus is doing amid the pageantry of the pin board, and then I think of fragrance and its crucial role in releasing the licentious spirit of a bacchanal; as Matthew Arnold wrote in the openings stanzas of his poem on the subject: "In puffs of balm the night-air blows / The perfume which the day forgoes."[2]

The Last Days of Disco feels to me like pure fragrance—the kind of sensual overload induced by a naively enthusiastic dose of wasabi that leaves all your orifices streaming. The primary tone is Permanent Rose: a violet pink with the richness of a ripe peony. The color was introduced by Windsor & Newton in the 1950s and has a kind of Funny Face (1957) femininity to it. There are thin glazes of apricot and cream and lilac, the marks frothing up from the lower right and seeming to emit a glow of warm light. A bubble is forming above this teeming mass adding to the uncertainty of what exactly we are looking at. A writhing of petal and flesh, perhaps, much like a first-person account from one of Elagabalus's ill-fated guests, facing death by rose?

When the Romans were revived in later periods of art it was often with a degree of disquiet about their debauchery. The Romans in their Decadence by Thomas Couture is a prominent protagonist on the pin board and a good example of this unease. It debuted at the Paris Salon in 1847 just a year before the revolution that toppled the July Monarchy, leading to the founding of the Second Republic. Alexis de Tocqueville said shortly before the revolts, "We are sleeping on a volcano," which has The Last Days of Disco written all over it.[3] In Couture's painting, an array of exhausted bacchantes lie in a state of post-coital abandon, framed by the classical architecture of Corinthian columns; here's the structure of what has been, enclosing the chaos of what has come to pass.

Lest anyone miss the political implications of his painting, the Jacobin artist included a quote from the Roman poet Juvenal in the exhibition catalogue: "Crueler than war, vice fell upon Rome and avenged the conquered world."[4] Recently Vanity Fair (of all places) ran a story on "Bacchanalia 2.0" with an illustration of Couture's painting updated with laptops and velvet pink stilettos and preening selfies and tech boi hoodies. The strap line reads: "Some of the most powerful men in Silicon Valley are regulars at exclusive, drug-fueled, sex-laced parties—gatherings they describe not as scandalous, or even secret, but as a bold, unconventional lifestyle choice. Yet, while the guys get laid, the women get screwed. In an adaptation from her new book, Brotopia, Emily Chang exposes the tired and toxic dynamic at play."[5] Perhaps these days it's easier to condemn a few bad princelings than to acknowledge that something might be rotten in the state of Denmark.

A year or two ago there was a trend on TikTok to ask a man in your life how many times a day he thinks about Ancient Rome. To be fair, the Empire endured for a thousand years and at its height spread over 1.7 million square miles so there's much on which to cogitate: aqueducts, newspapers, concrete, underfloor heating, sanitation, surgical instruments, not to mention the A10 road in London. For me, I can't think about it without thinking about Monty Python's Life of Brian (1979) and its depiction of the sheer pomp and silliness of Caesar's Rome, epitomized by the lisping Pontius Pilate: "The little wascal has spiwit," he says of the condemned Brian. Back in October 2019, the then-45th President of the United States spoke at a press conference with Italian President Sergio Mattarella about their two countries' "shared cultural and political heritage dating back thousands of years to ancient Rome," so I'd hazard a guess that He has an embarrassingly high mental search rate—if a thin grasp on actual historical events.

Now it's July (a month named in honor of Caesar) and the air is humid, heavy. He managed to squeeze His "big beautiful bill" through the House of Representatives by a majority of 215 to 214 on the eve of Independence Day, and it is hard to know what to do with that; now the bluster is being enshrined in law. My brother used to say that he loved the phrase "late Capitalism" because it implied such optimism about the possibility of a state beyond ruthless market-driven economics. But Rome did fall. The wisdom of the ancients is that luxury quickly cedes to corruption and chaos and from the wreckage a phoenix could arise. What is a painter to do but submerge in the whorl of revelries and see what might emerge?

1. Samuel Beckett to Thomas McGreevy, September 8, 1934, in The Letters of Samuel Beckett: Volume I, 1929-1940, eds. Martha Dow Fehsenfeld and Lois More Overbeck (Cambridge: Cambridge University Press, 2009), 222.
2. Matthew Arnold, “Bacchanalia” (1867), The Poems of Matthew Arnold, 1840-1867 (London: Oxford University Press, 1922), 419.
3. Mayer, J. P. Alexis de Tocqueville: A Biographical Study in Political Science (New York: Harper & Brothers, 1960), 42.
4. Explication des ouvrages de peinture, sculpture, architecture, gravure et lithographie des artistes vivants, exposés au Musée Royal le 16 Mars 1847, (Paris: Vinchon, 1847). Originally, “Plus cruel que la guerre, le vice s’est abattu sur Rome et venge l’univers vaincu.”
5. Emily Chang, “BACCHANALIA 2.0,” Vanity Fair, February 2018, 66.

Yukhnovich's statements about her research-based practice that appear in the following pages came out of a conversation with Jake Brodsky at her studio in Long Island City, New York, on June 12, 2025. The photographs of her studio, by Dan McMahon, were taken during this same visit.

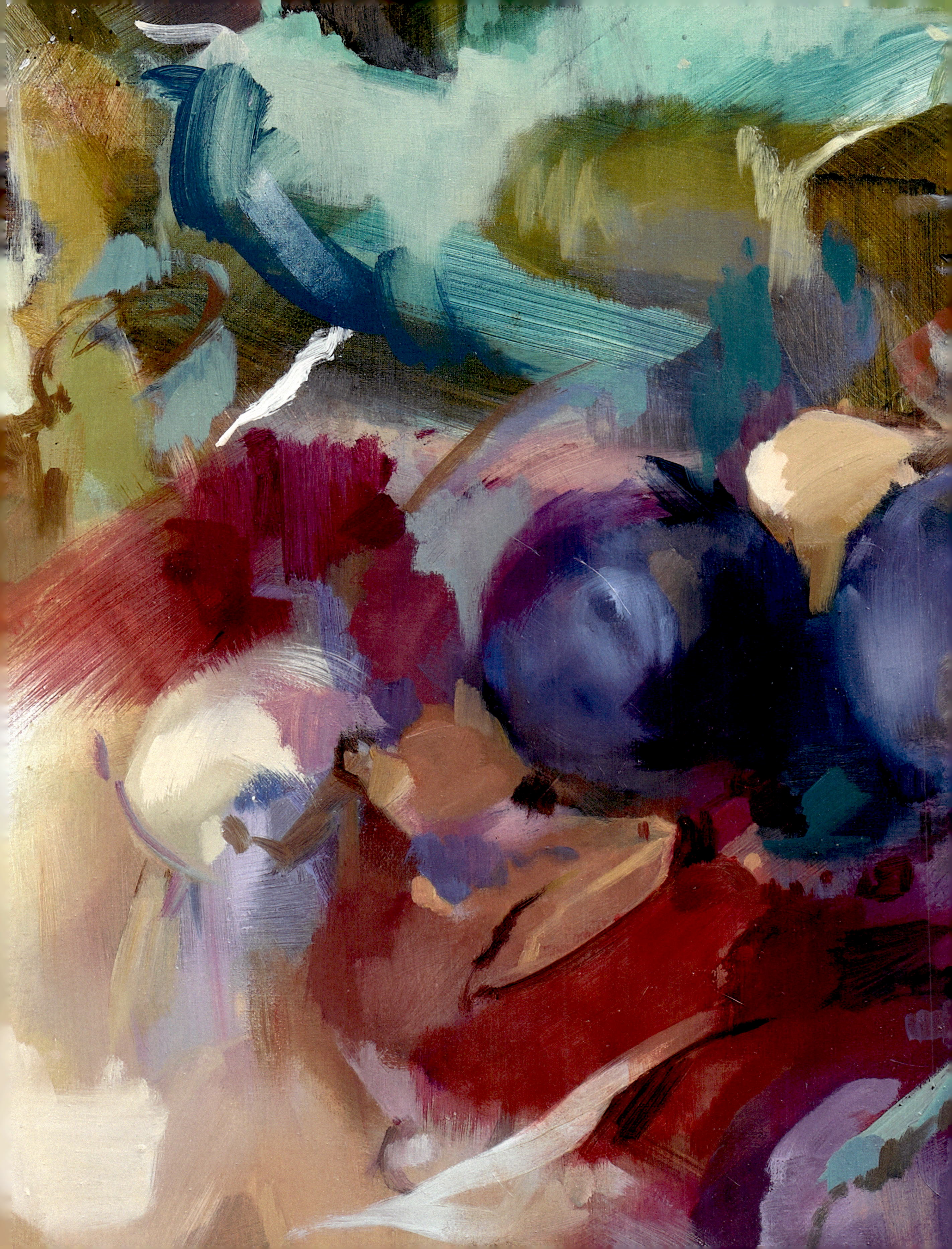

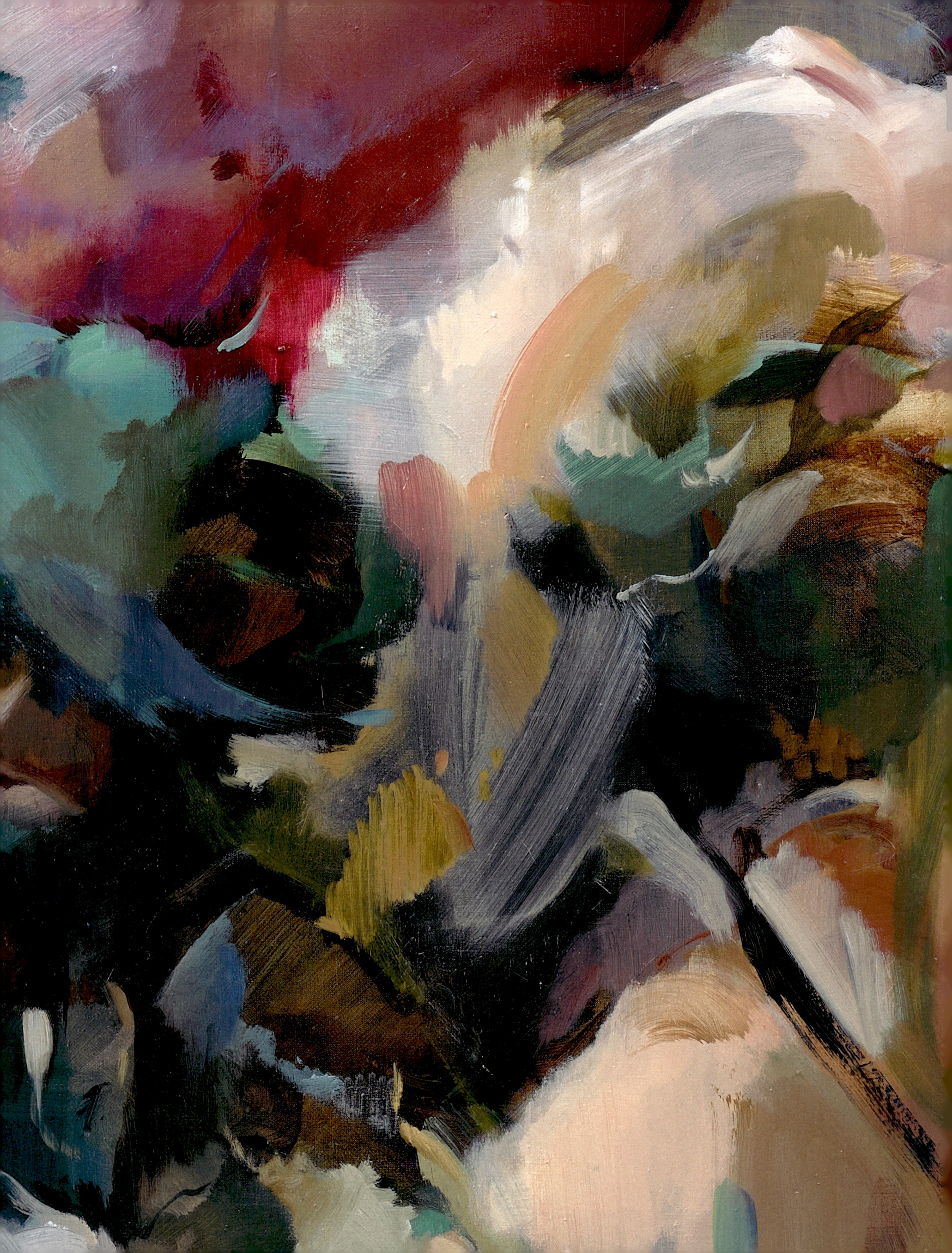

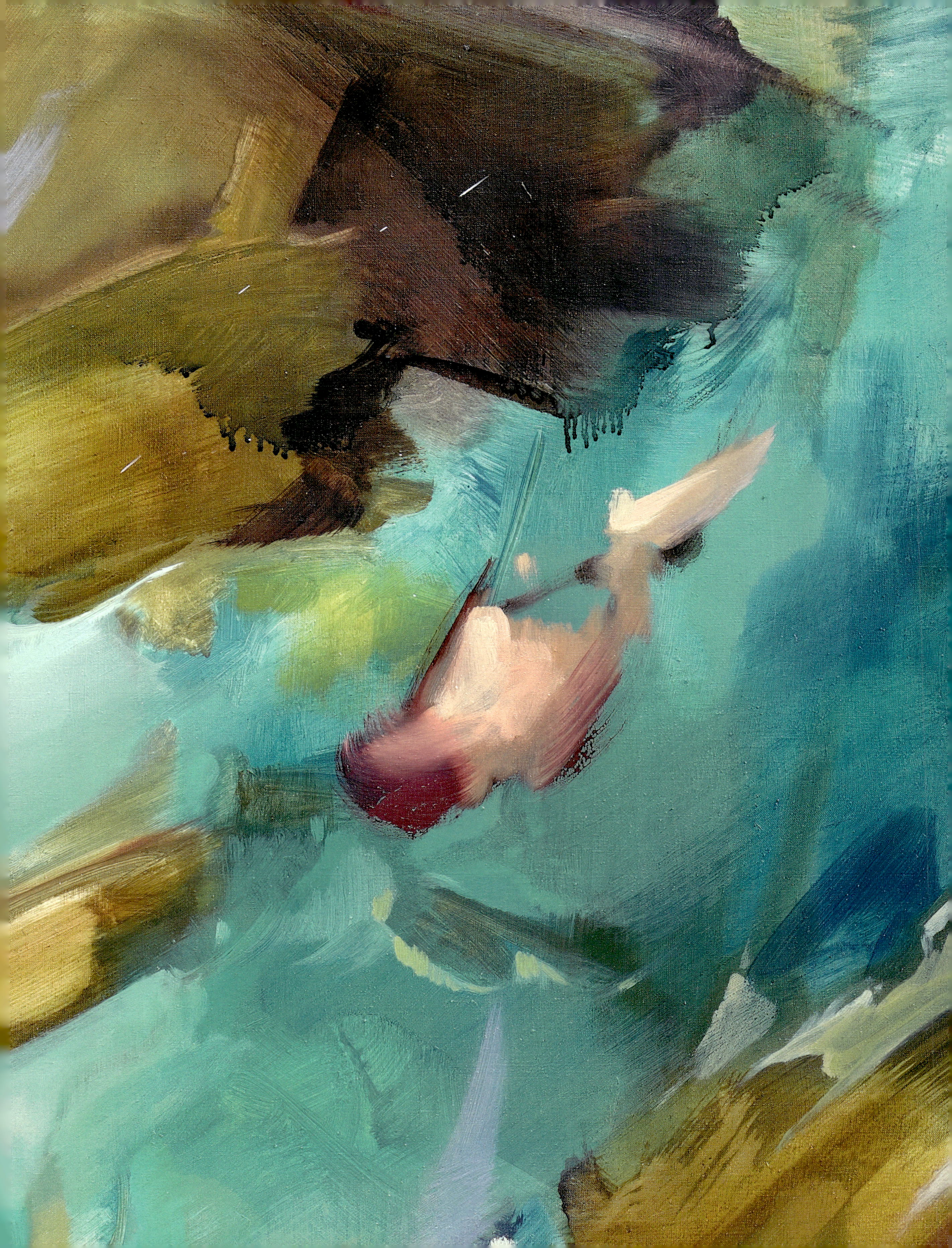

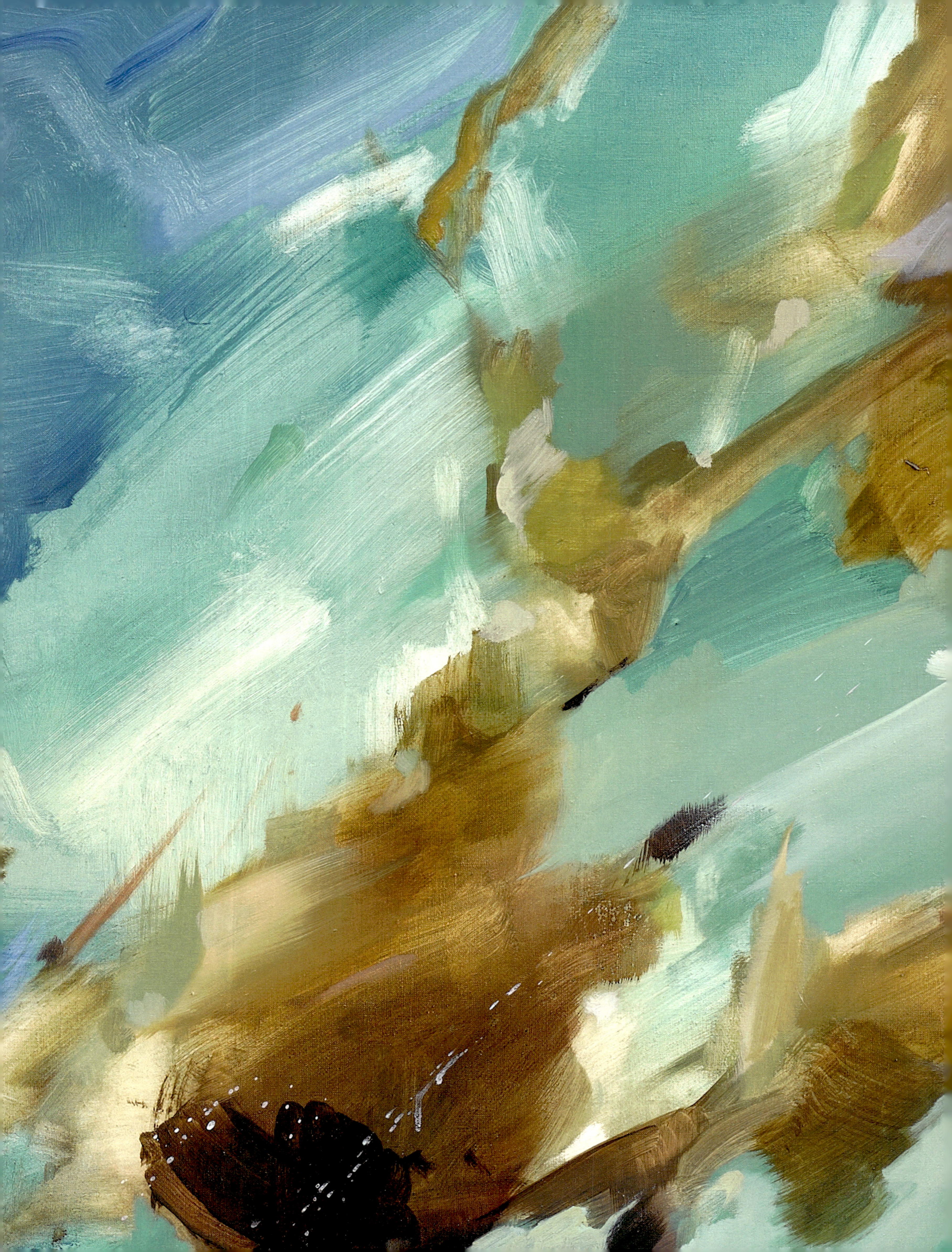

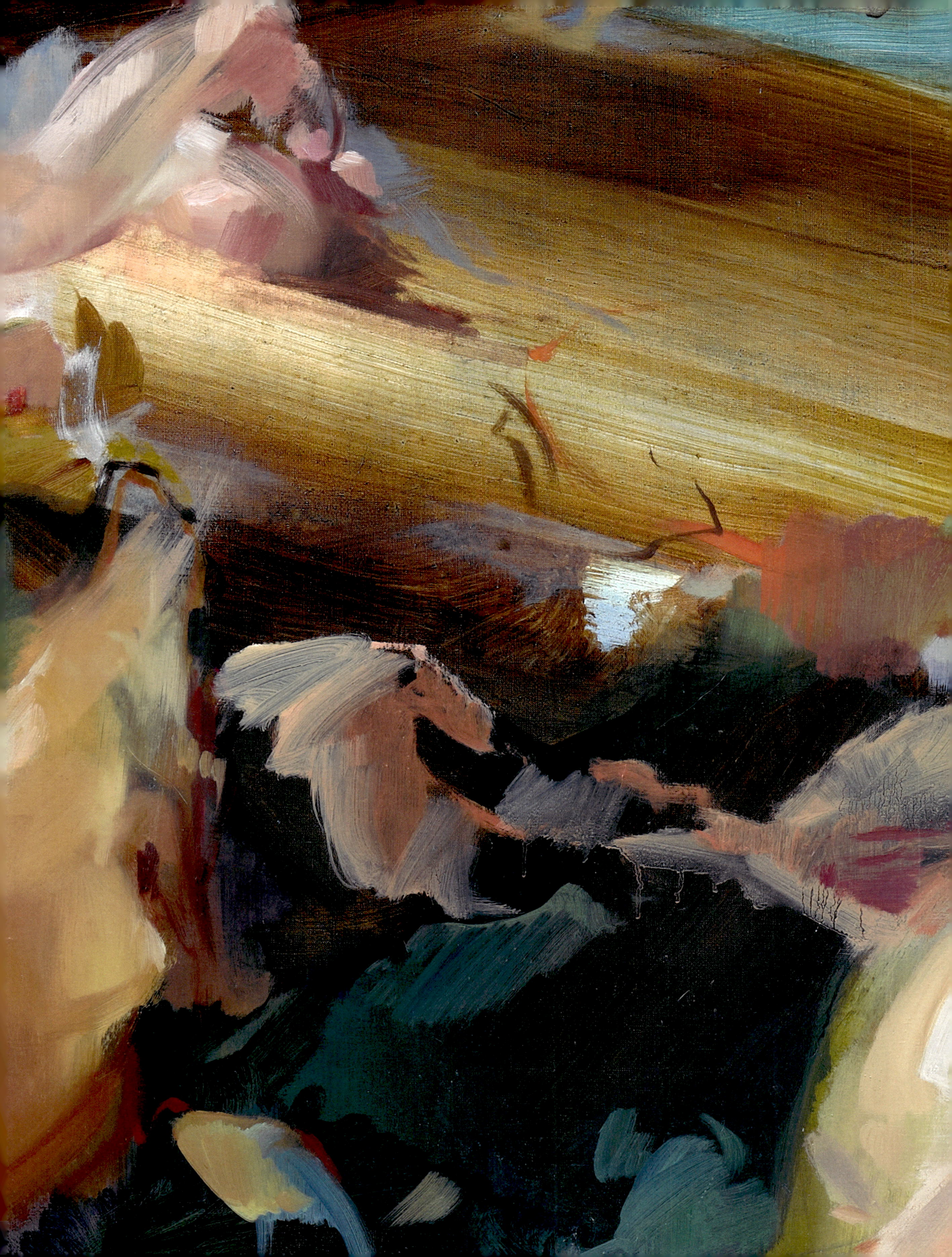

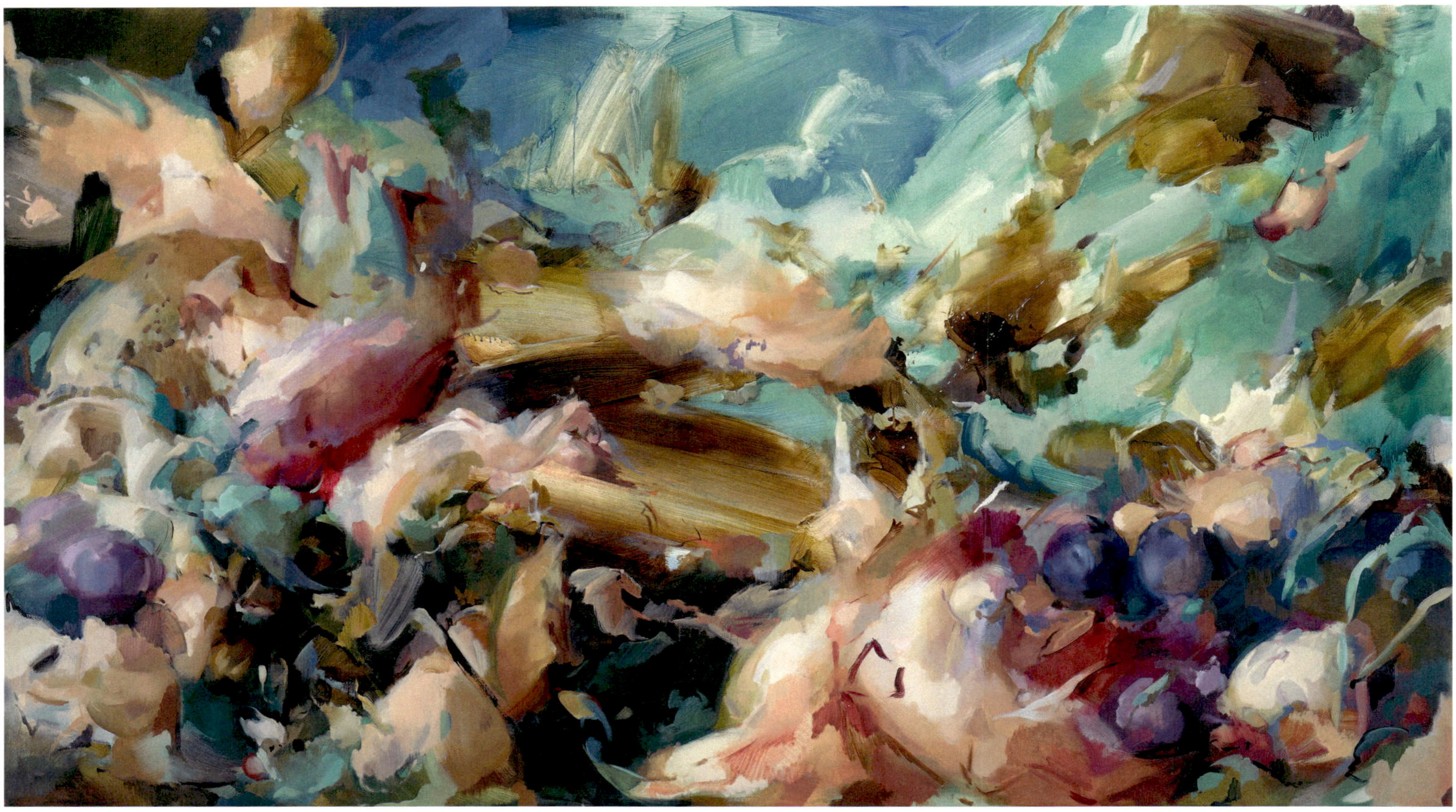

FAST AND LOOSE
2024. Oil on linen, 63 × 110¼ in. (160 × 280 cm)

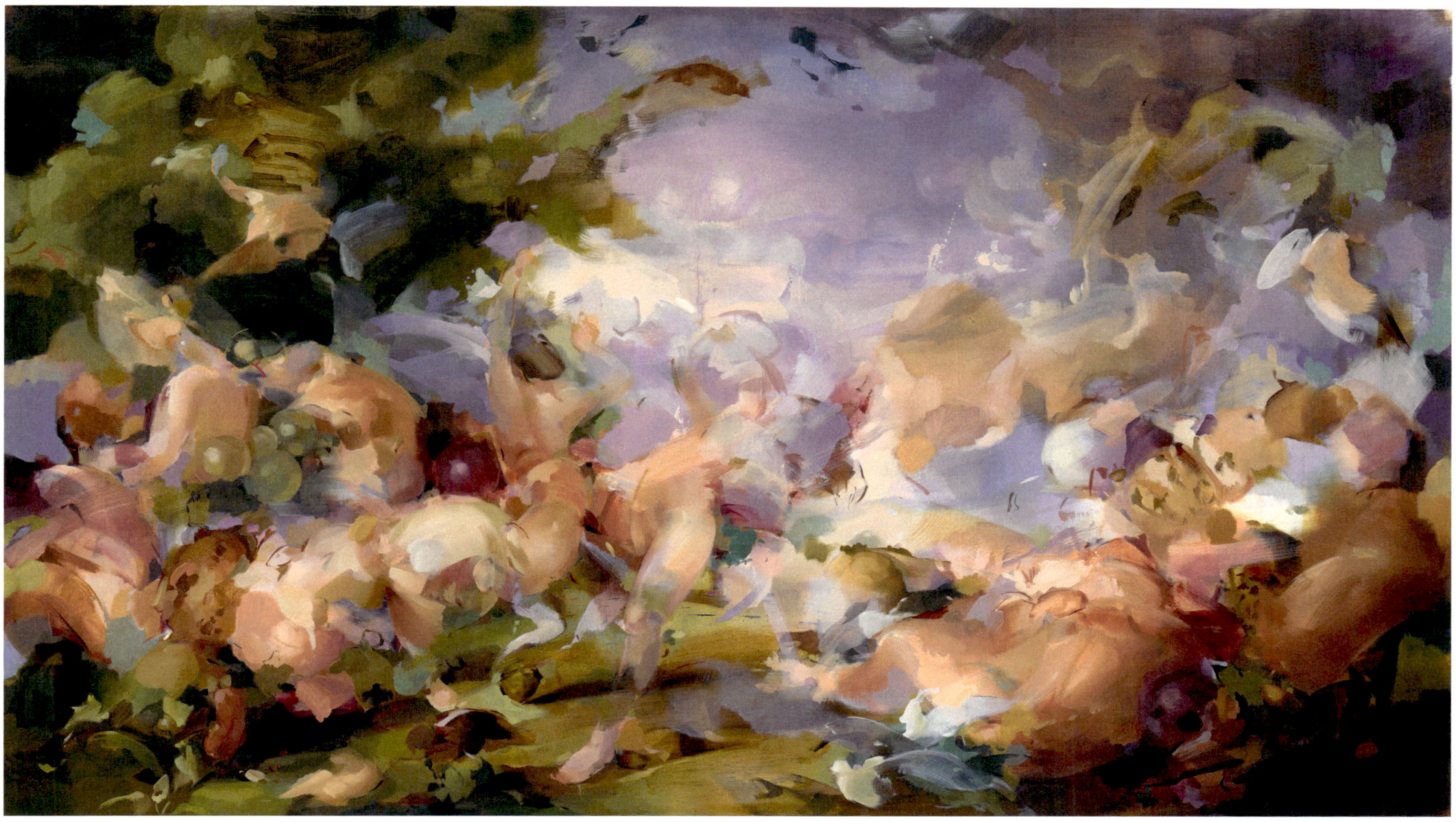

BACCHANALIA
2023. Oil on linen, 72⅞ × 126 in. (185 × 320 cm)

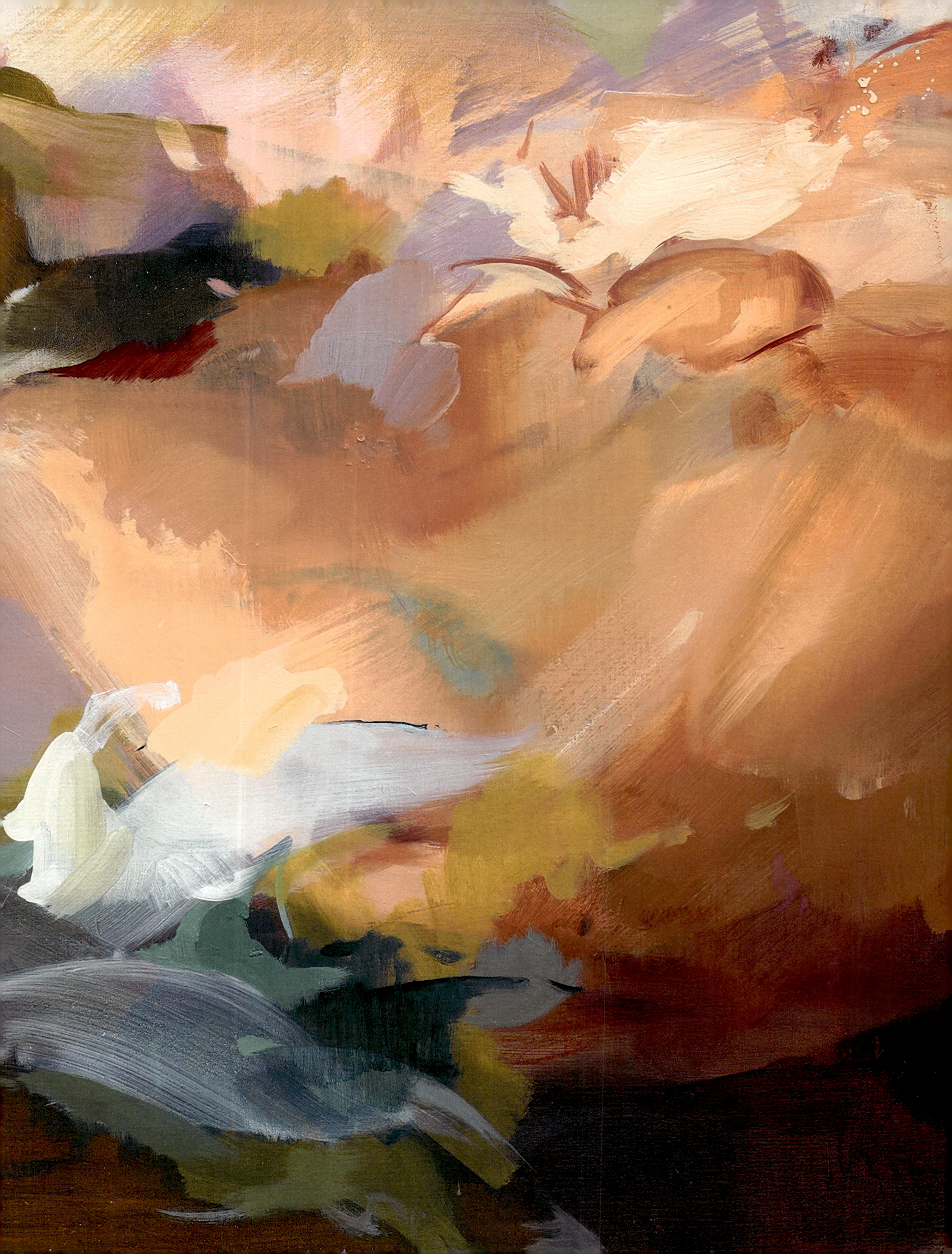

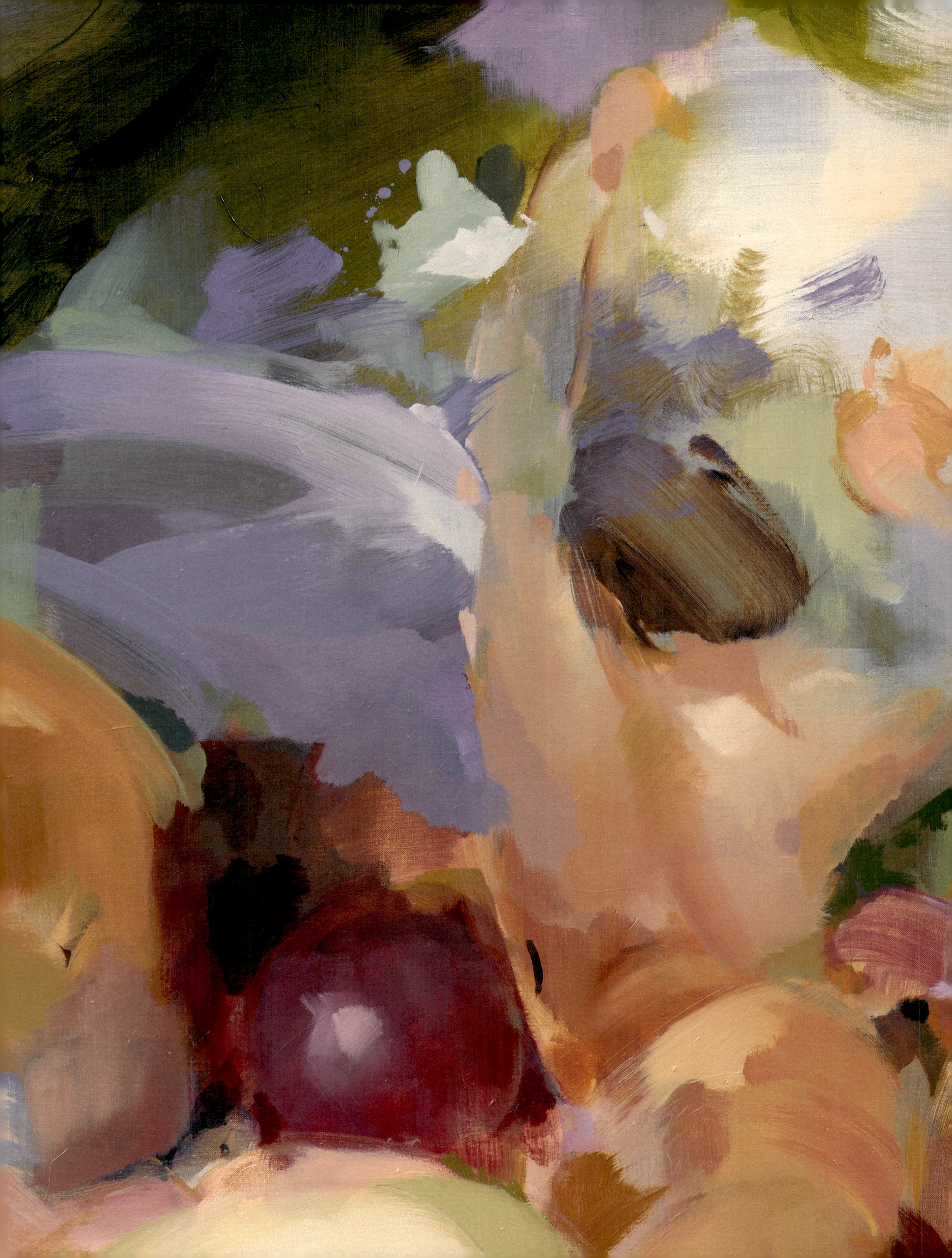

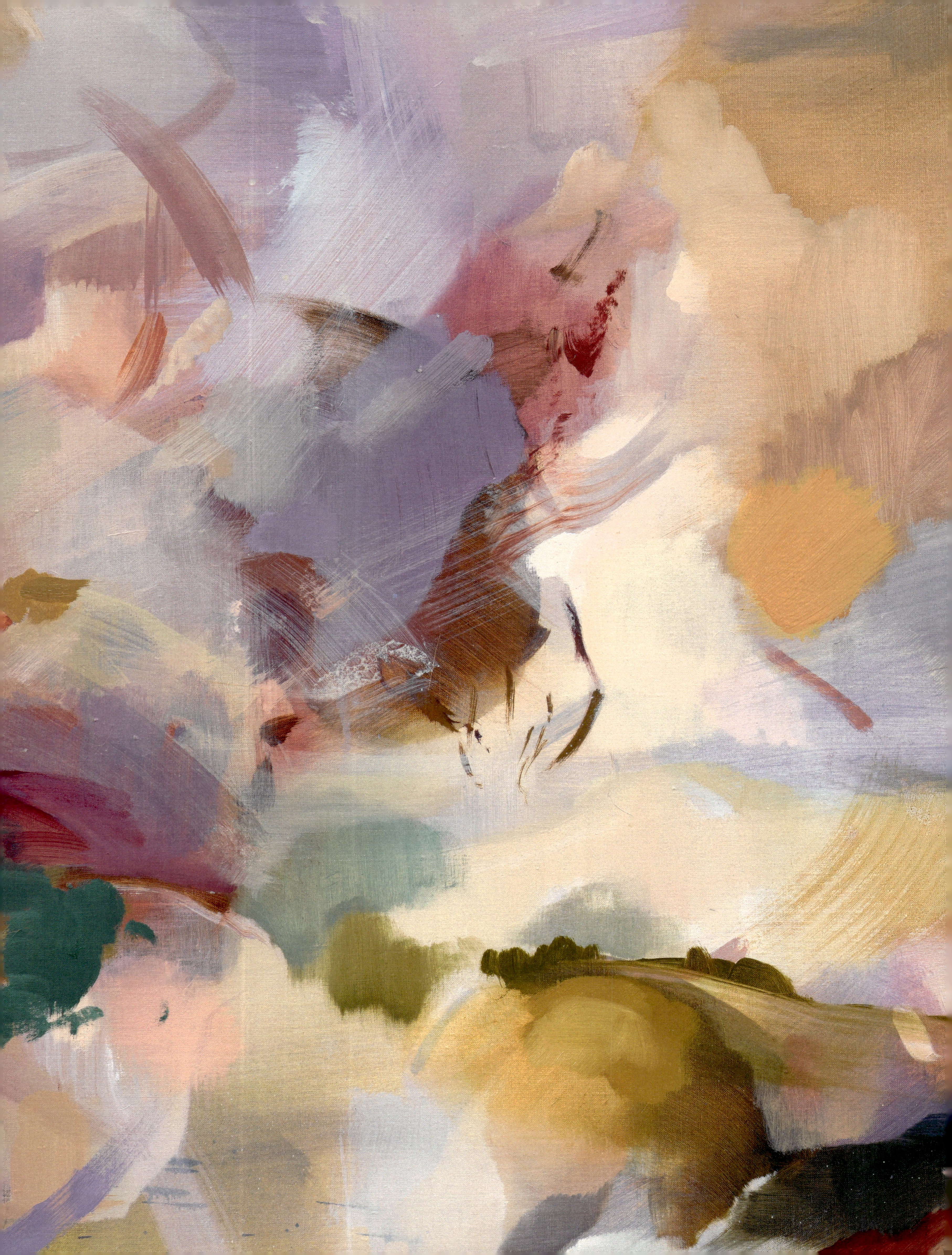

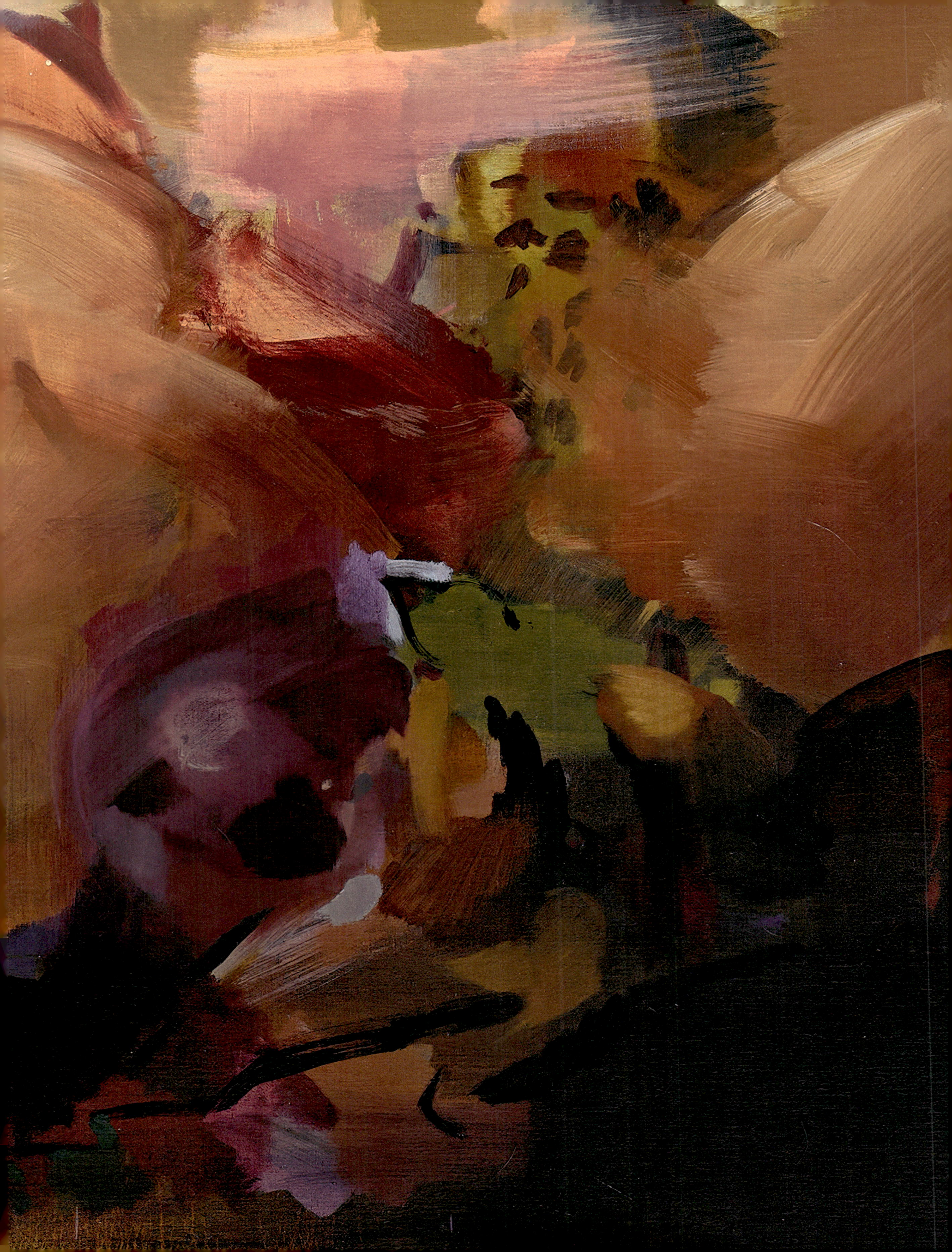

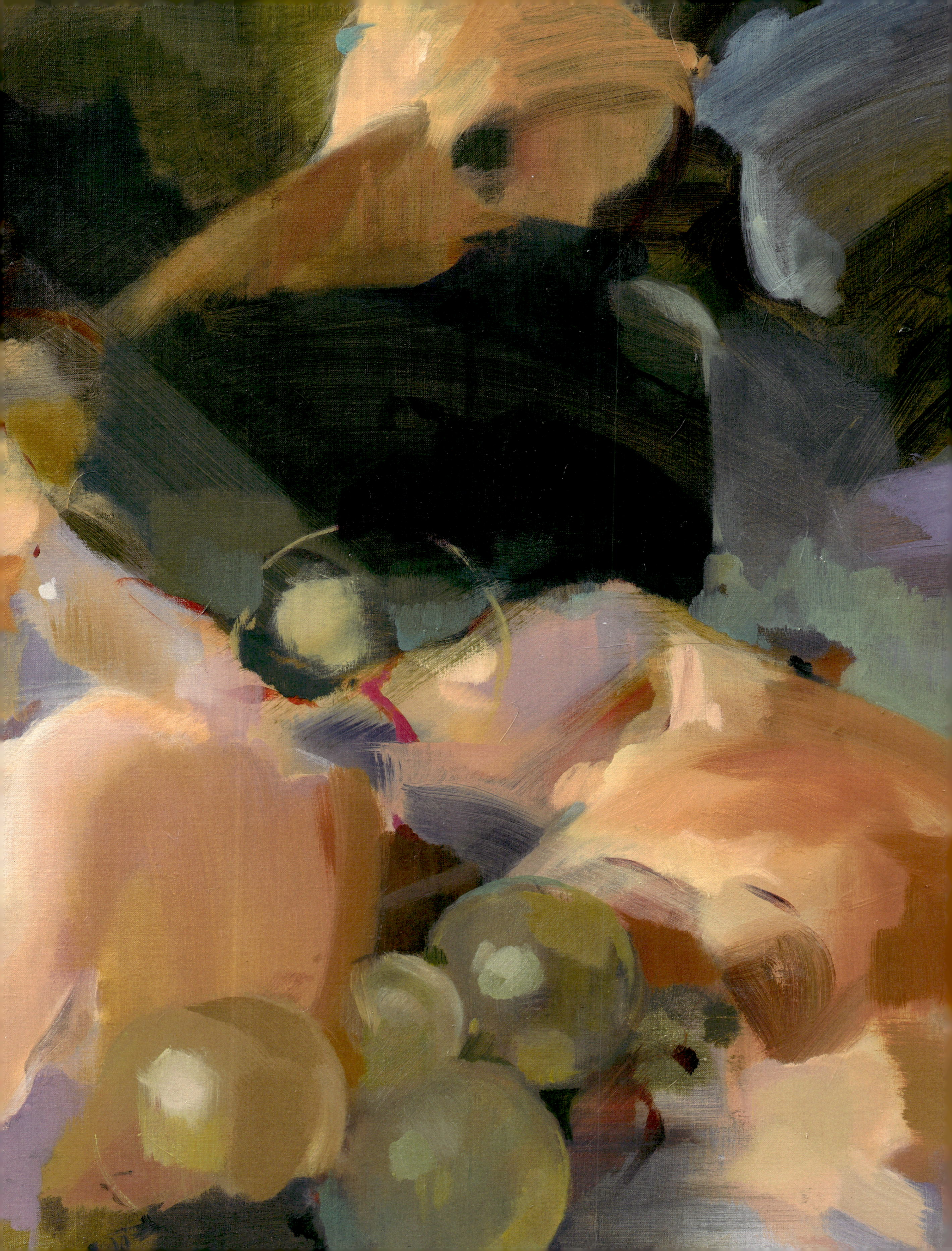

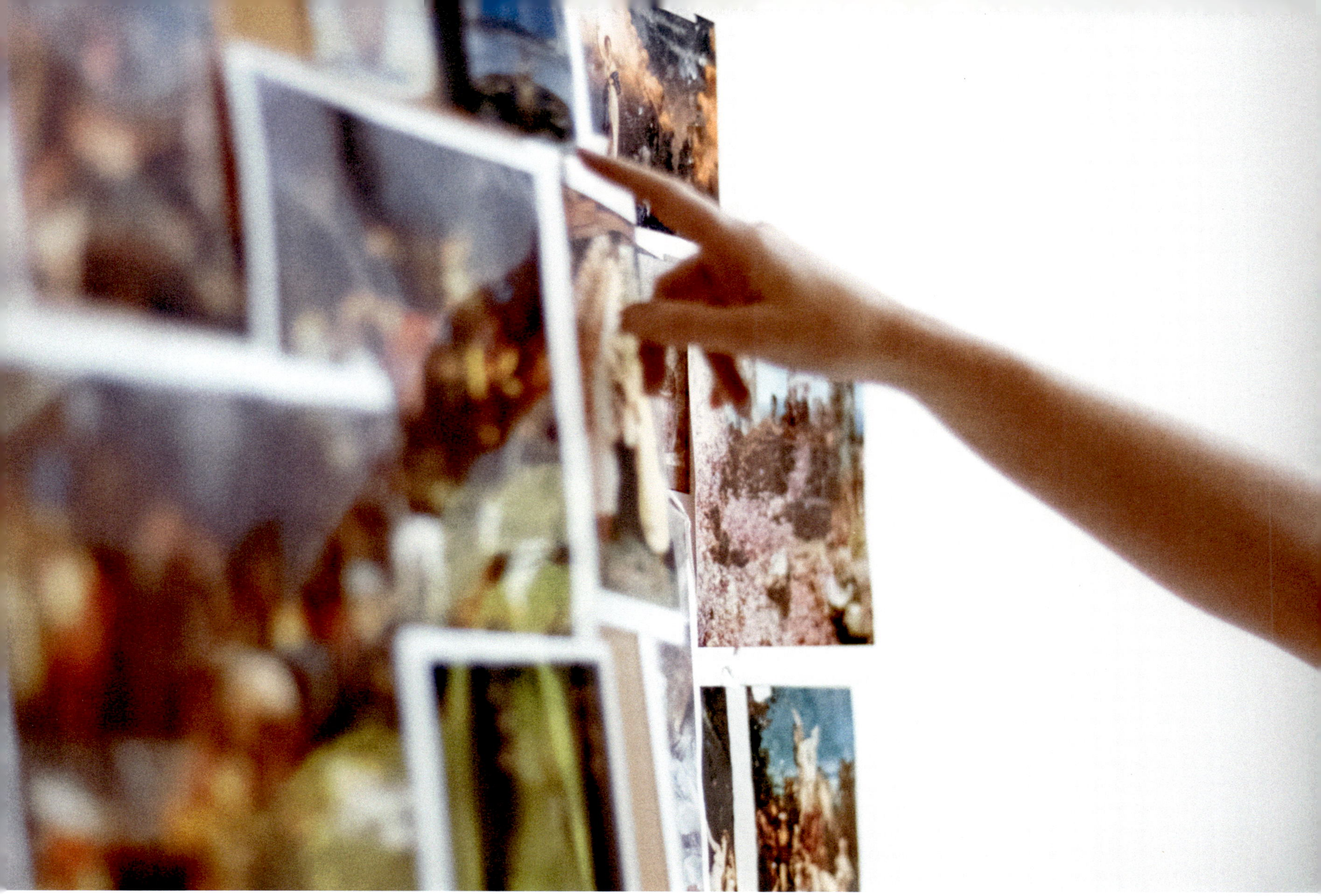

I like to begin a painting by collecting images—snippets from books, magazines, museums, films, pinning them up around the studio. I'm looking for a through line, a red thread. For me, painting lives in the squishy, imprecise space between images, the familiar feelings that flicker through the fast-thinking mind before logic catches up. Mood boards help me pin down this shadowy feeling before I begin painting. As I work, I stay on the lookout for new images that speak the same language. The boards grow alongside the paintings, evolving with them.

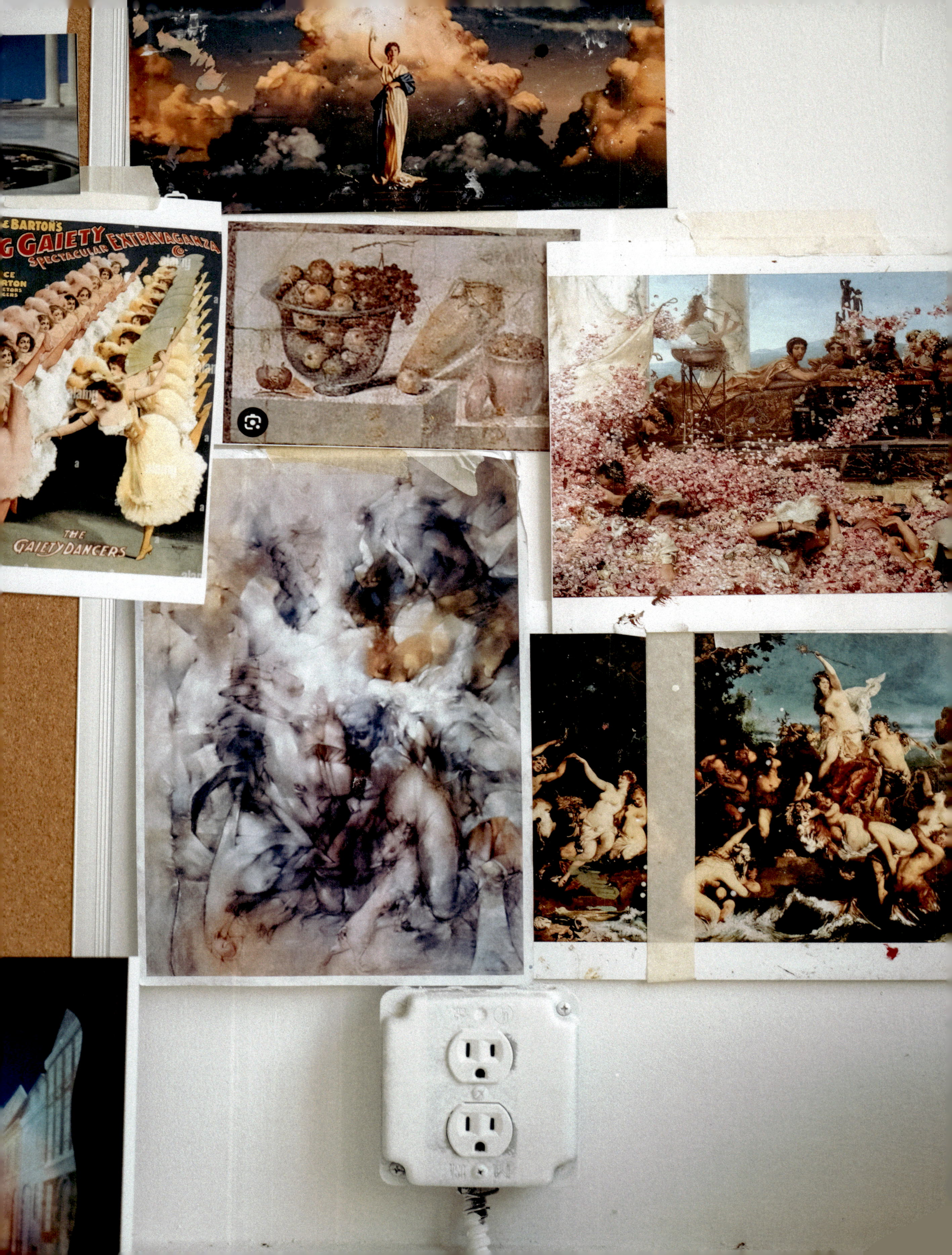
SPECTACULAR EXTRAVAGANZA
THE GAIETY DANCERS

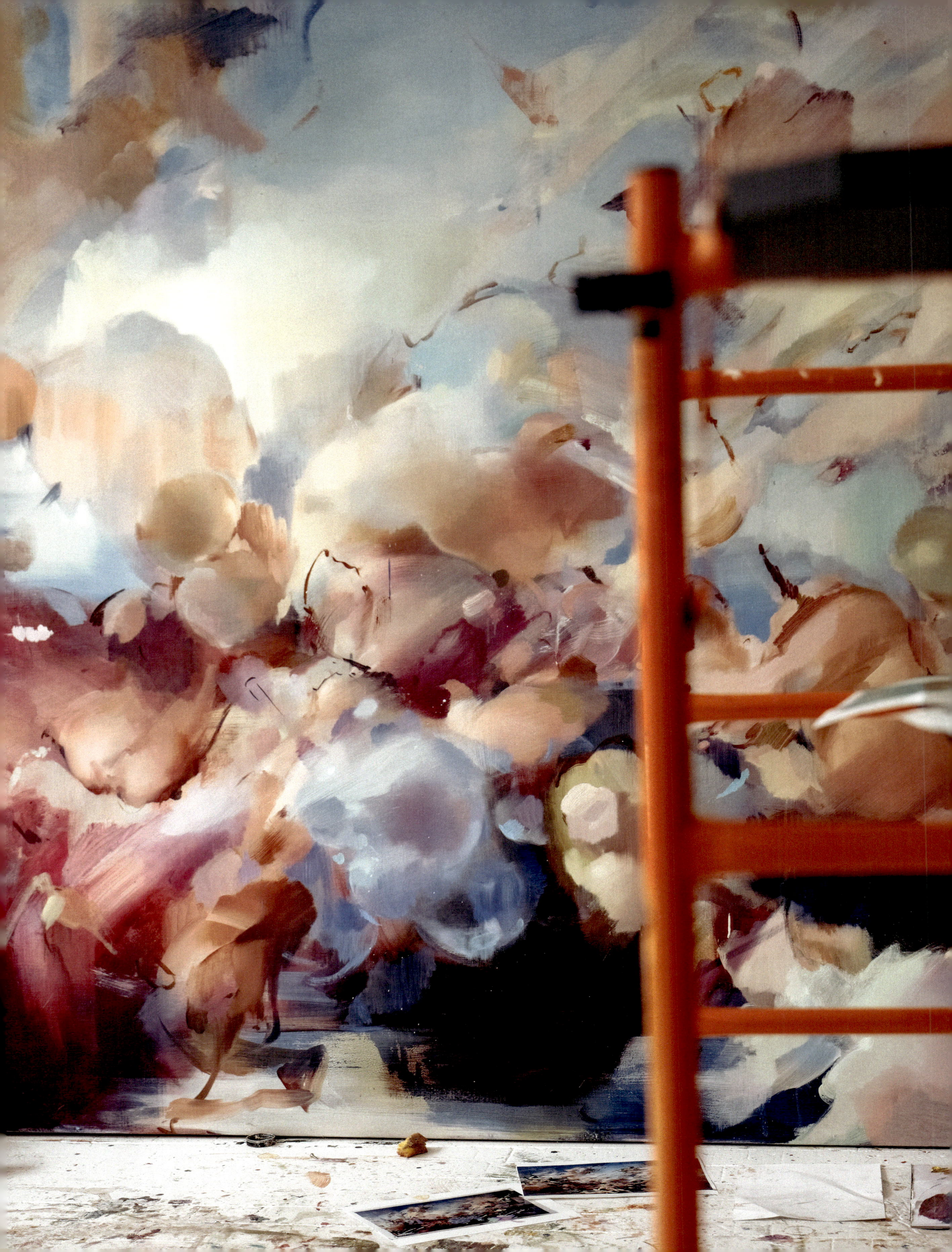

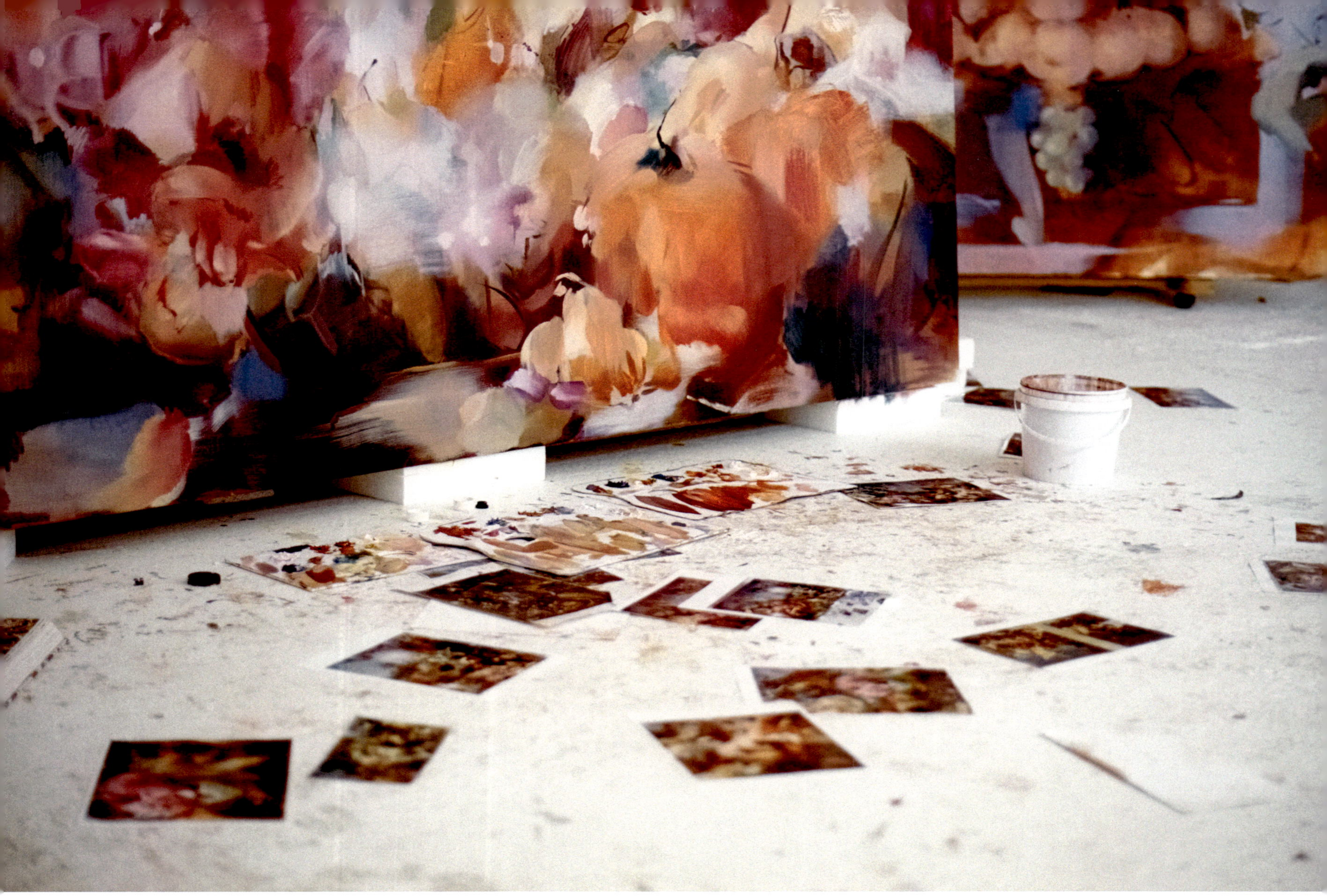

We are living in a time that is excessive. There is more information out there than we can possibly take in. The concept of bacchanalia resonates with this moment in history, its frenetic energy. I was looking at the Rococo period and at Dutch still life paintings and thinking about how they manifest their excess in different ways. I was also thinking about screens—how our lives, work, and relationships are all mediated through phones and computers. I had initially planned to make paintings about the body, movement, and rhythm—excess through paint. But I became more interested in the layering of imagery—the point where excess obscures, rather than delivers, information. It's less about the visceral ecstasy of bacchanalia and more about spectacle—about collective hallucination.

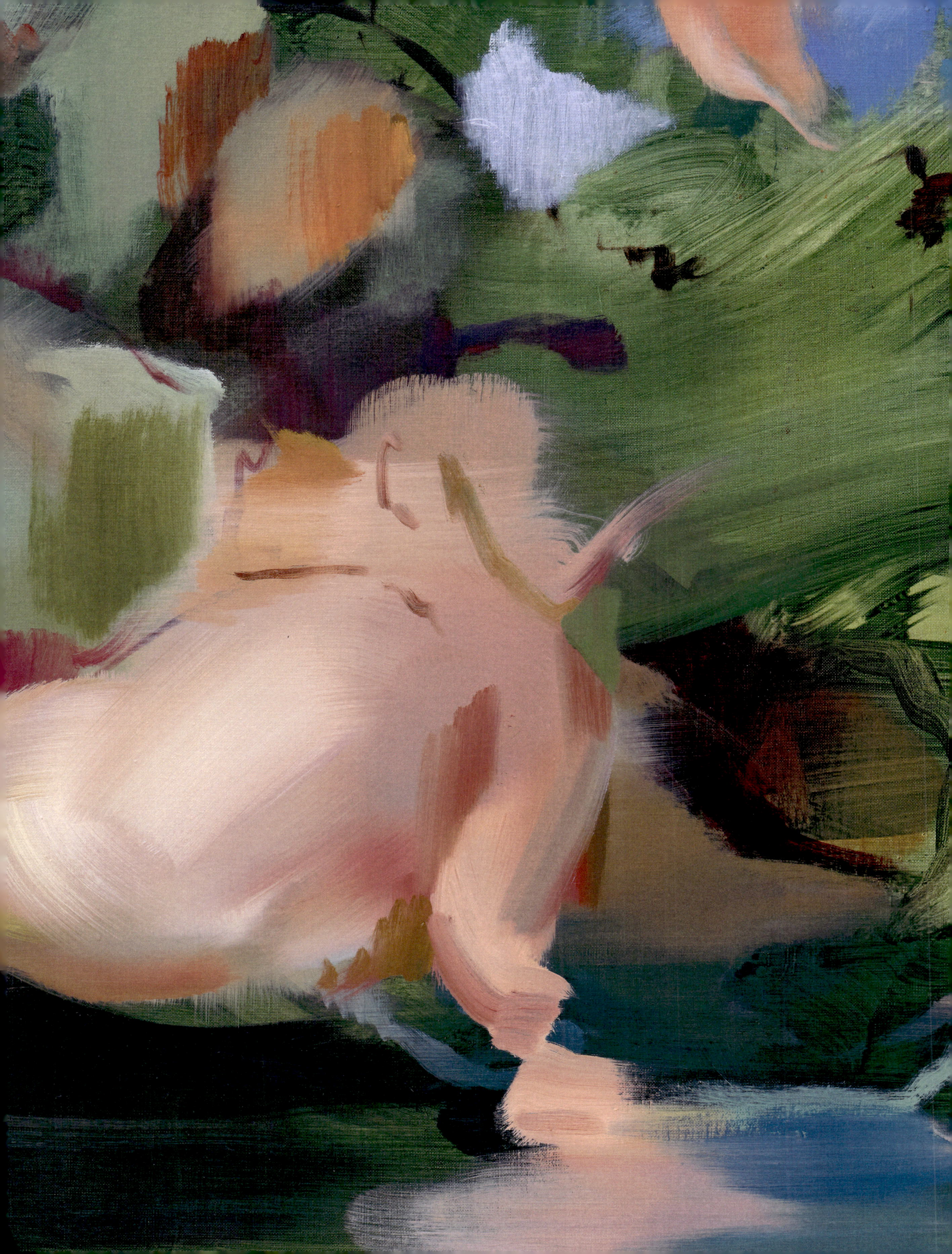

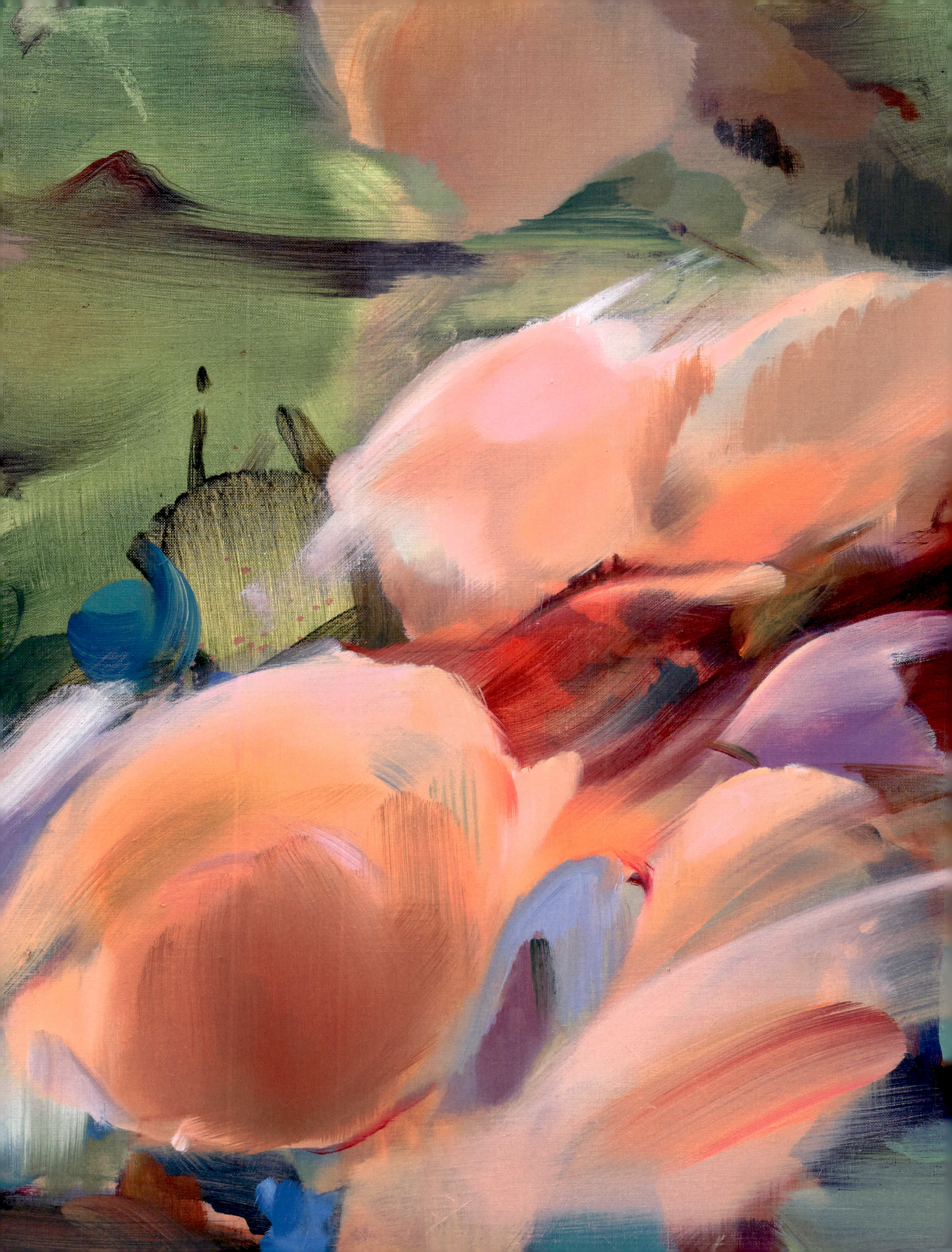

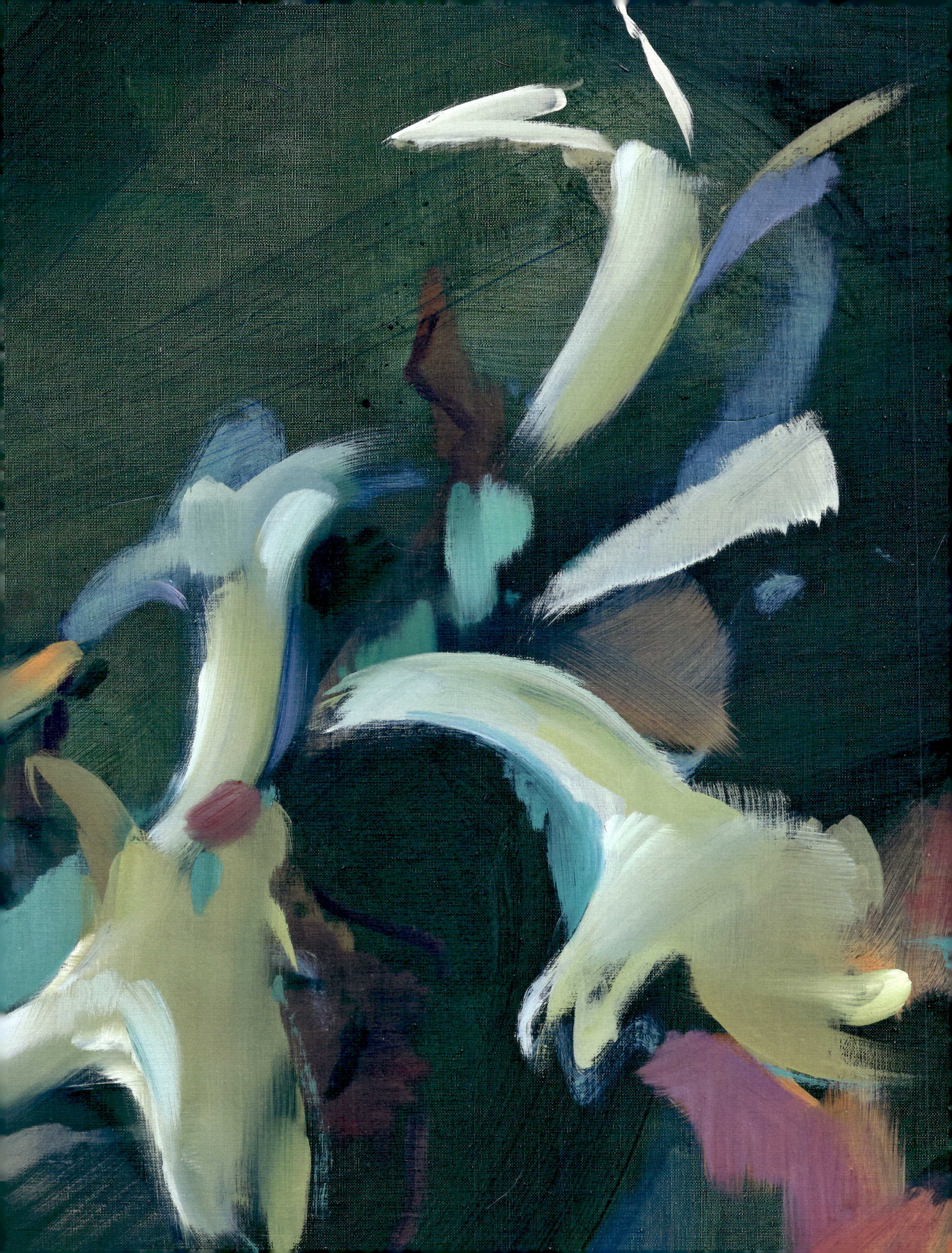

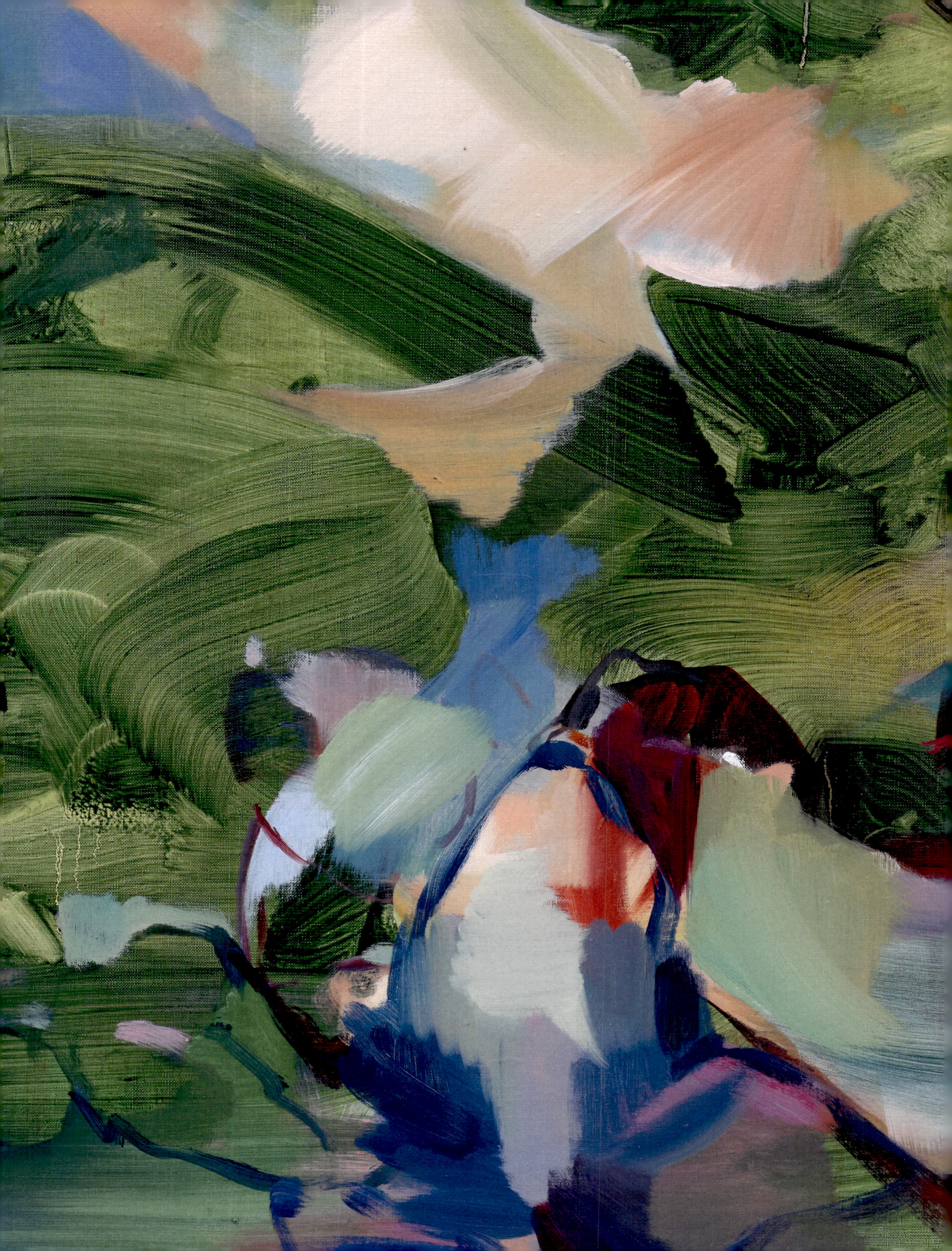

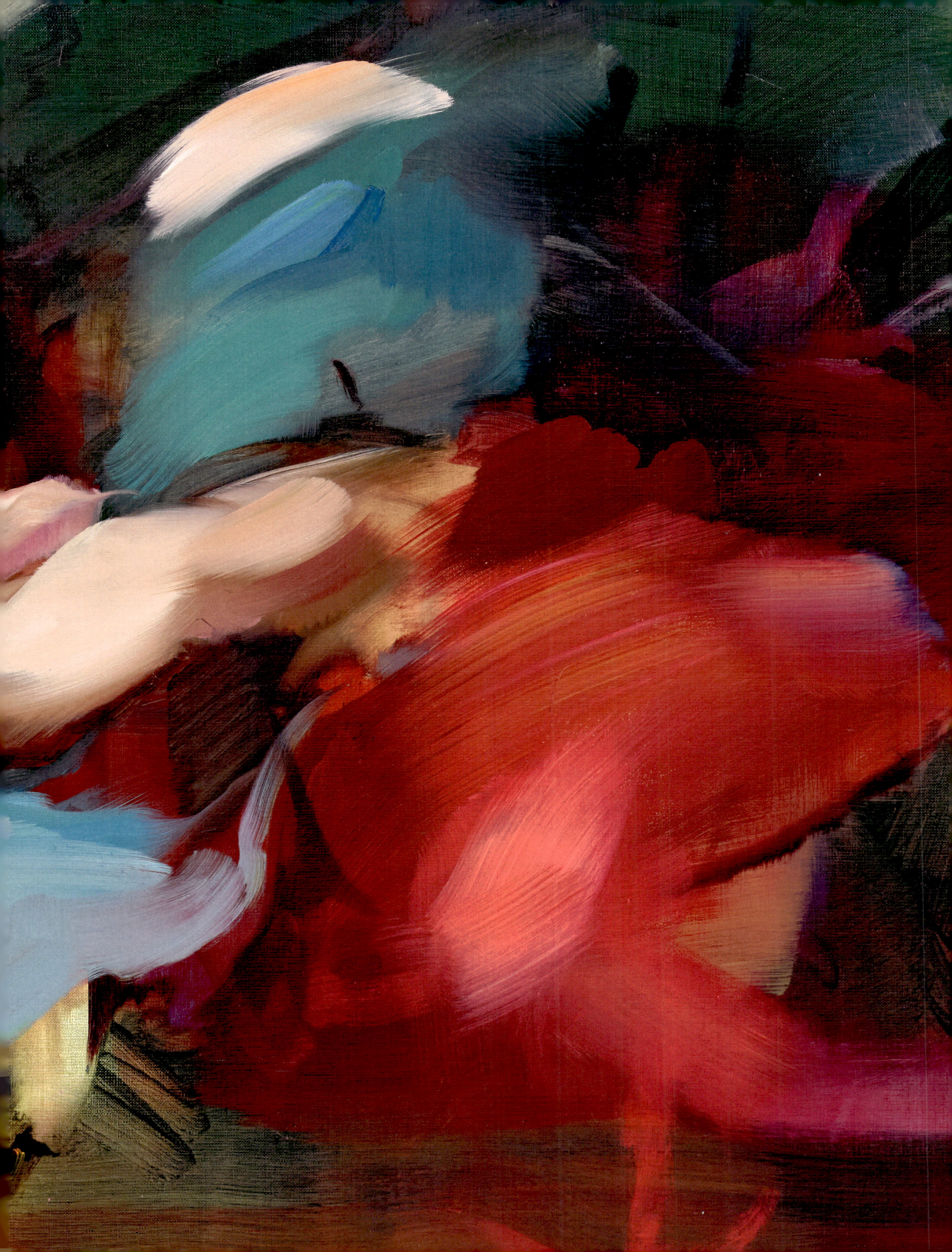

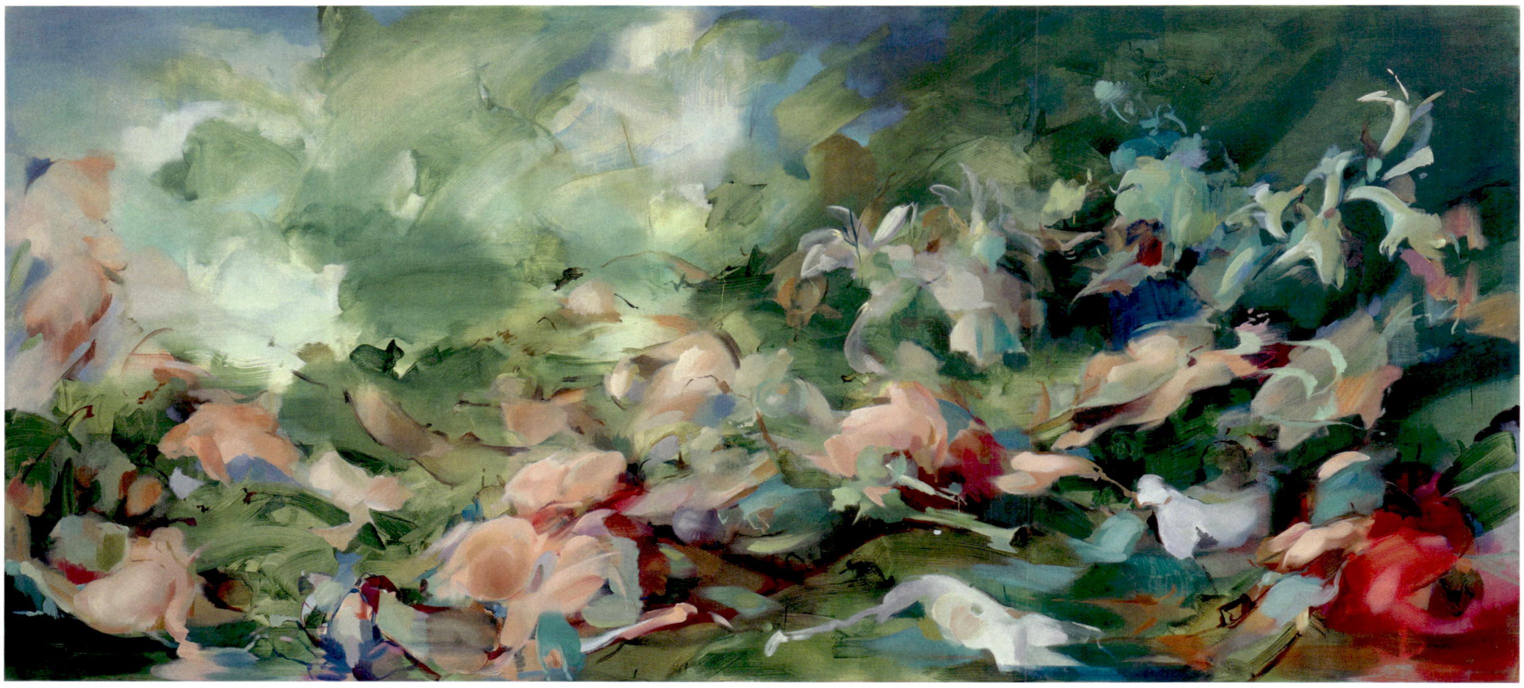

SEEING PINK ELEPHANTS
2025. Oil on linen, 82½ × 179 in. (209.5 × 454.6 cm)

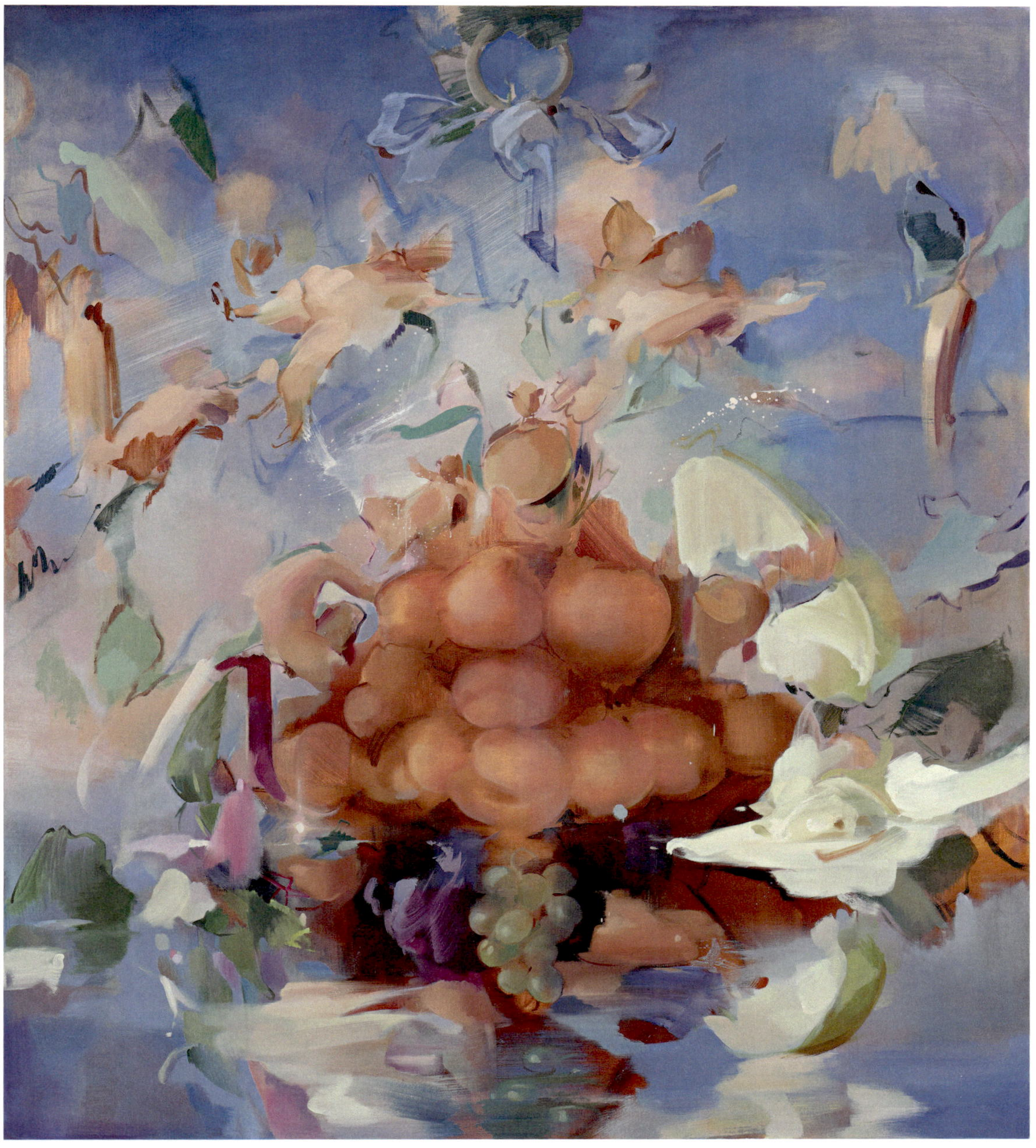

TRIFLE
2025. Oil on linen, 79 × 69 in. (200.6 × 175.2 cm)

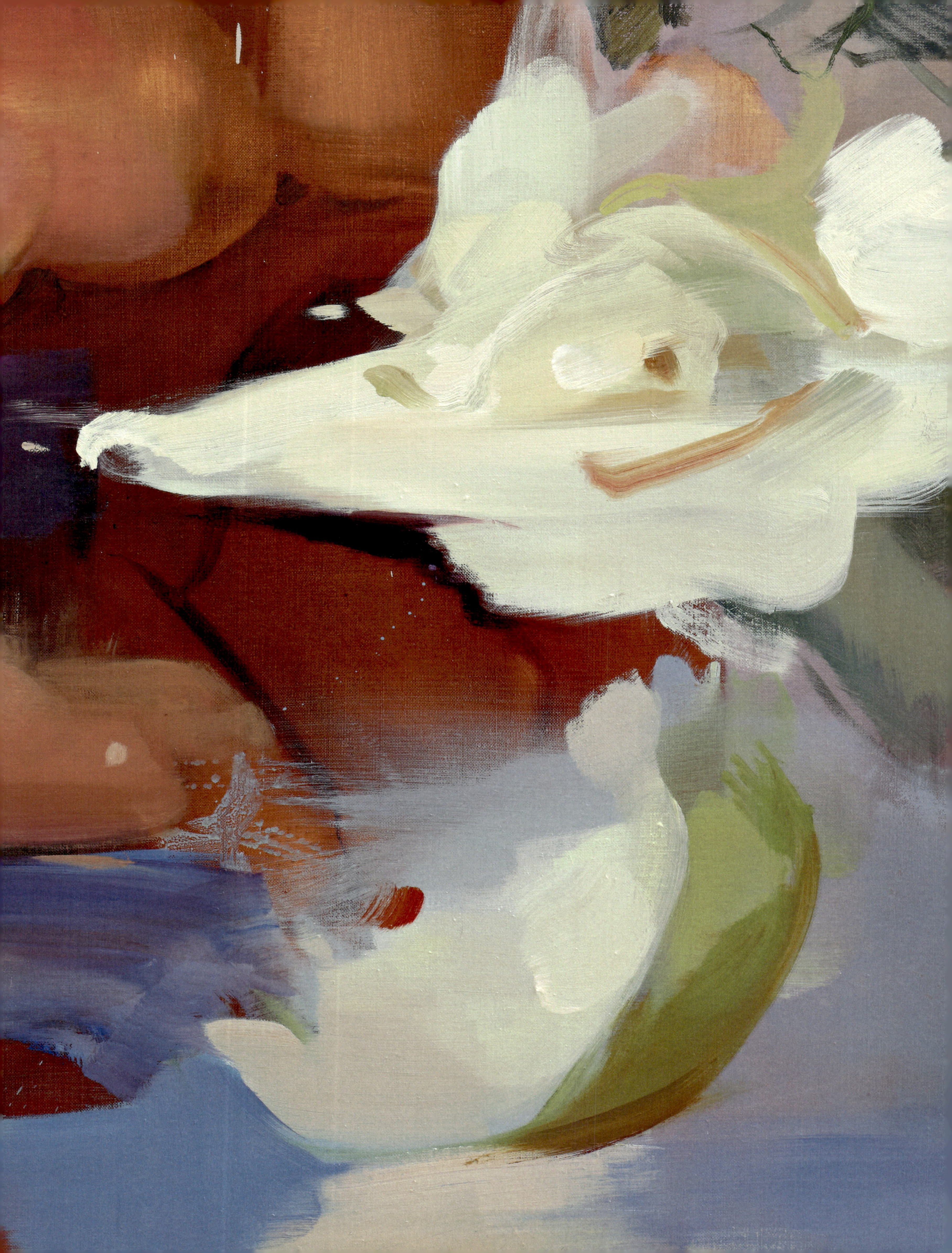

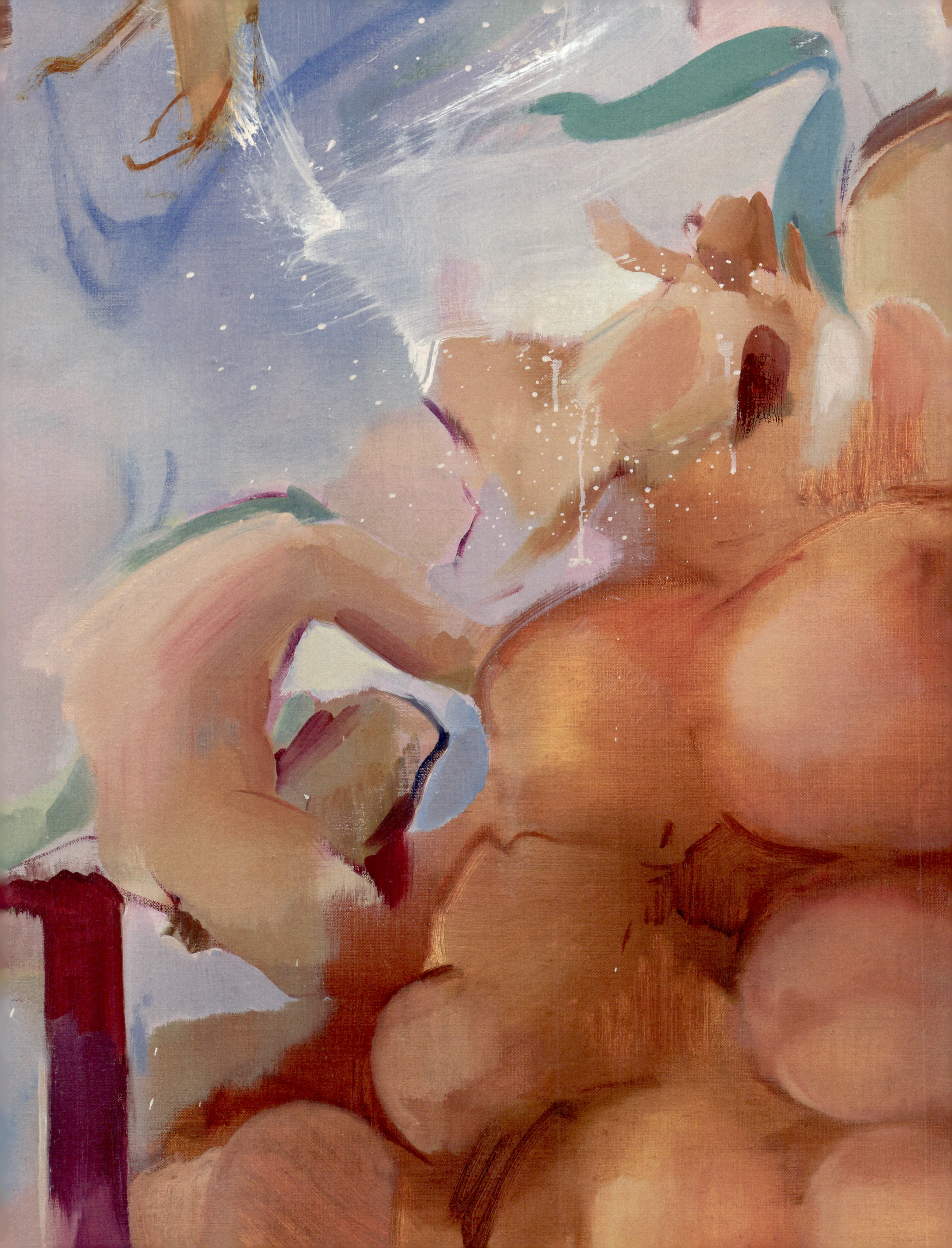

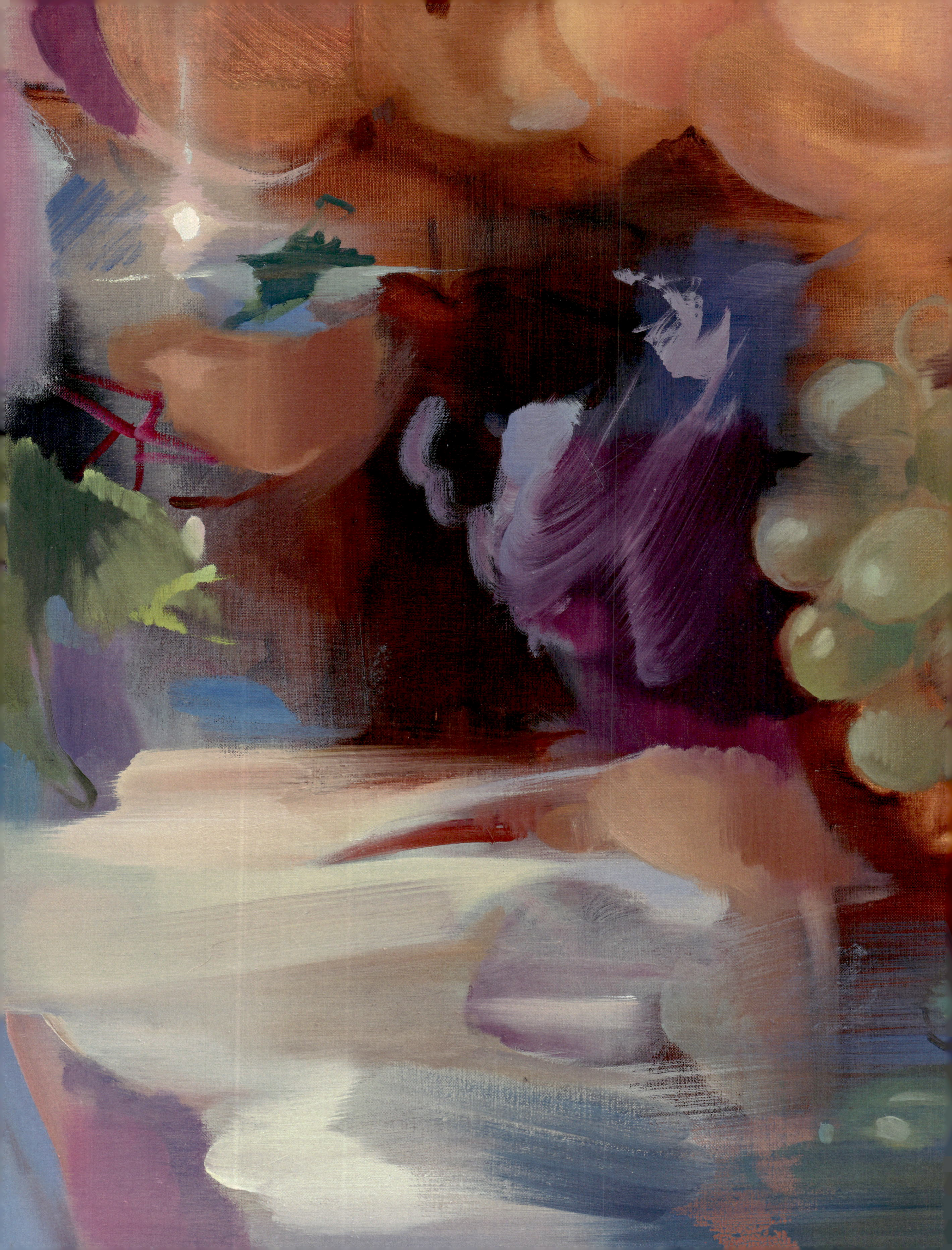

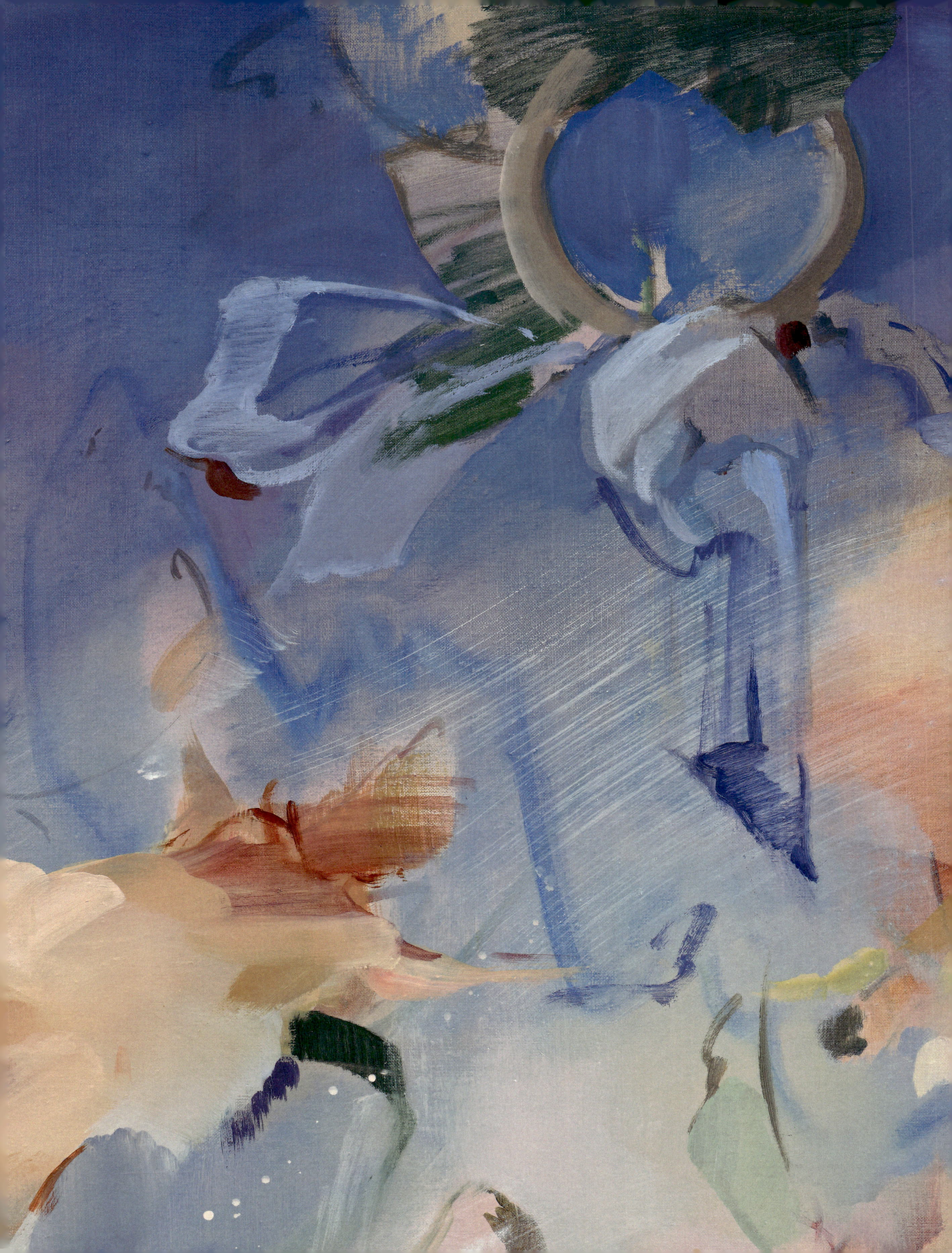

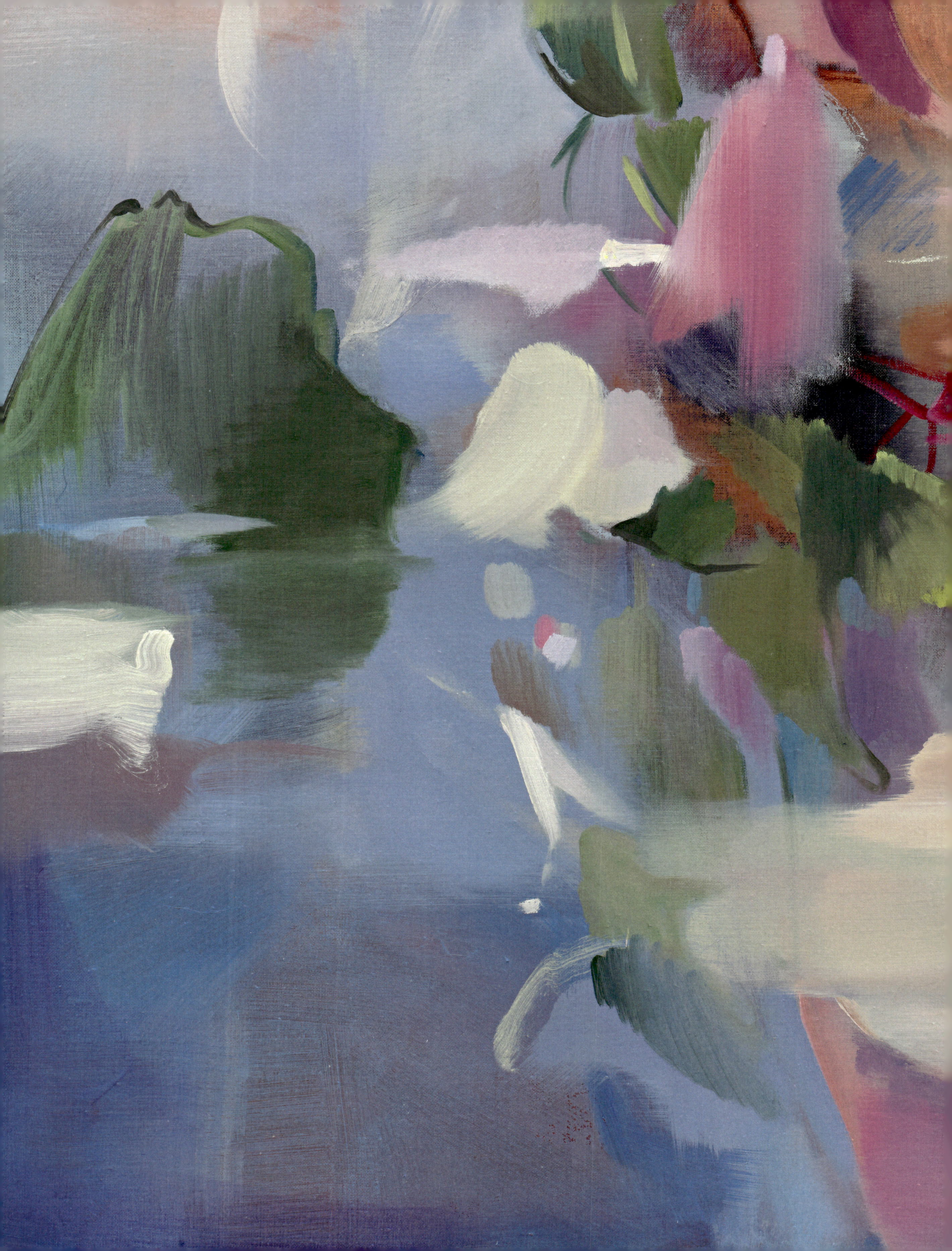

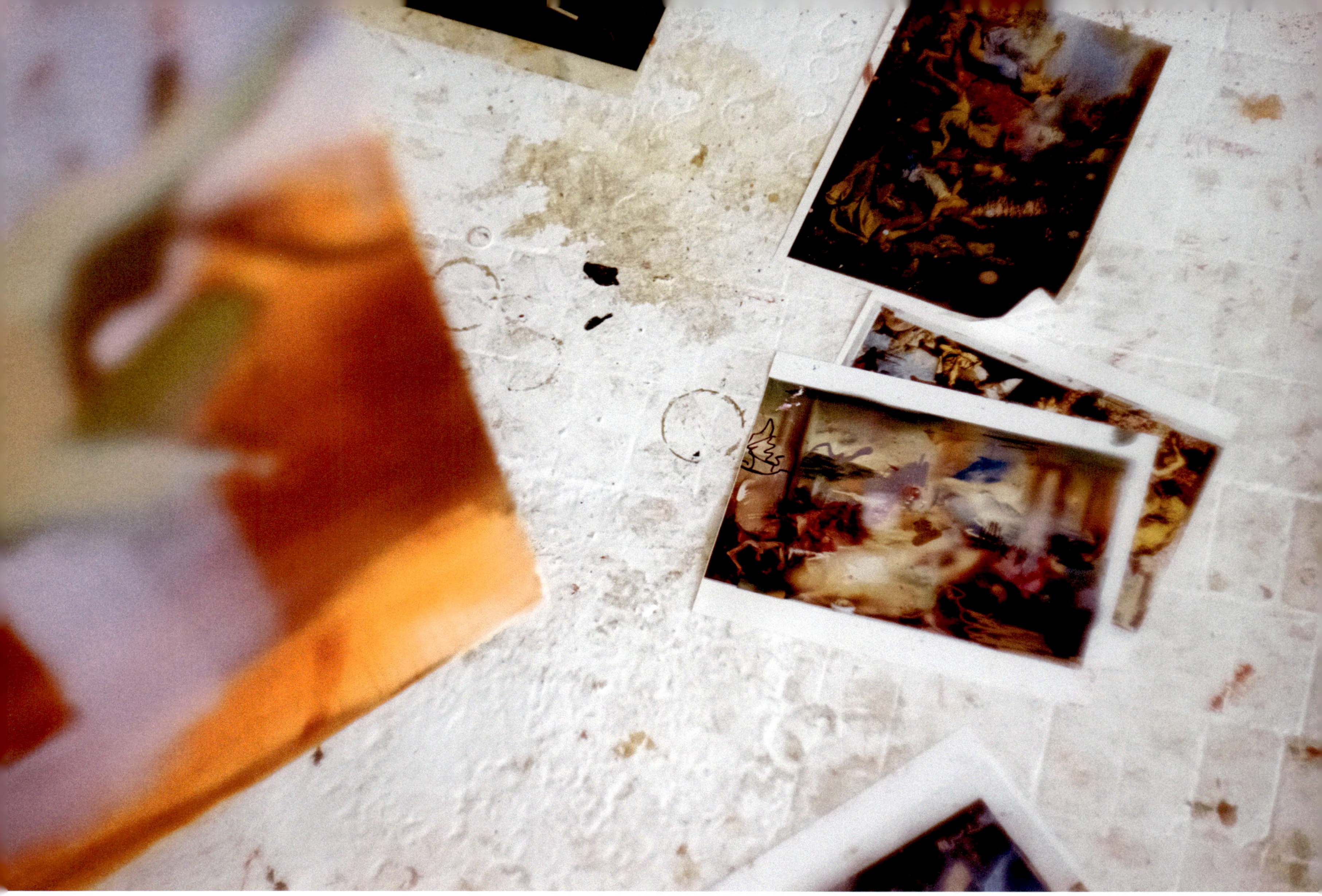

I work between painting and digital collaging. The collage is a guide for structuring paintings and getting a sense of space. Sometimes it is an off-canvas medium to experiment with meaning and help reshape the composition around another piece of imagery. Painting is so intuitive and sensory, it's all about color and speed and wetness. It's helpful to compartmentalize the process. Digital collaging gives me room to think about the "what" (which imagery, which specific references) as opposed to the "how." Thinking through ideas with images and collage feels useful, partly because painting is so difficult. It helps me develop ideas more playfully, then there's less pressure when I'm facing the canvas.

I don't want to know what the works will look like at the end—that's not interesting. I like the way an accidental paint mark might lead to another idea. It might suggest a new shape or motif that could creep in. I like to be surprised by what emerges.

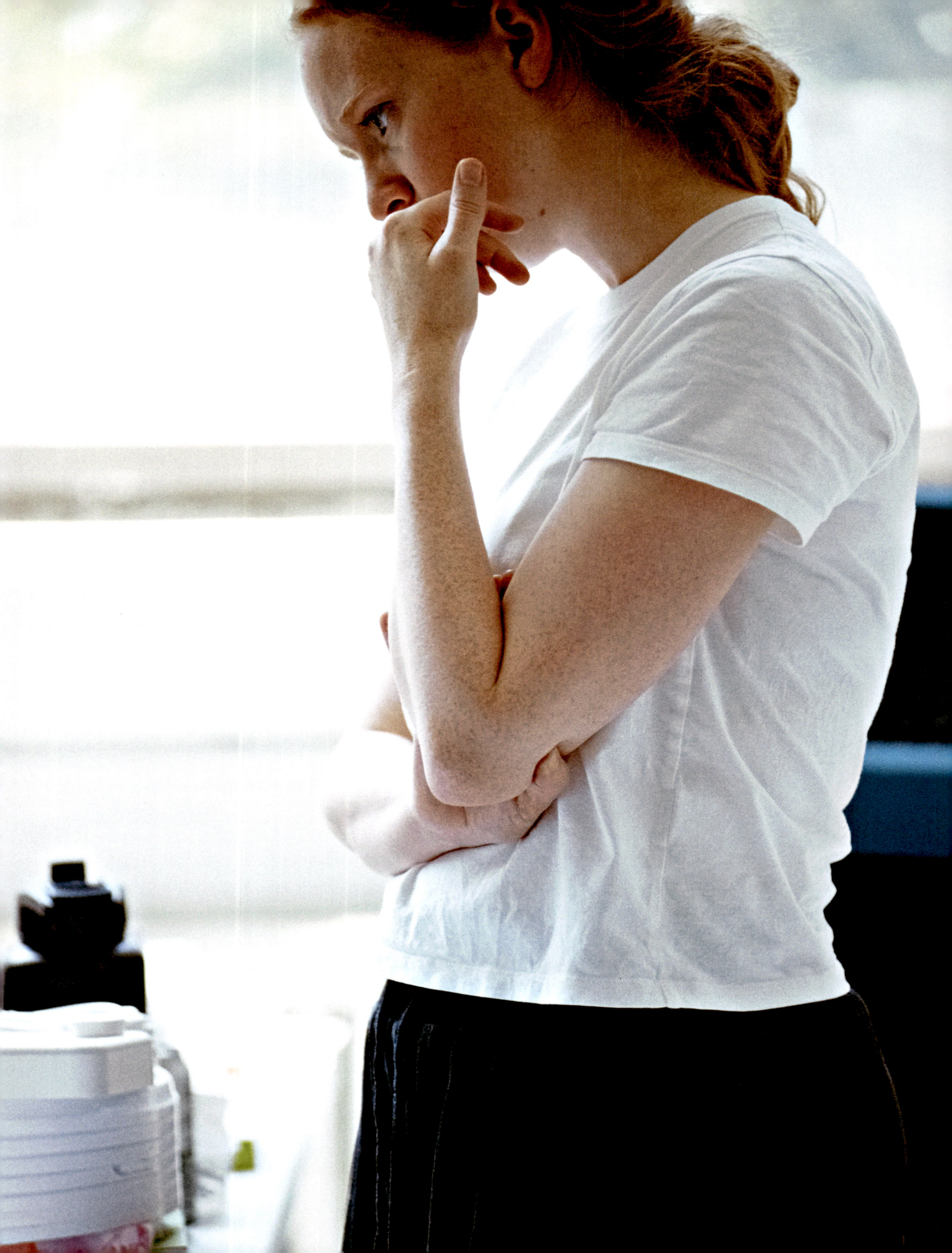

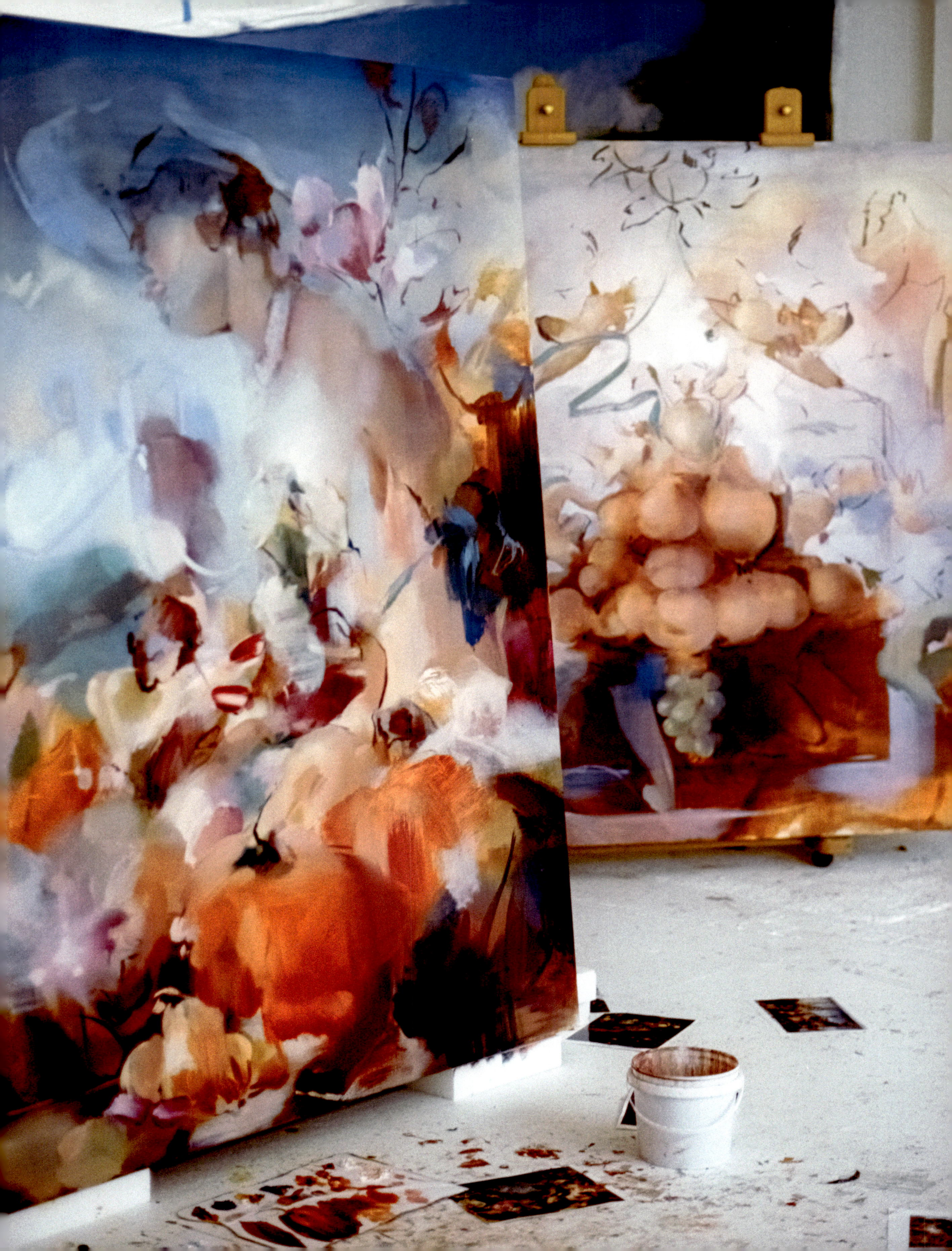

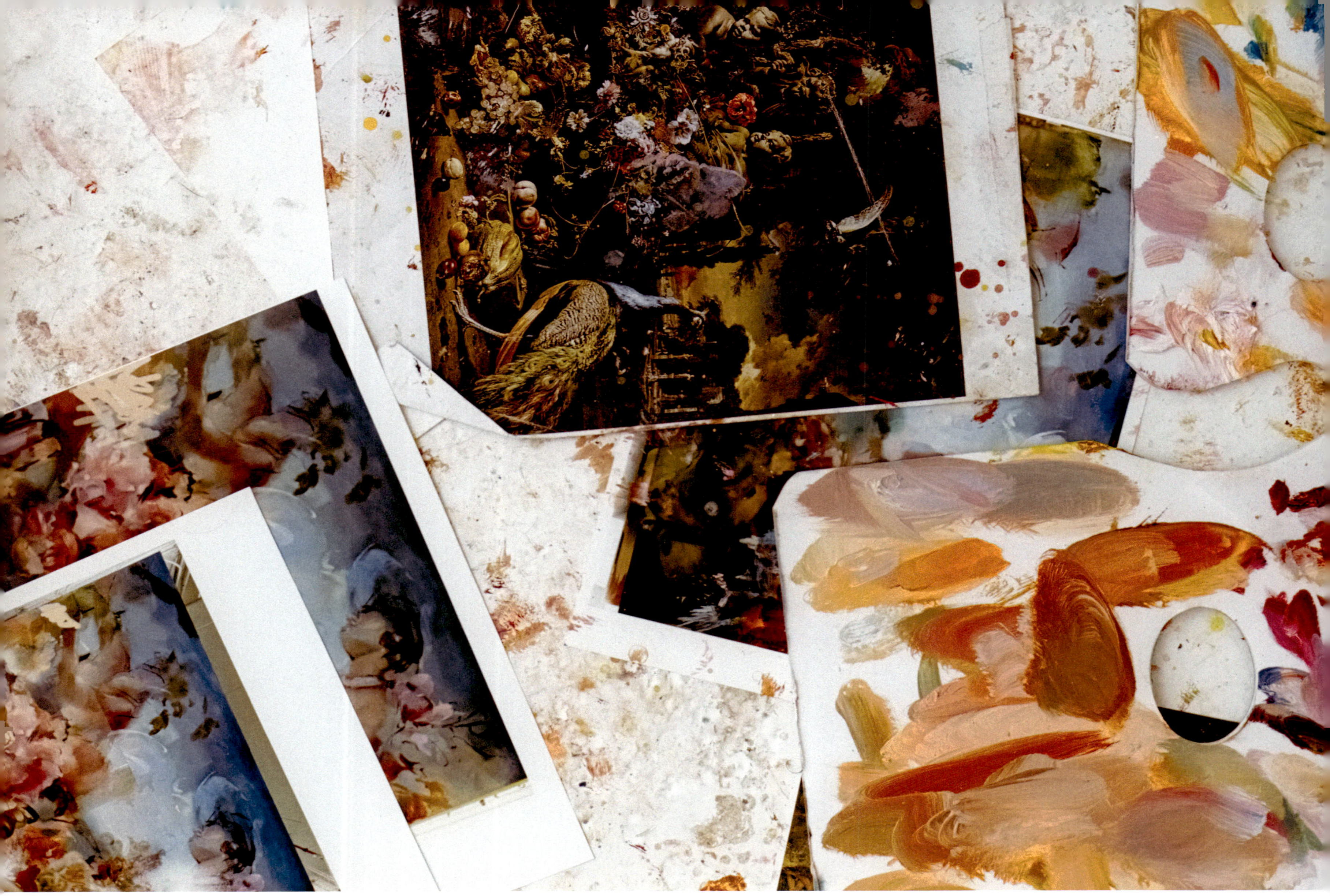

I wanted these paintings to lack a specific focal point where the eye could rest. The images are alluring but fragmented; there is a push and pull between something that is seductive but maybe alienating. These fragments are beautiful in some way, they shimmer—but you cannot quite pin them down. Shiny surfaces felt important, where light does not illuminate, it blinds you. So, too, did fetishized surfaces—things you want to linger on, like objects in a still life painting full of luxurious surfaces and textures.

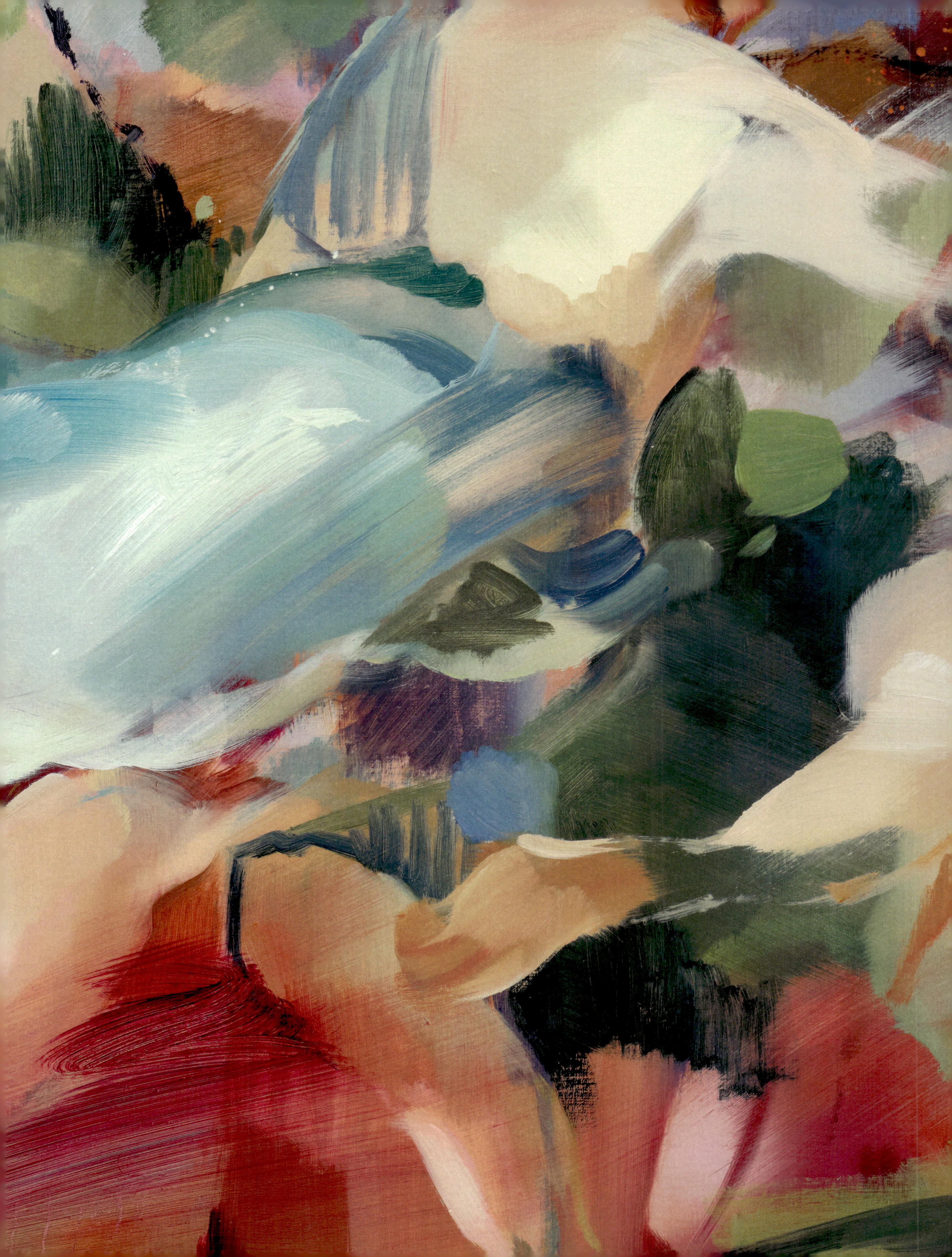

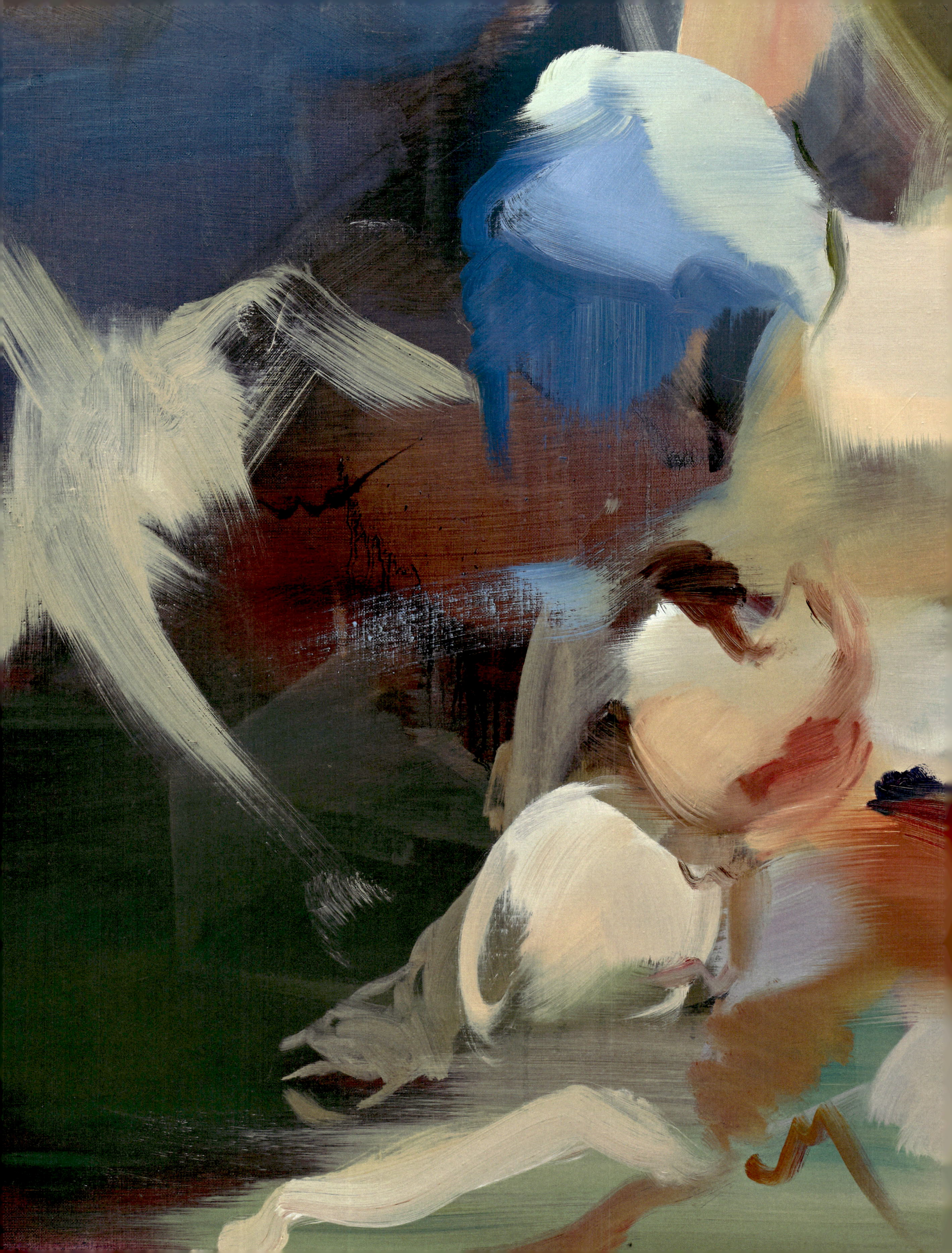

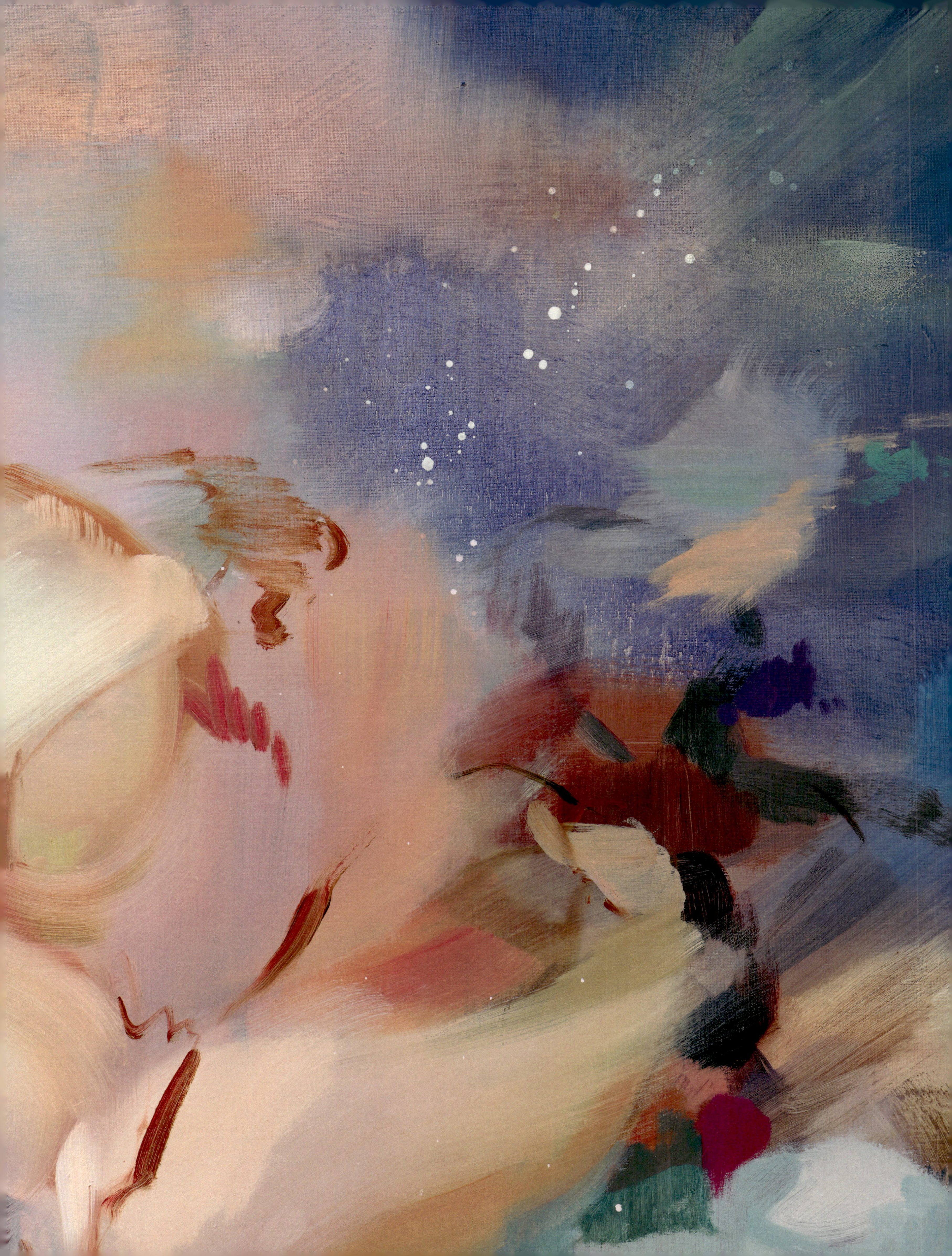

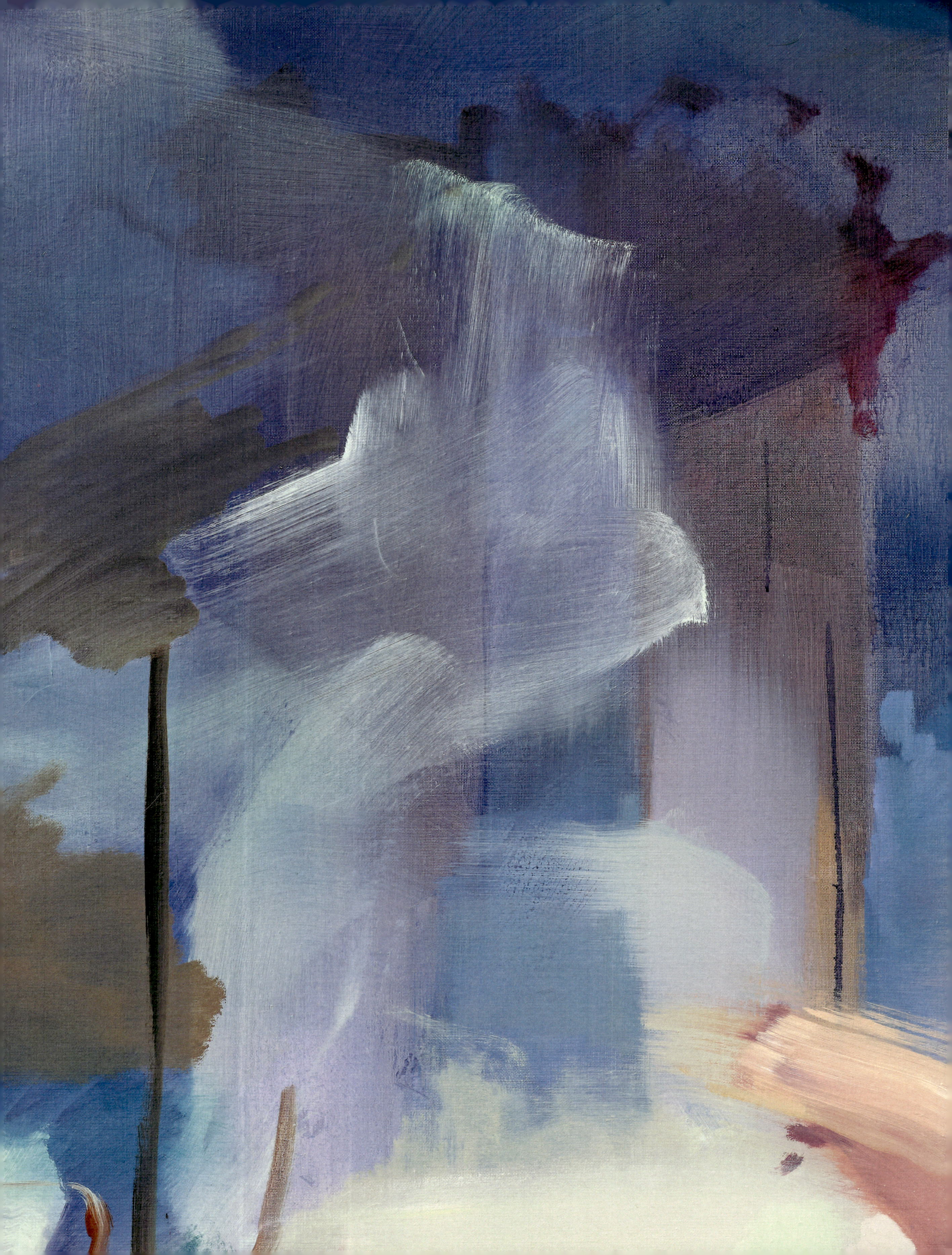

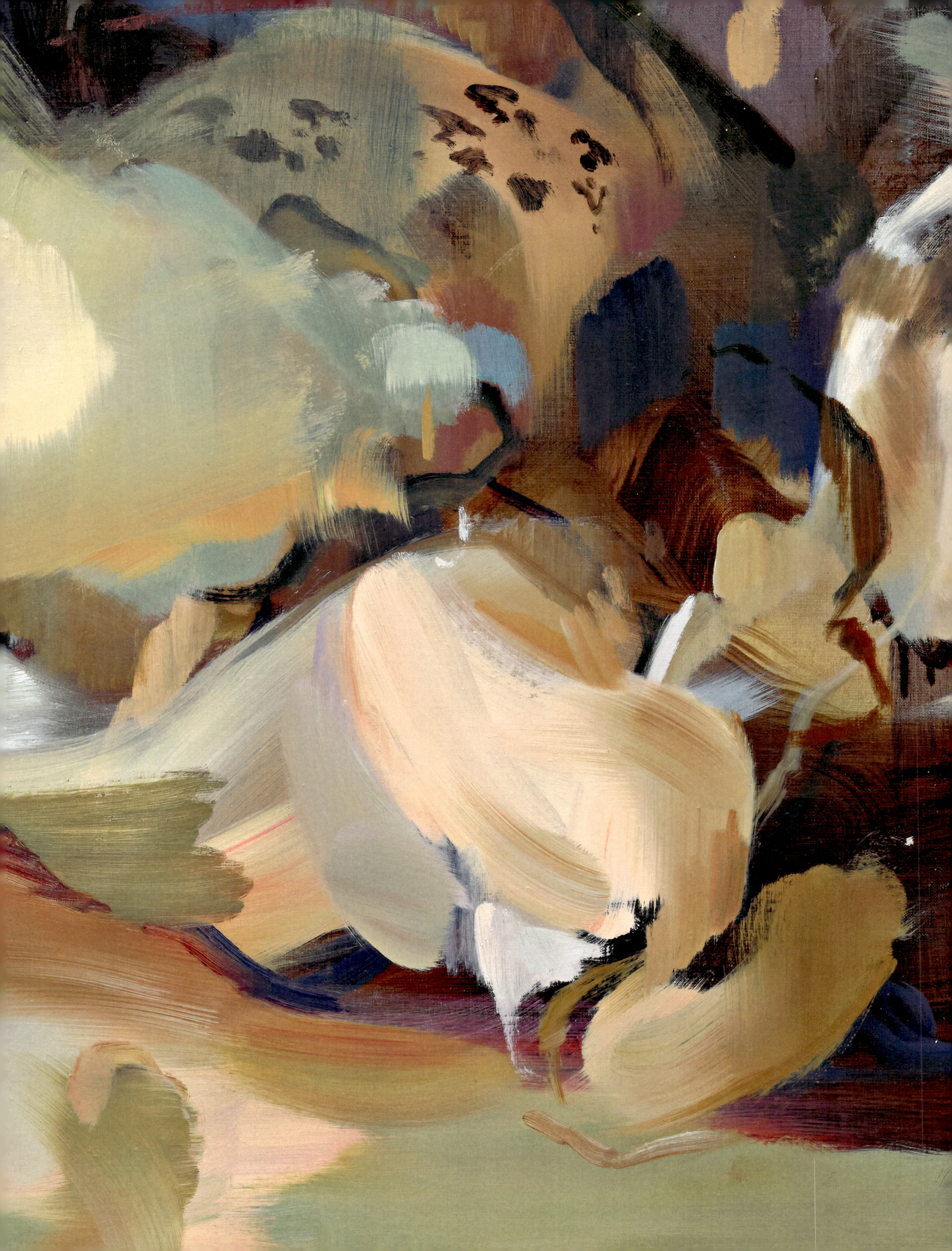

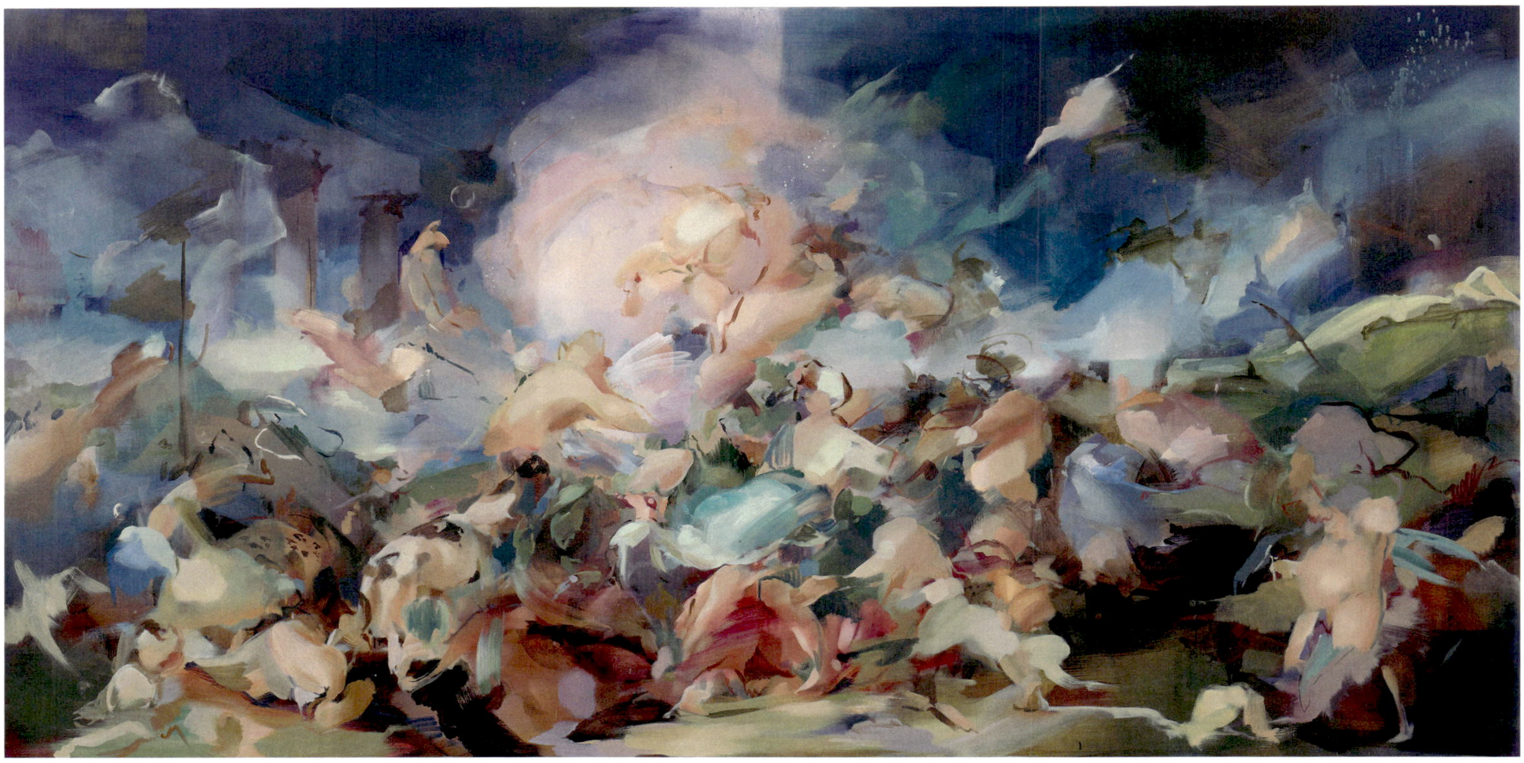

PARTY IN THE U.S.A.
2025. Oil on linen, 83 × 161 in. (210.8 × 408.9 cm)

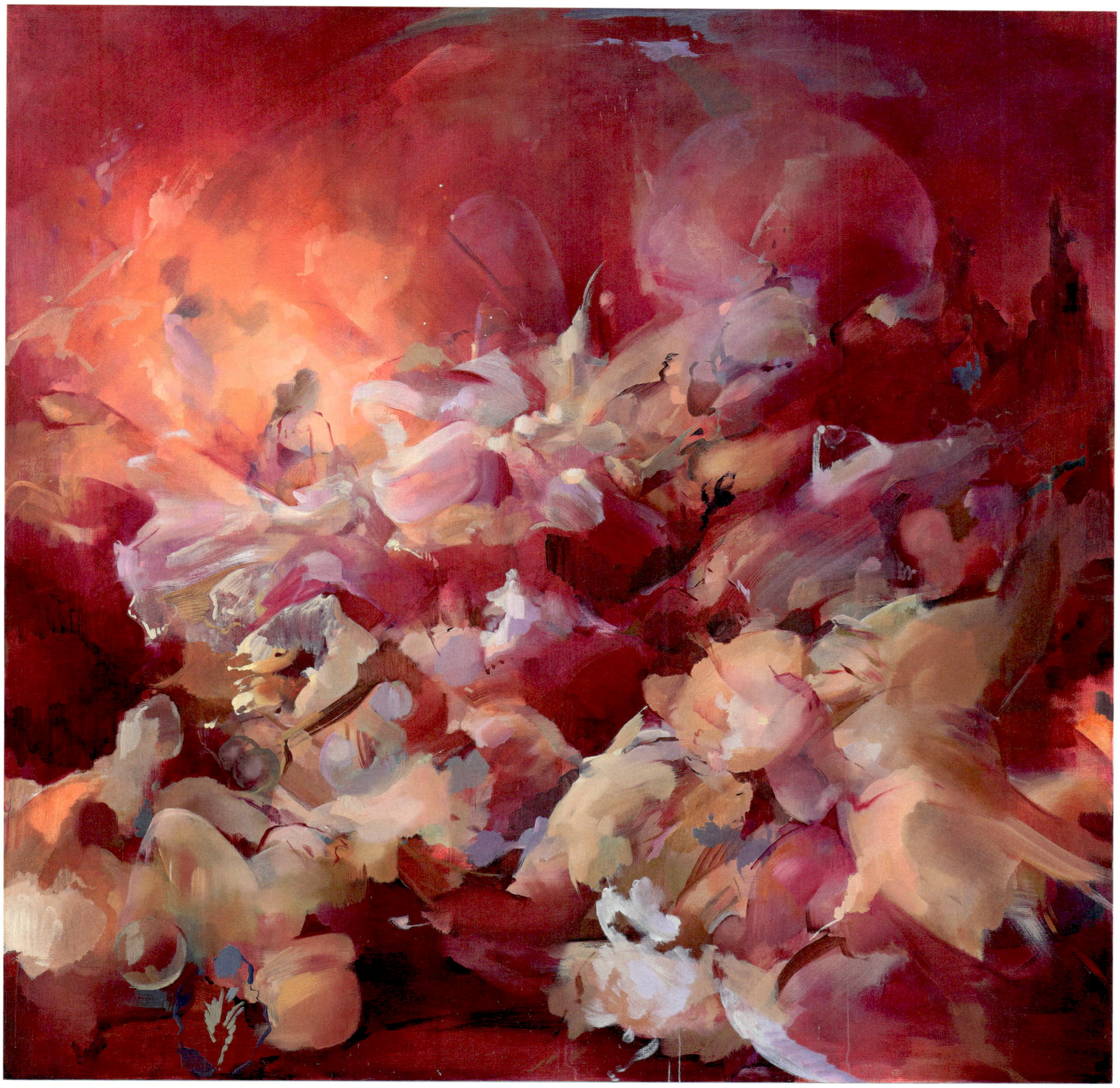

THE LAST DAYS OF DISCO
2025. Oil on linen, 98½ × 98½ in. (250.2 × 250.2 cm)

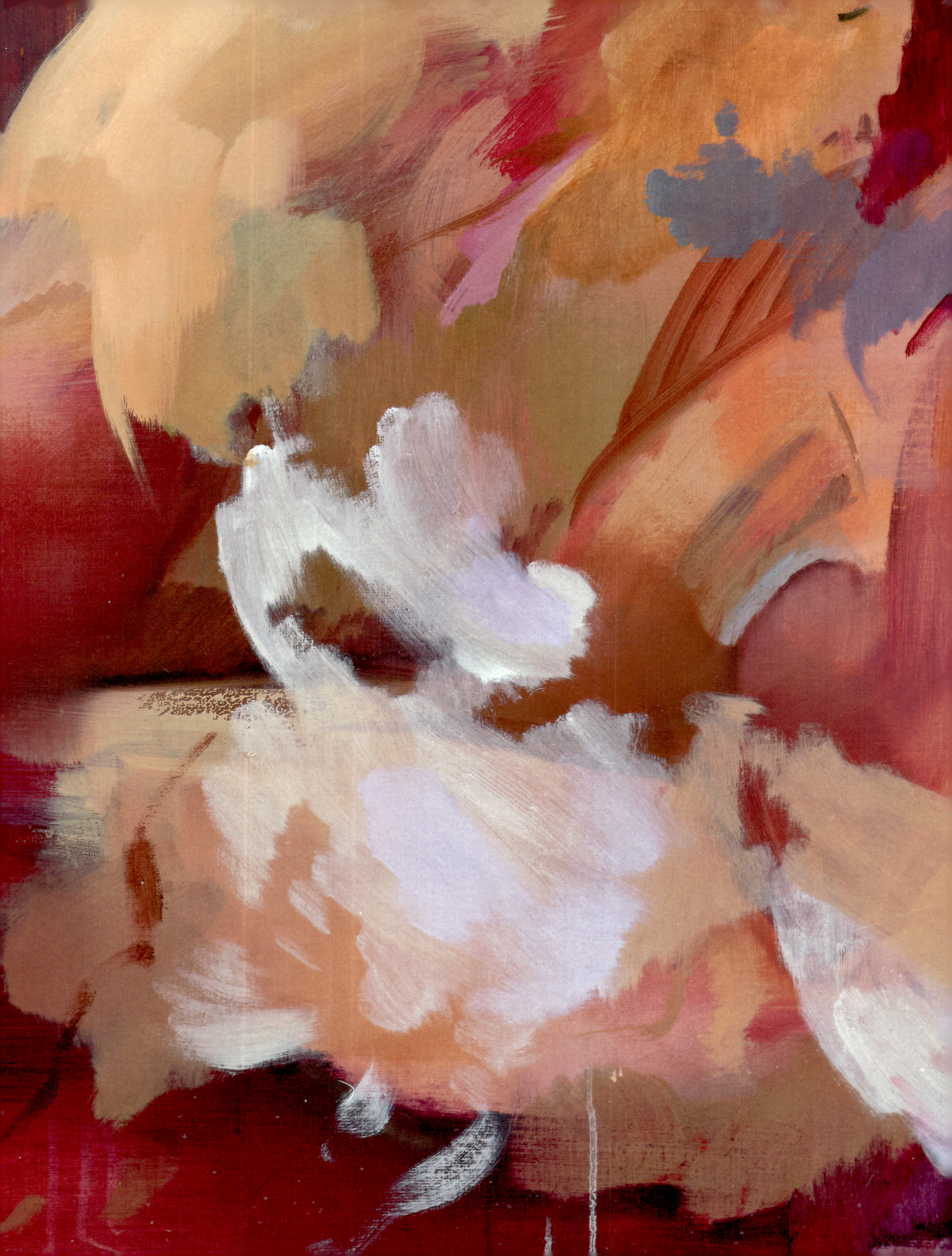

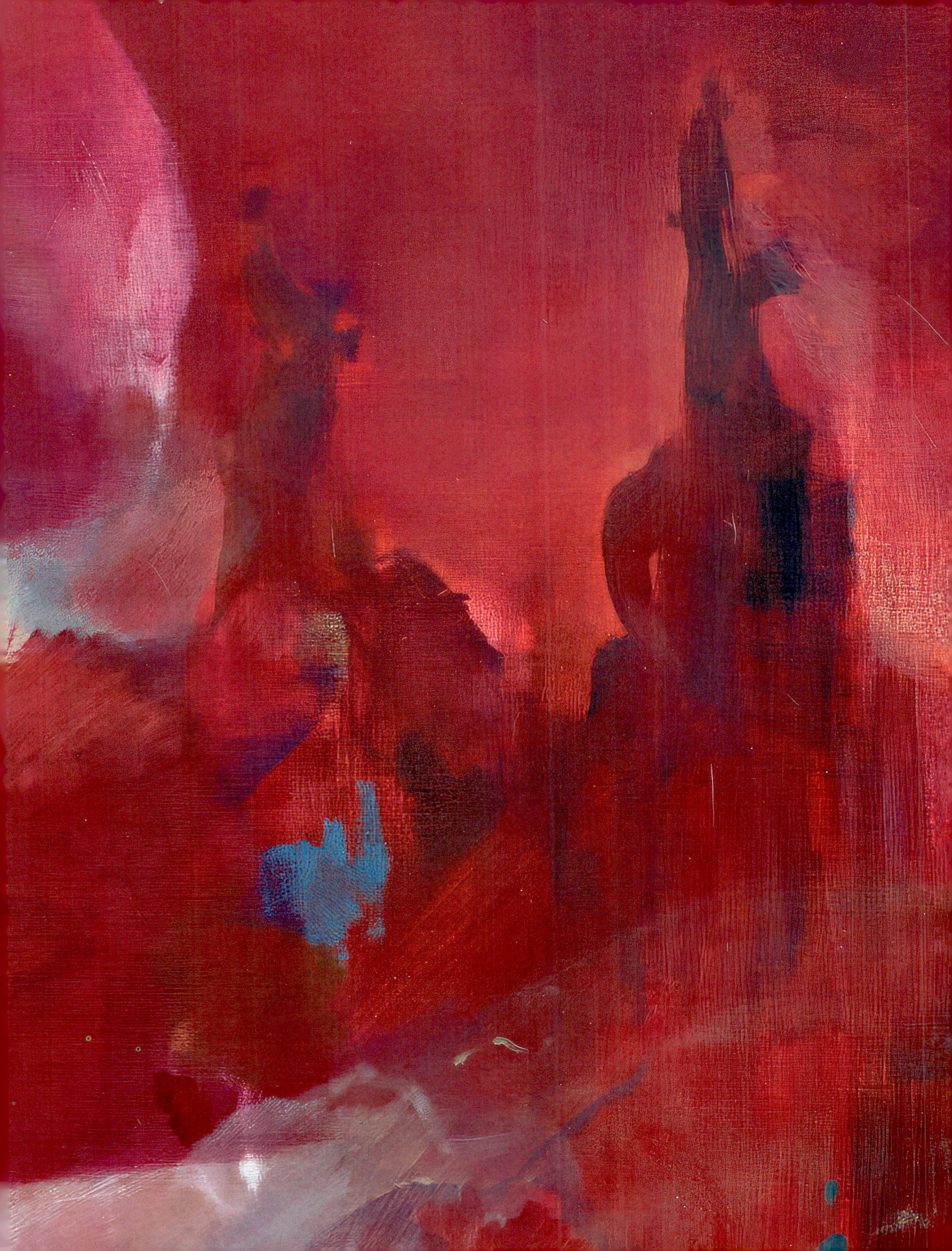

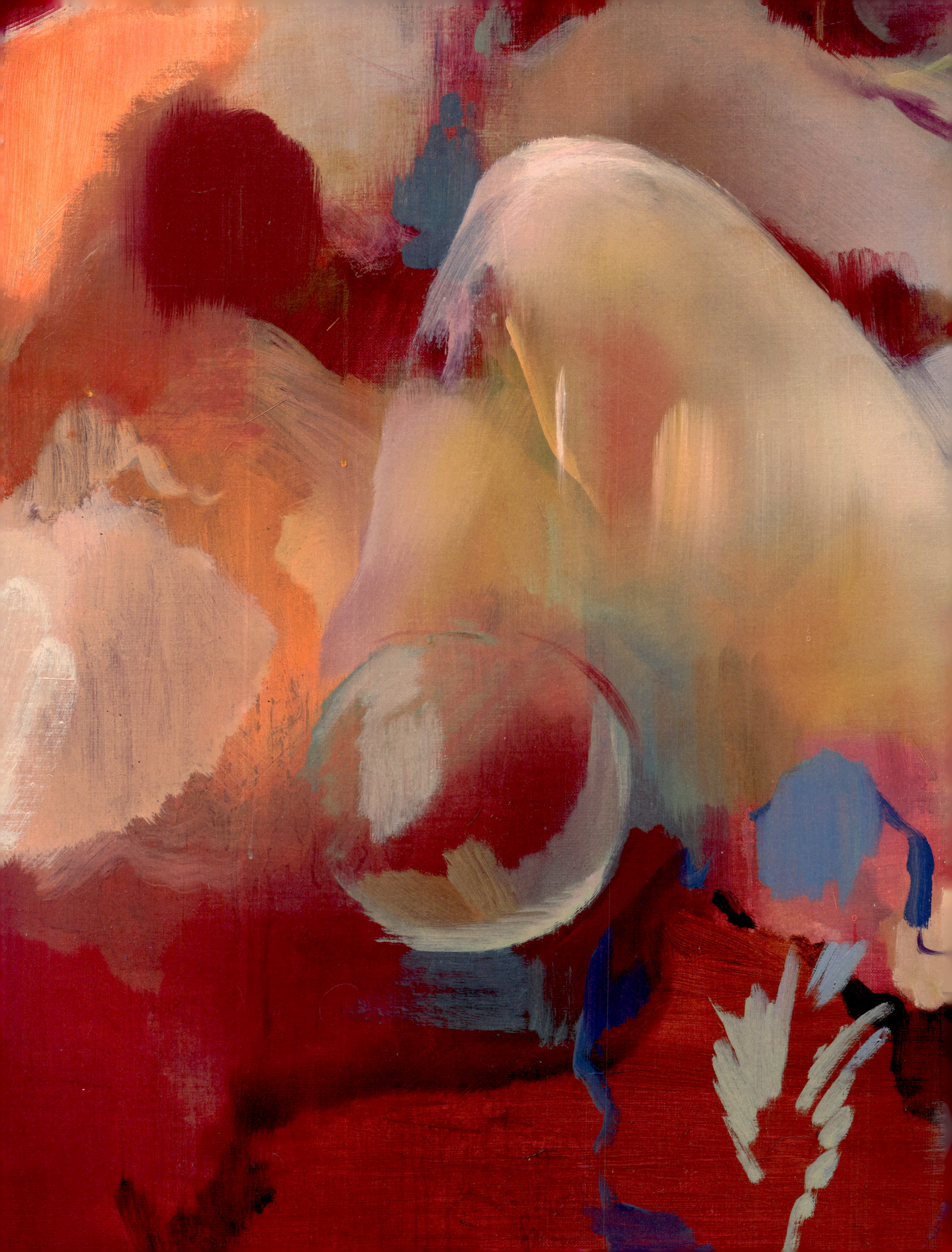

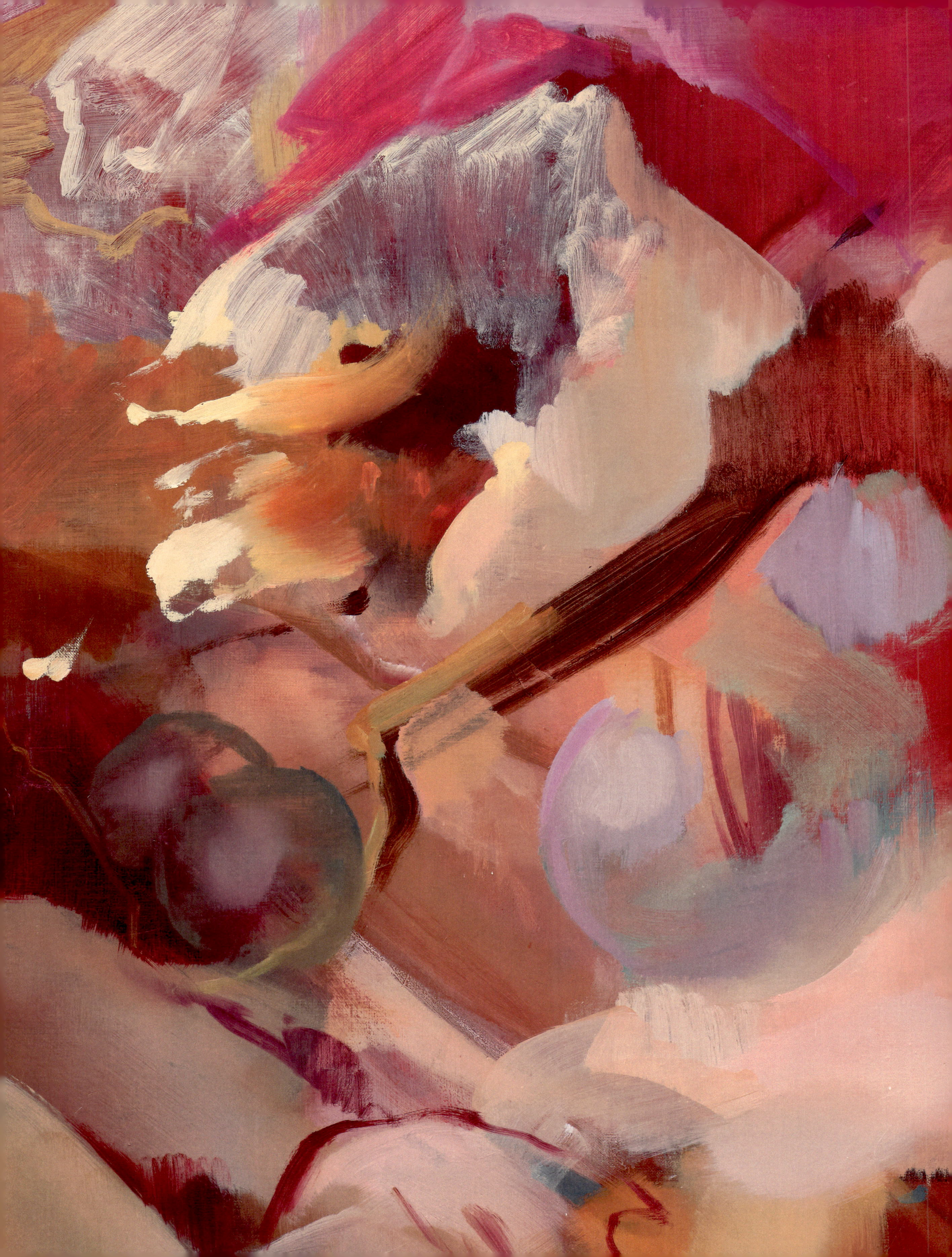

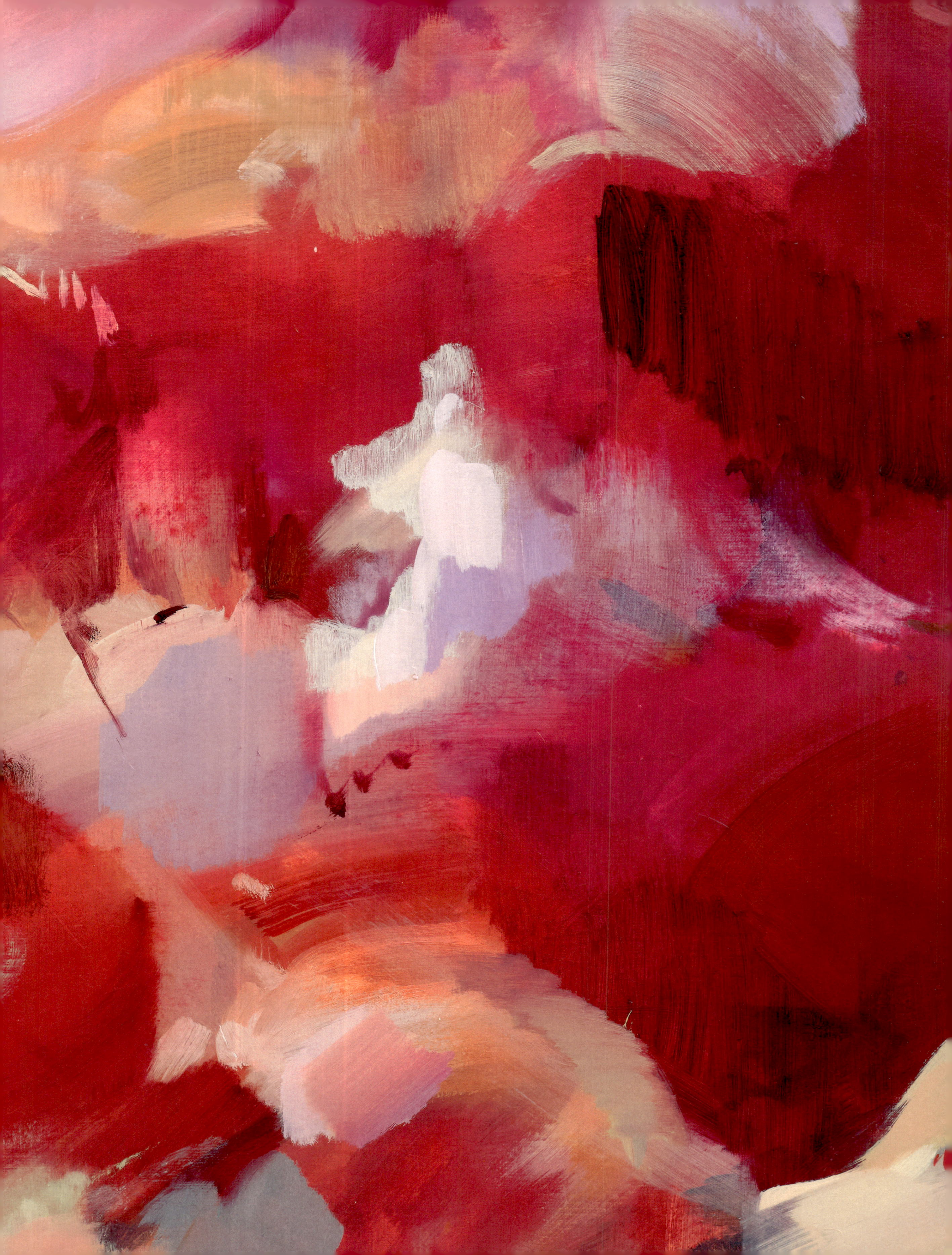

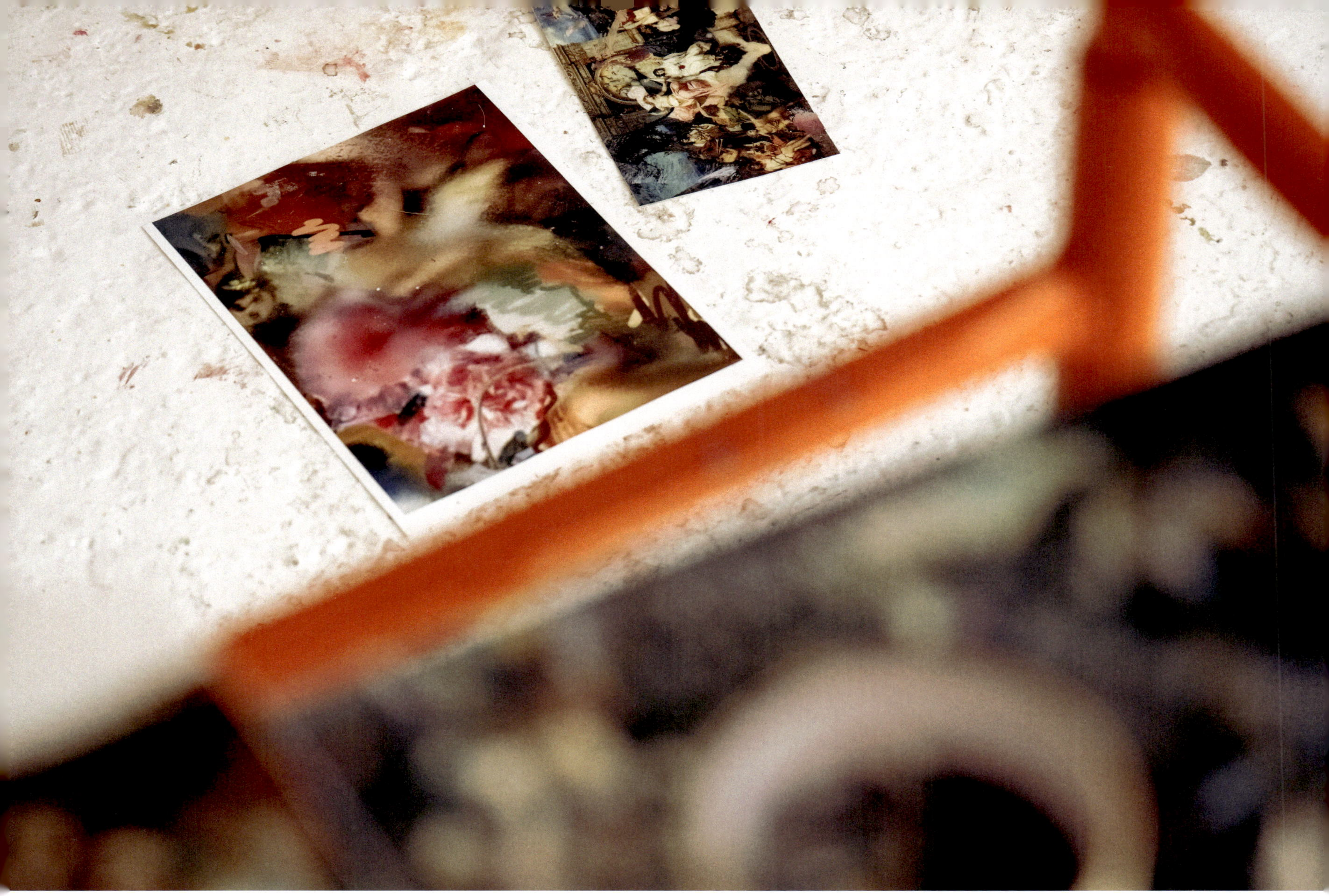

I have been looking at film studio title cards—the fleeting icons at the start of a movie that somehow hold the full weight of cinematic promise. I used the Columbia Pictures logo as a starting point for a painting; the "Torch Lady" dissolved through layering, but the clouds remain. The canvas's aspect ratio is meant to suggest widescreen projection. The "Torch Lady" also gestures toward classicism—her robes, her stance, the plinth. That language of power repeats across history: Roman temples, civic buildings, currency, dictators' homes, Vegas interiors. I'm interested in what happens when repetition drains symbolism—when something meant to signify order begins to feel unhinged. I'd like my paintings to capture that tipping point, layering imagery until structure gives way to excess. Like a bacchanalian unravelling or like a still-life just before the fruit starts to rot.

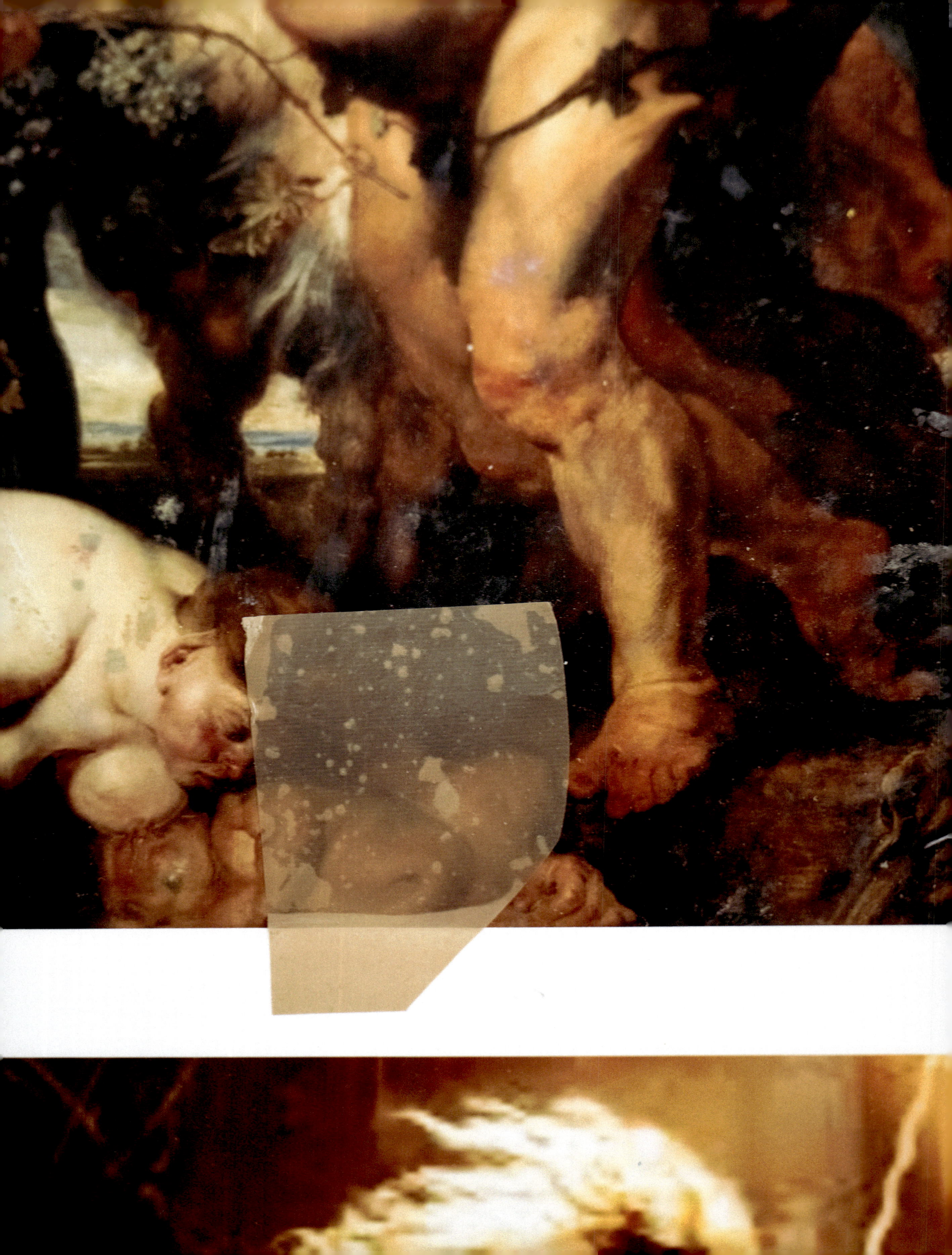

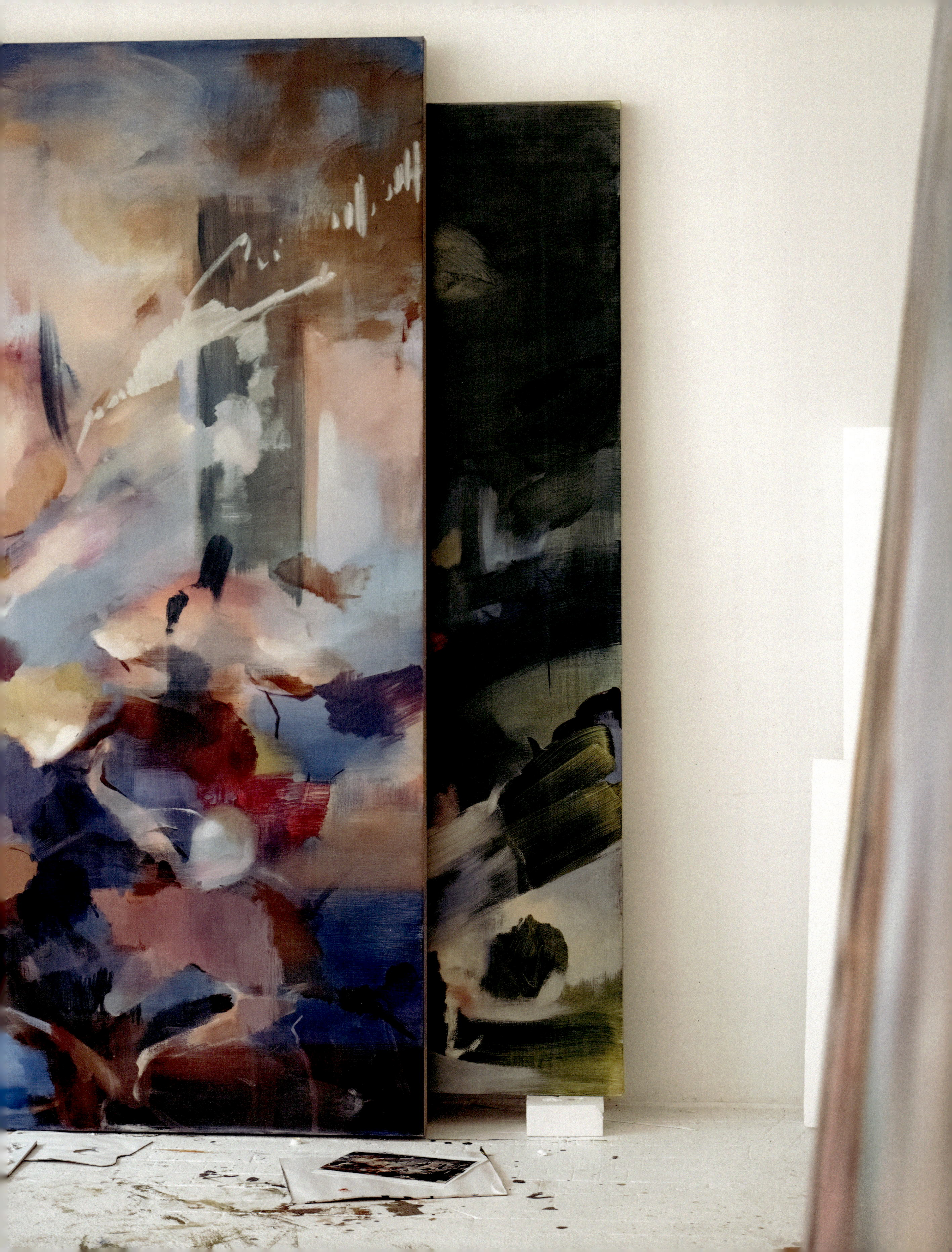

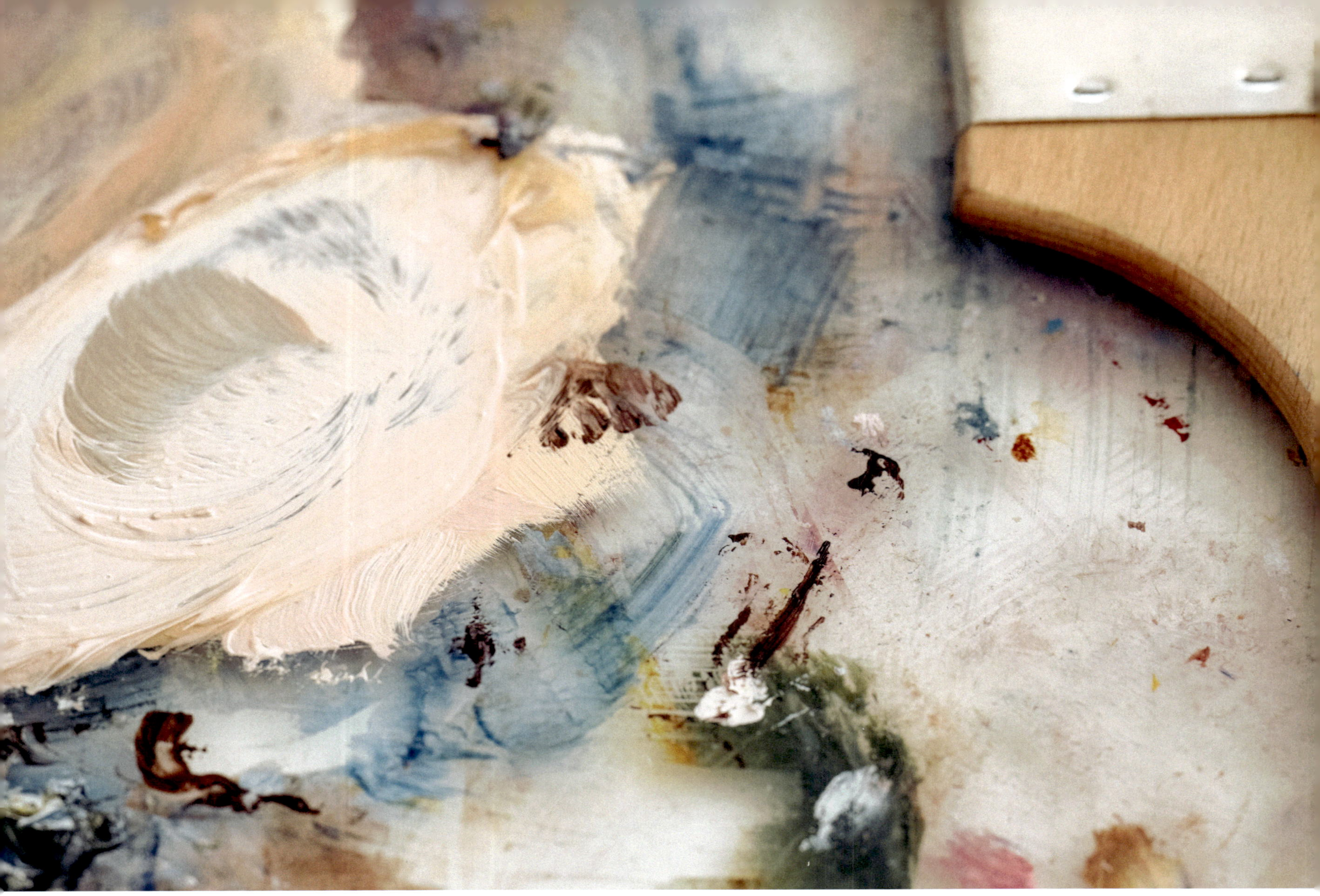

I have been referencing party scenes in films, the beginning of *Babylon* (2022), for instance, or *The Great Beauty* (2013)—I love the way the dance sequence is slowed down to show Jep standing alone amongst the frenzy. It's a sad film in a way—Jep watches the beauty in his life slip through his fingers. It felt like a helpful reference tonally. It is the slight emotional distance of looking through glass. I was also looking at *The Goldwyn Follies* (1938), this little series of vignettes which result in a very big fancy film. It was panned when it came out. It had a huge cast of famous ballet dancers and opera singers, but this star-studded spectacle flopped. It was just too much. Then Disney parodied it with *Fantasia* (1940).

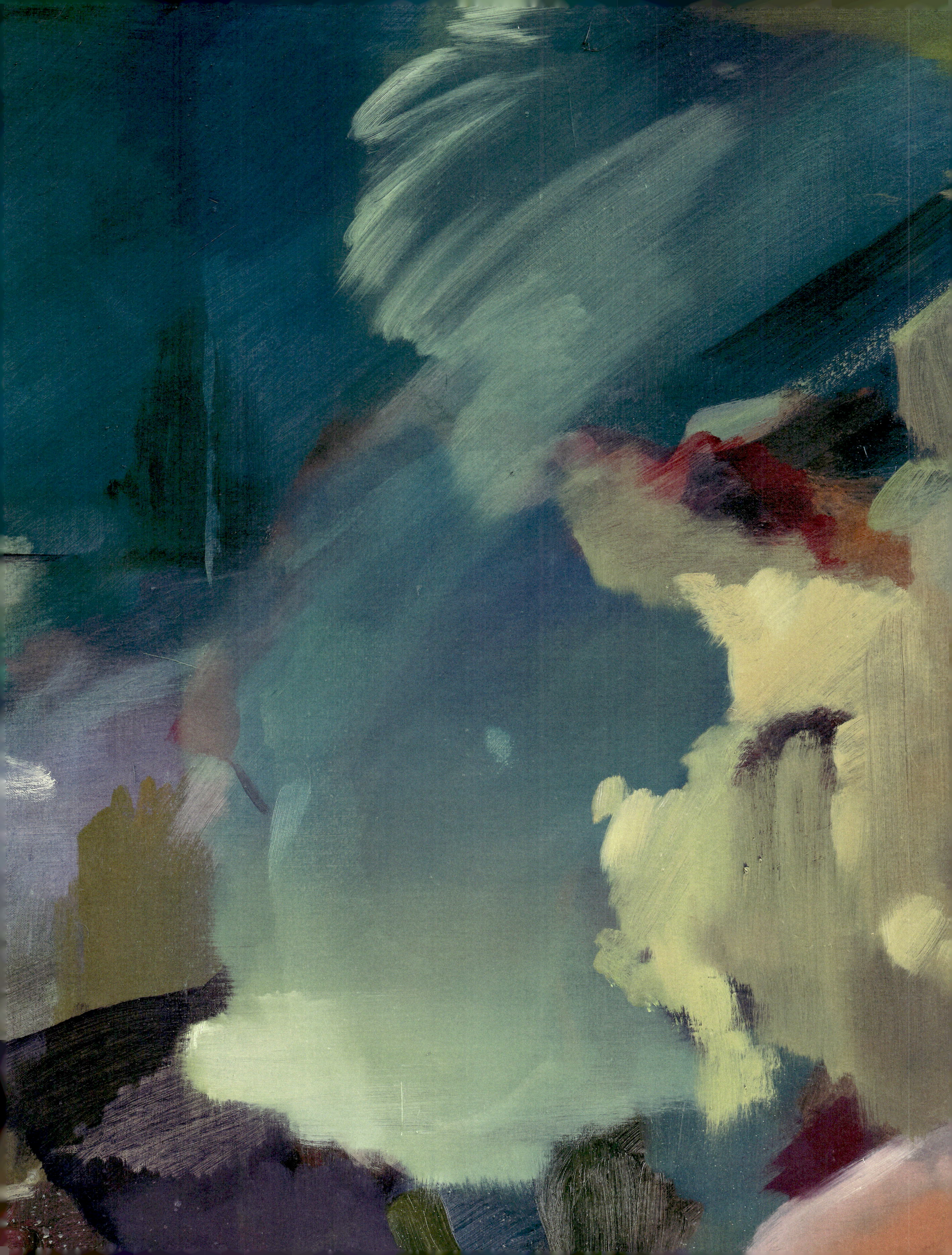

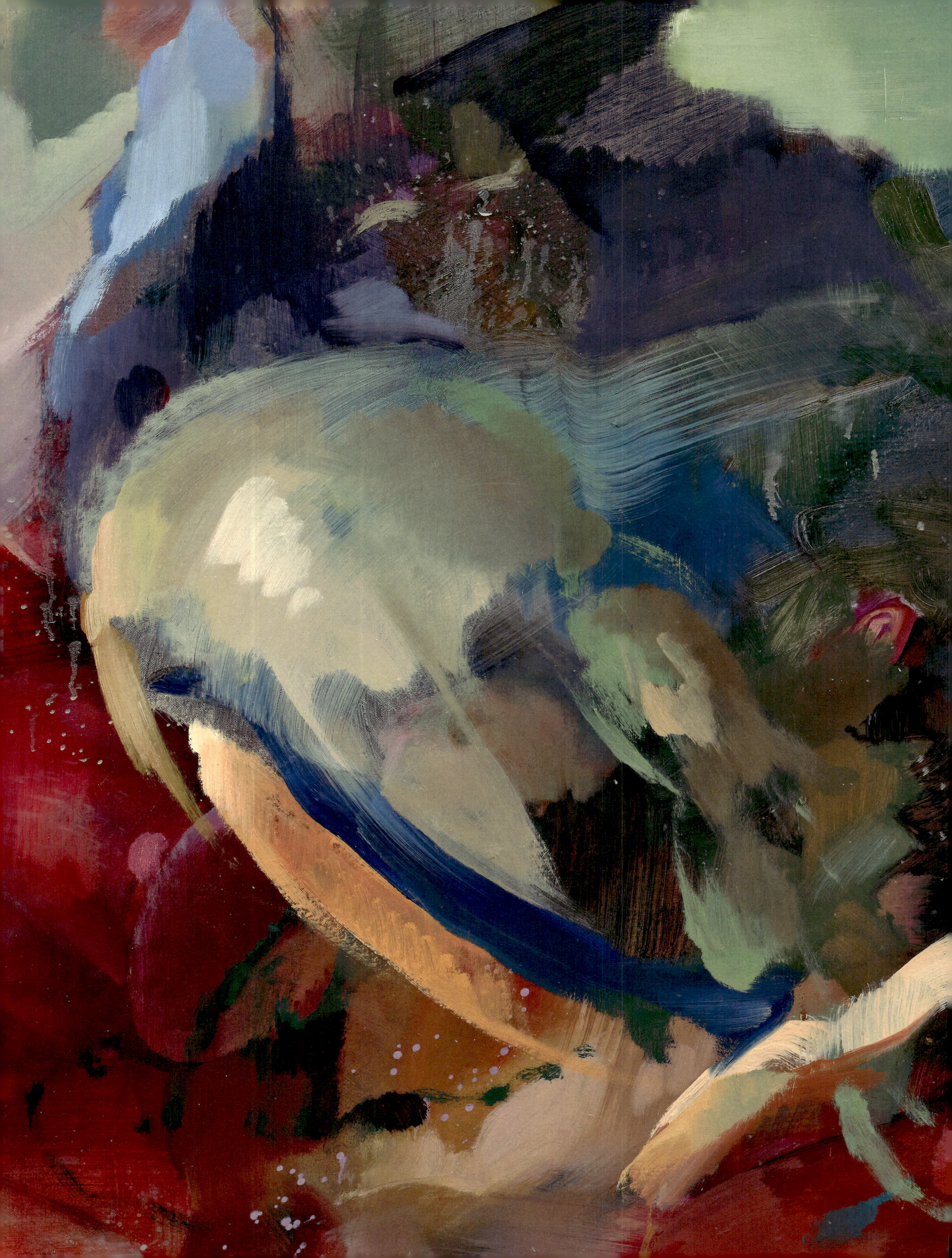

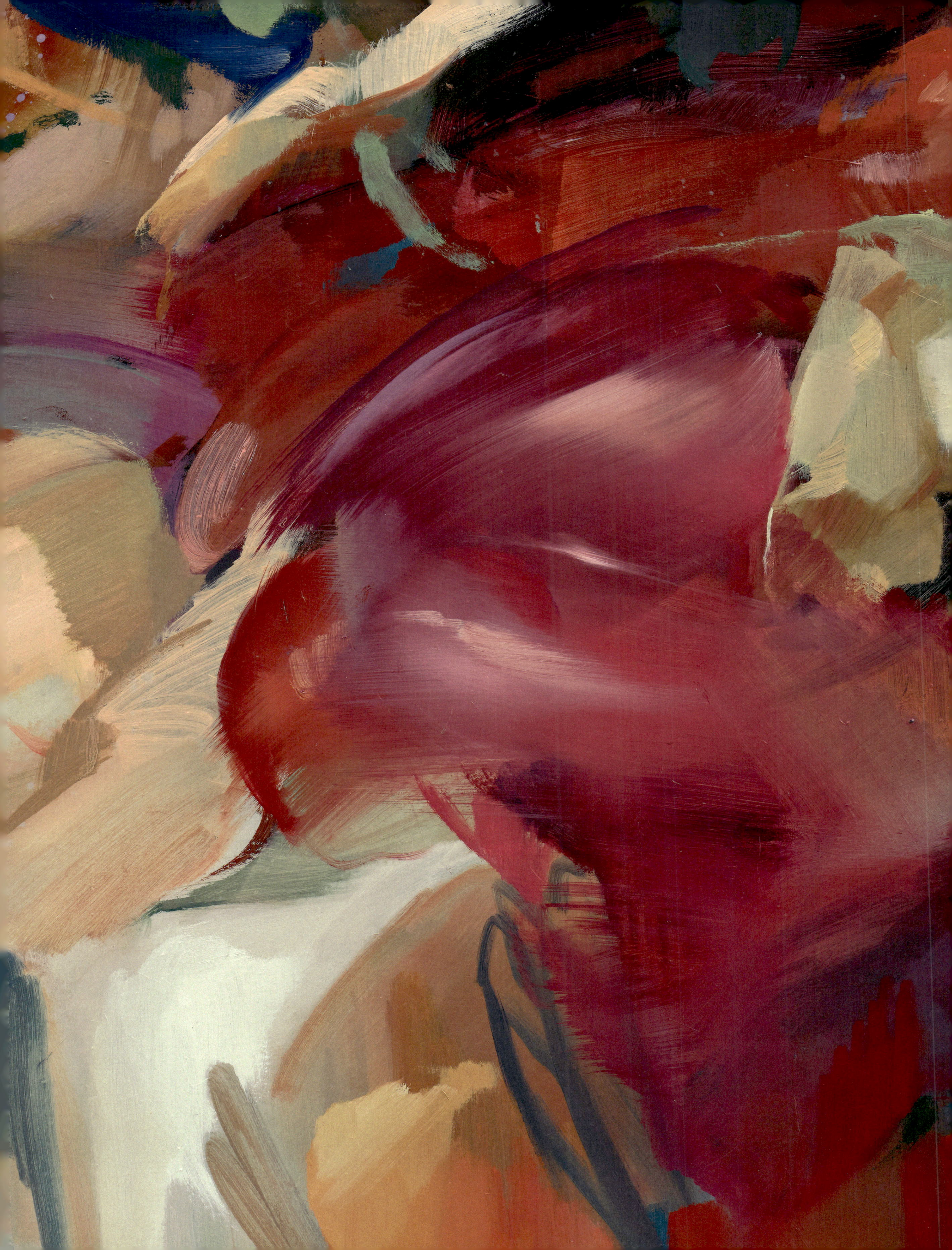

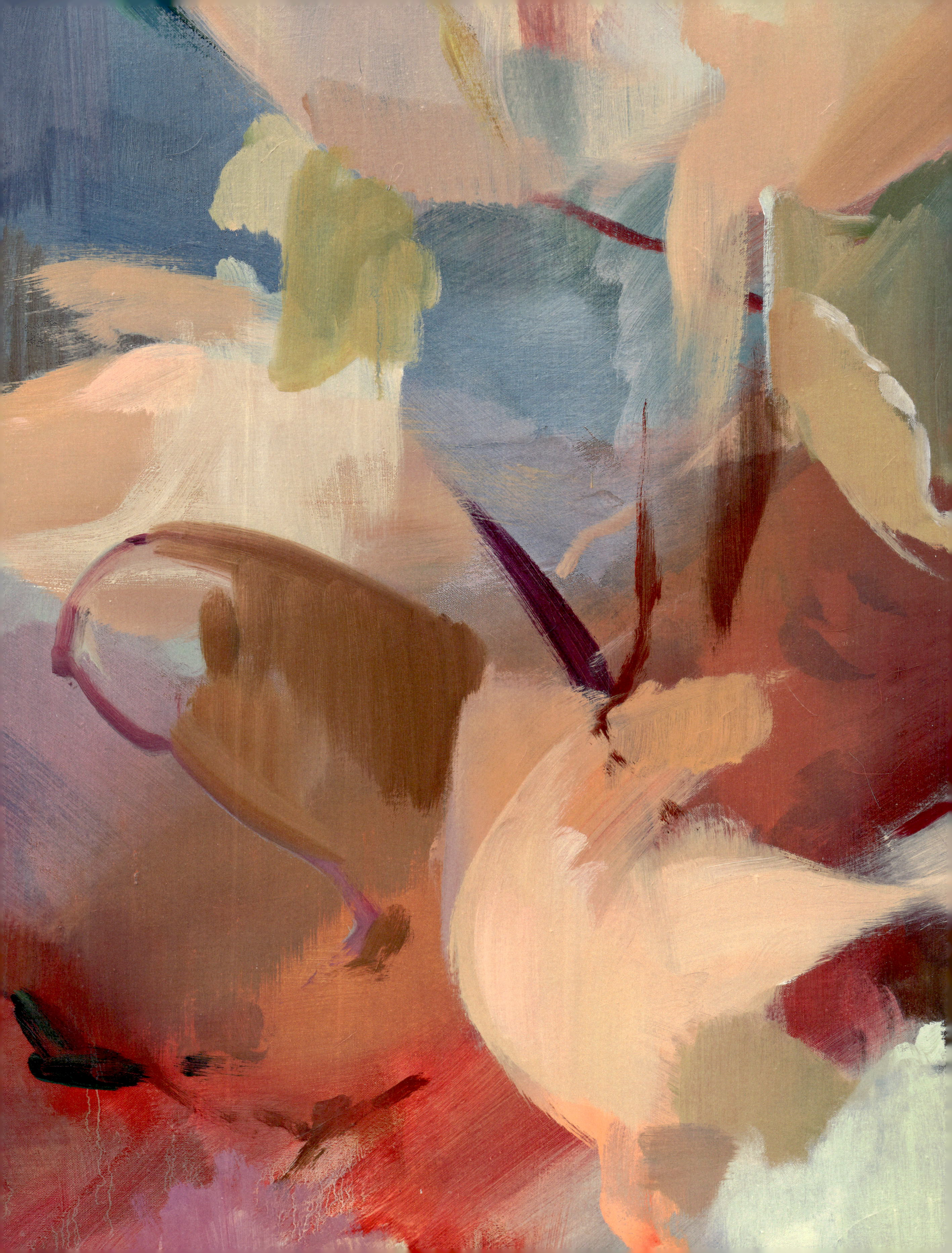

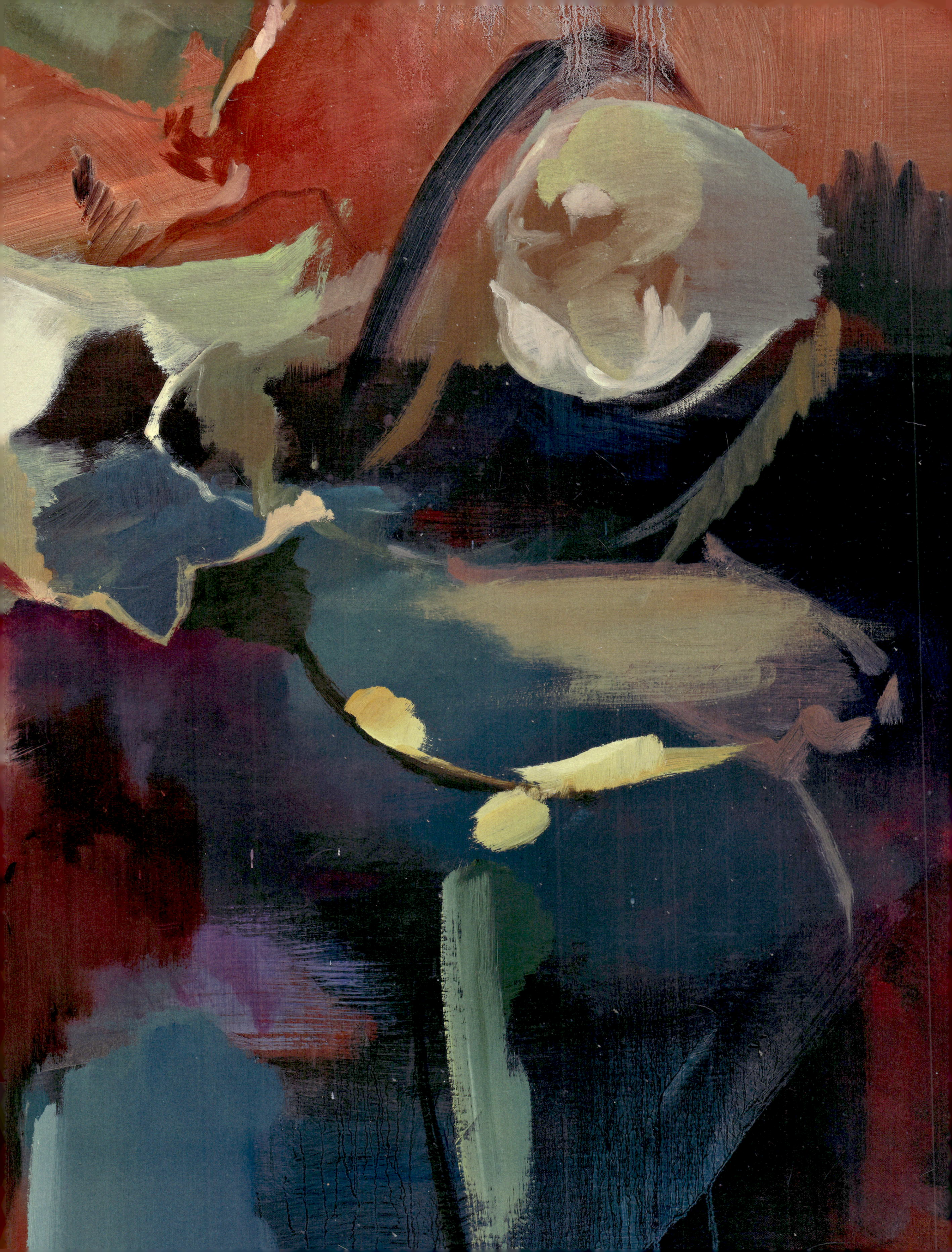

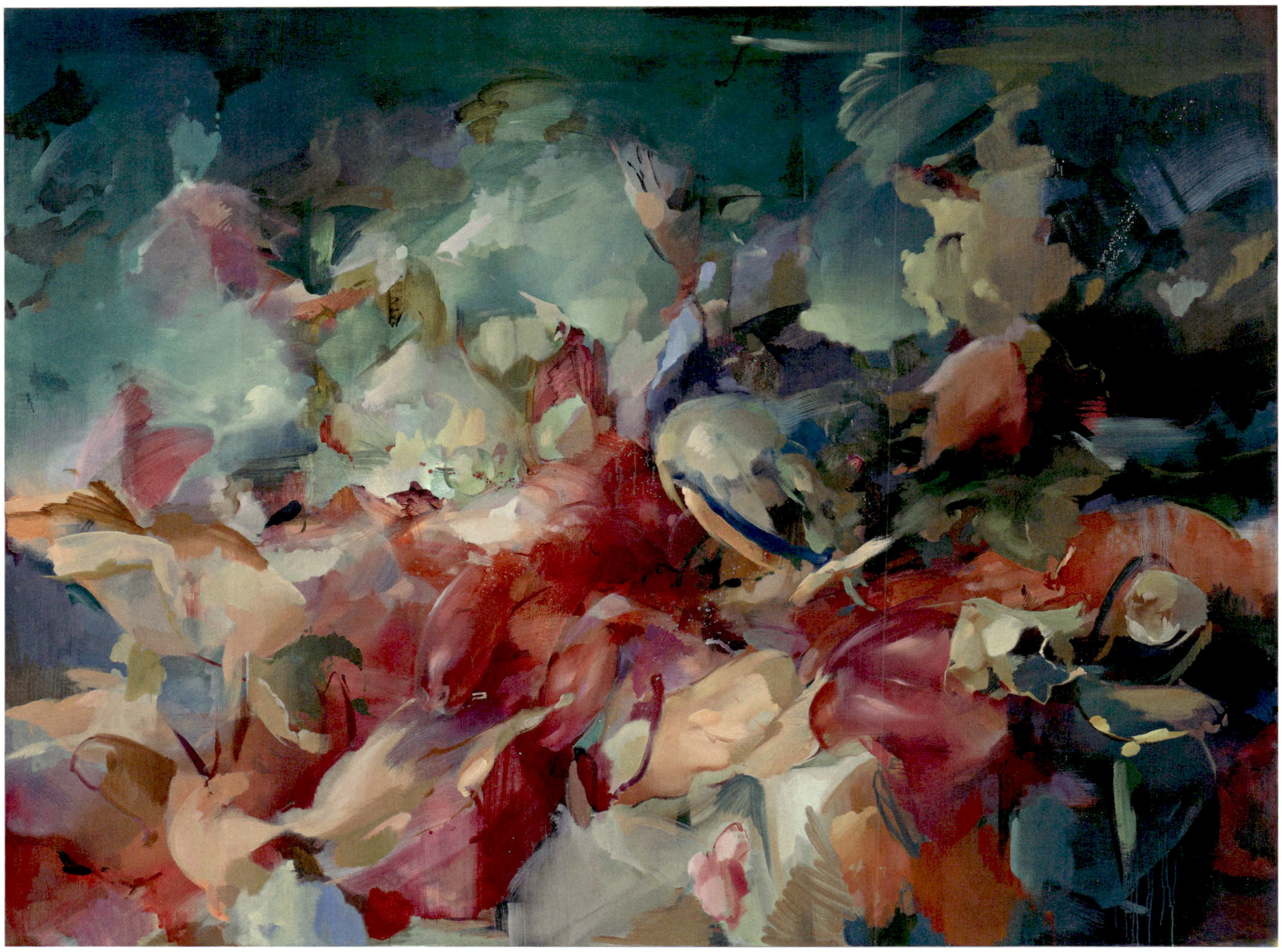

DON'T JUST STARE AT IT, EAT IT
2025. Oil on linen, 78½ × 102 in. (199.4 × 259.1 cm)

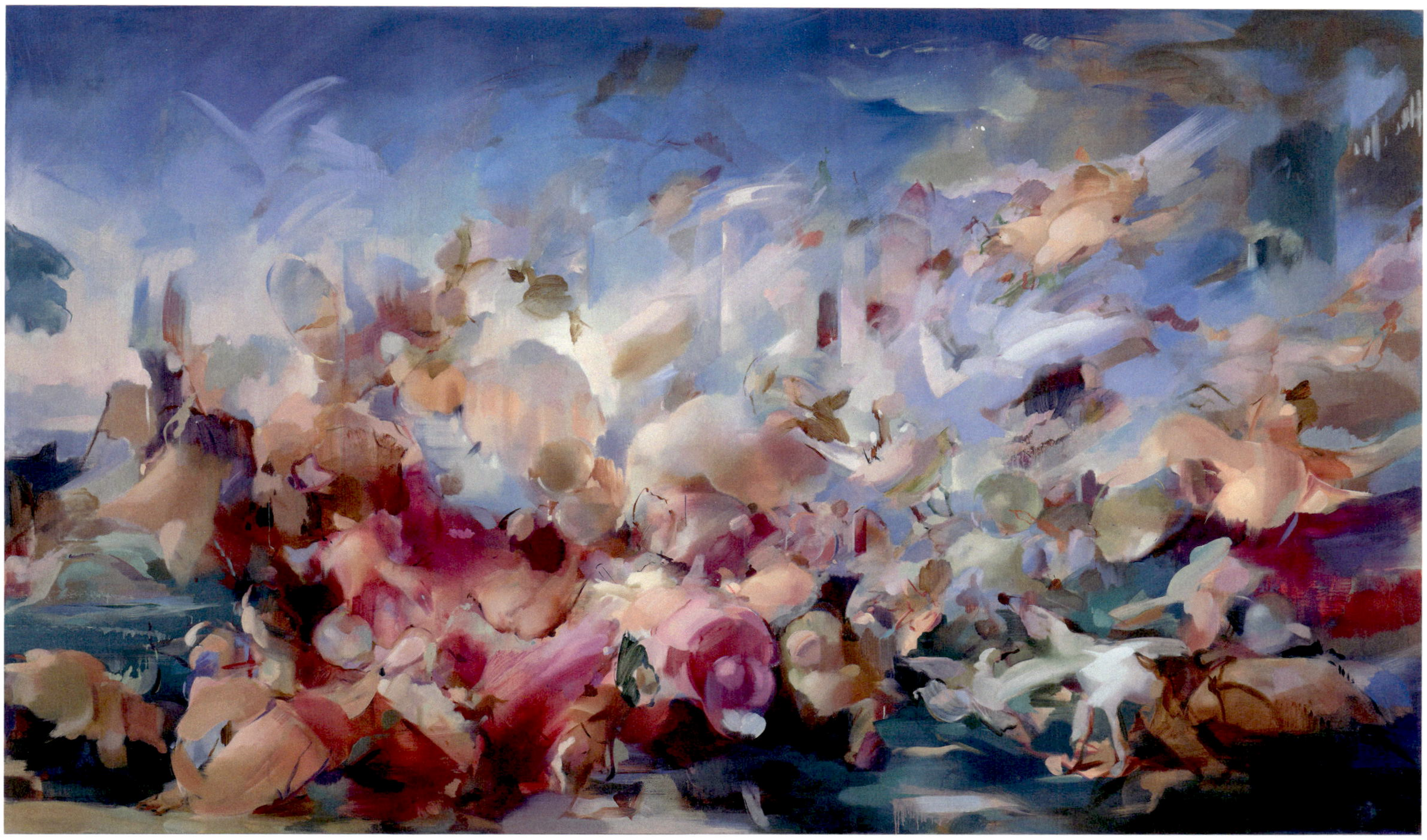

FEVER PITCH
2025. Oil on linen, 90½ × 150 in. (229.8 × 381 cm)

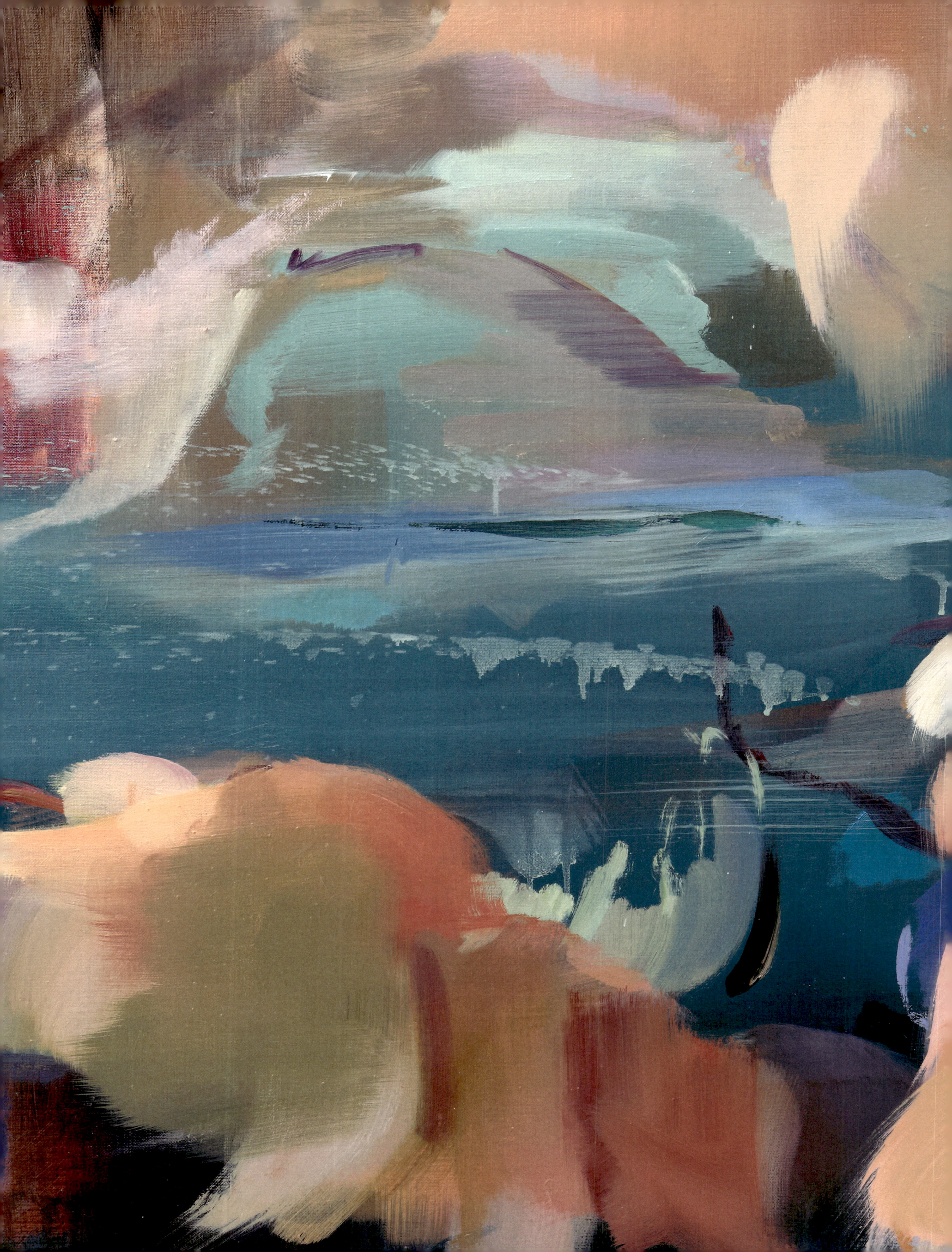

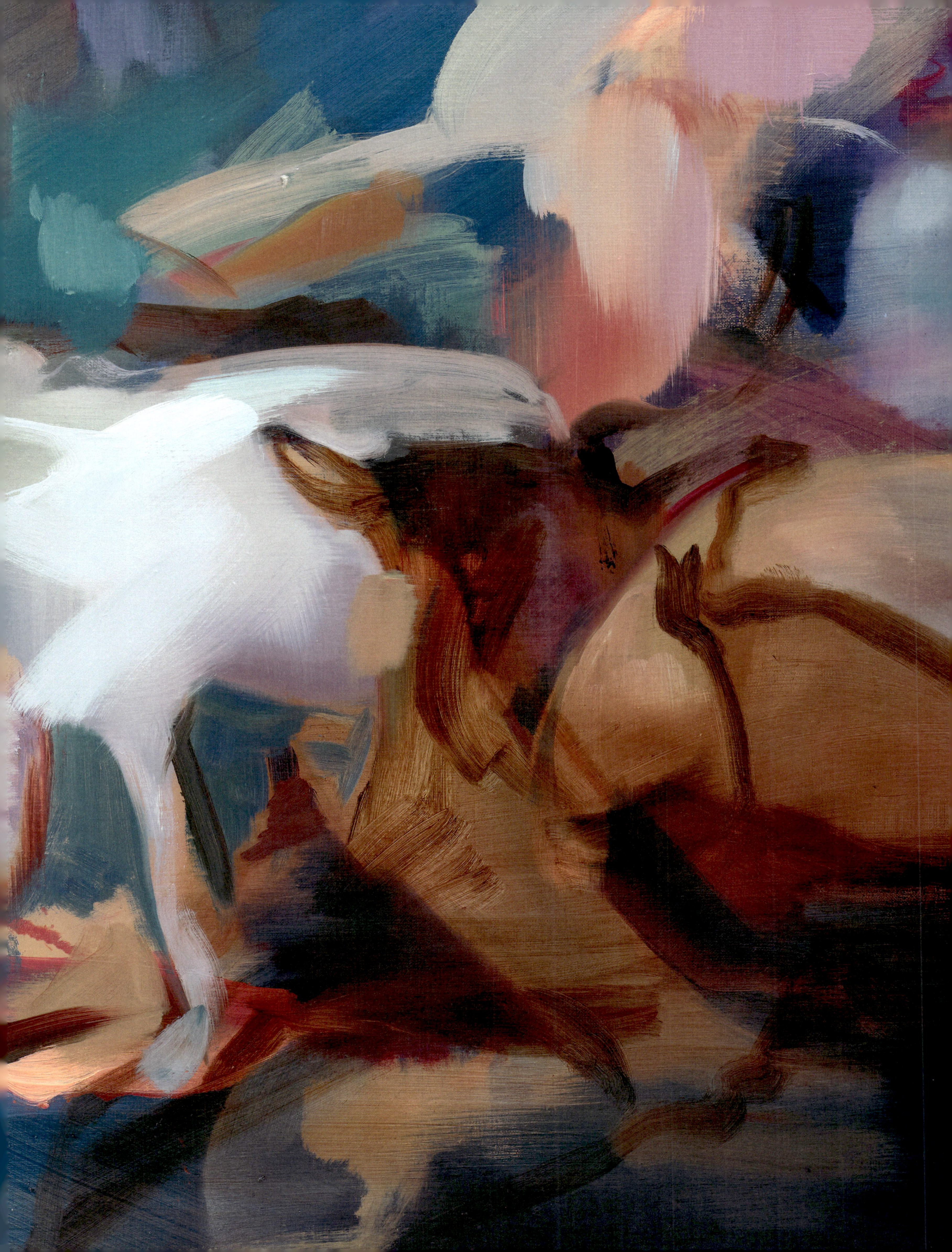

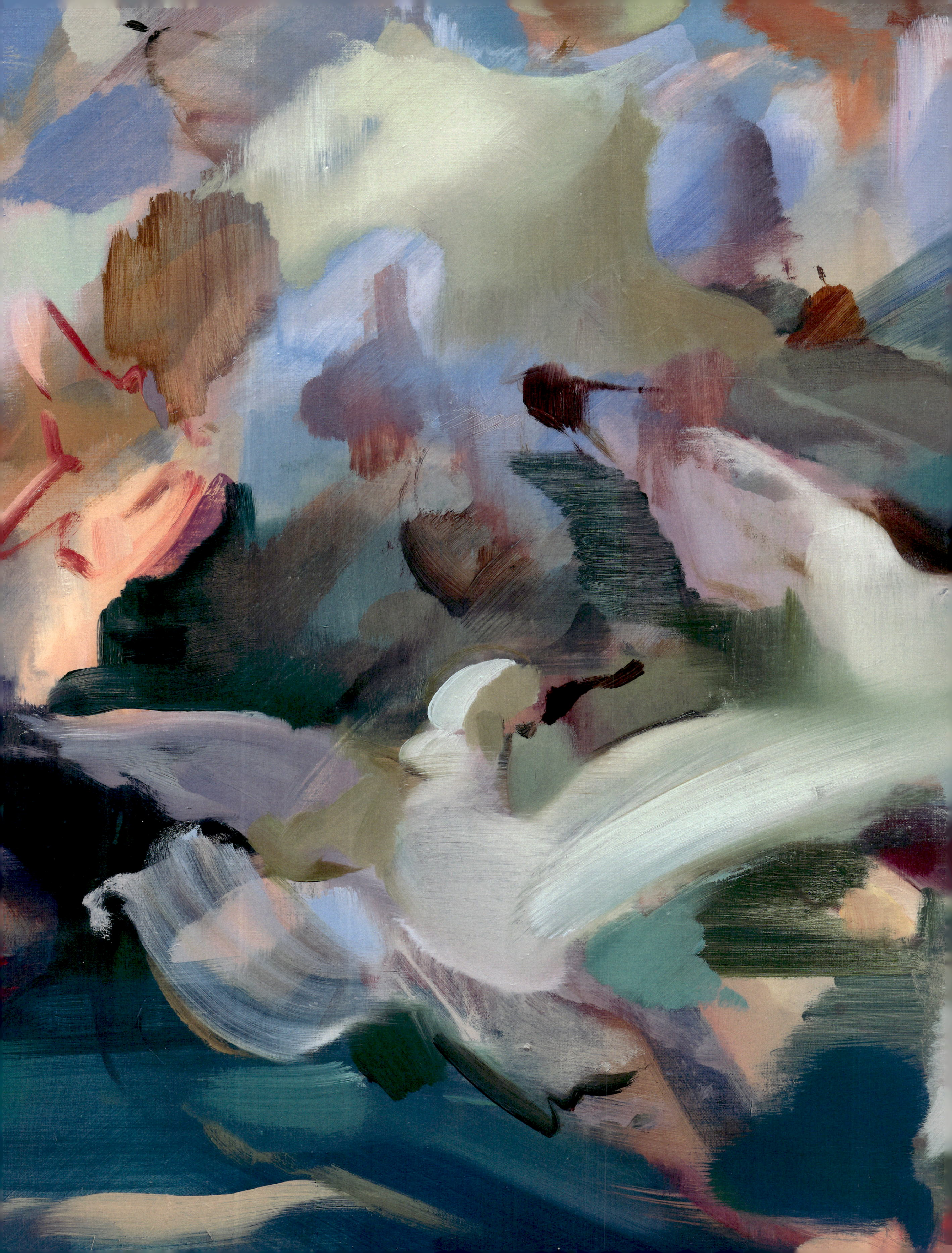

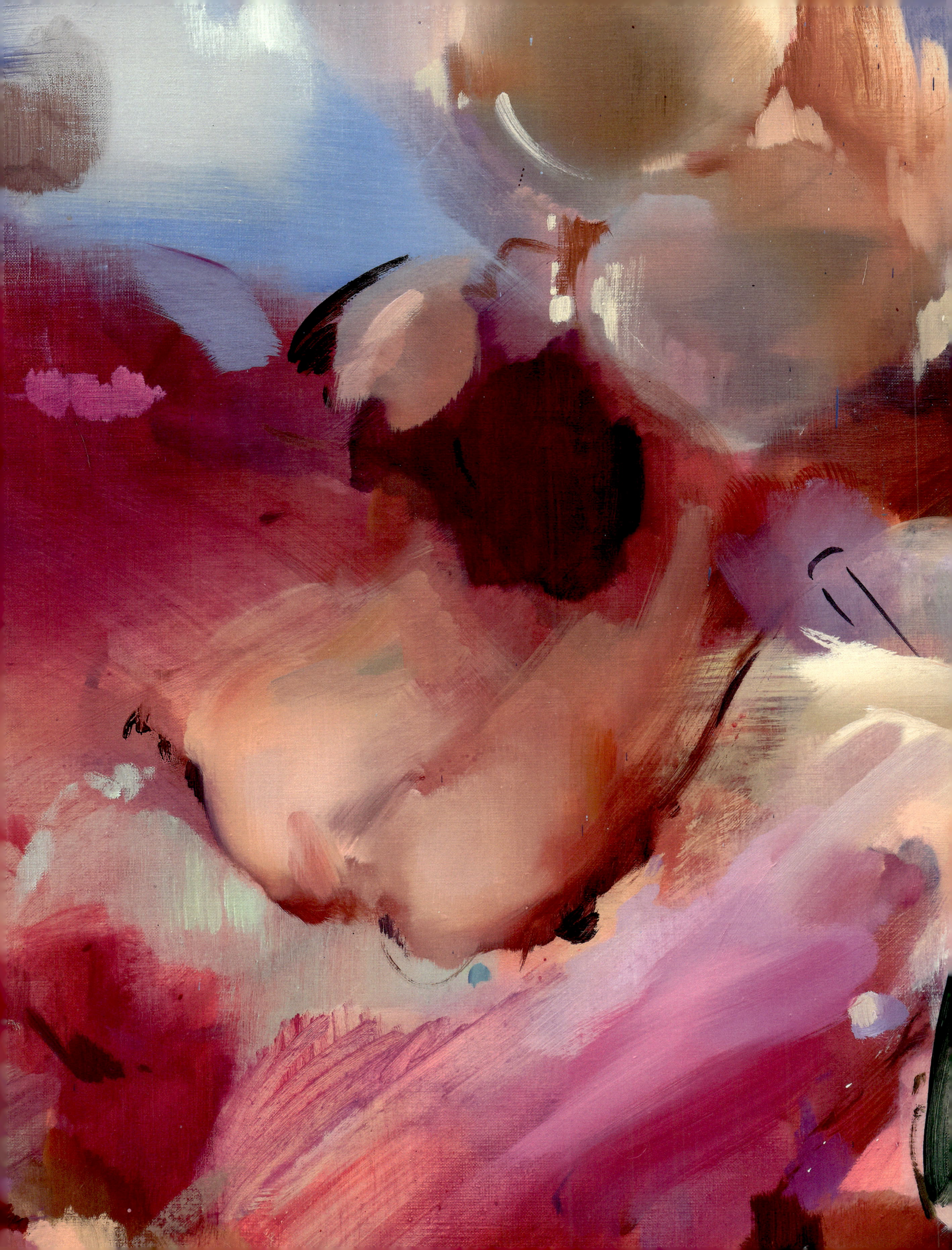

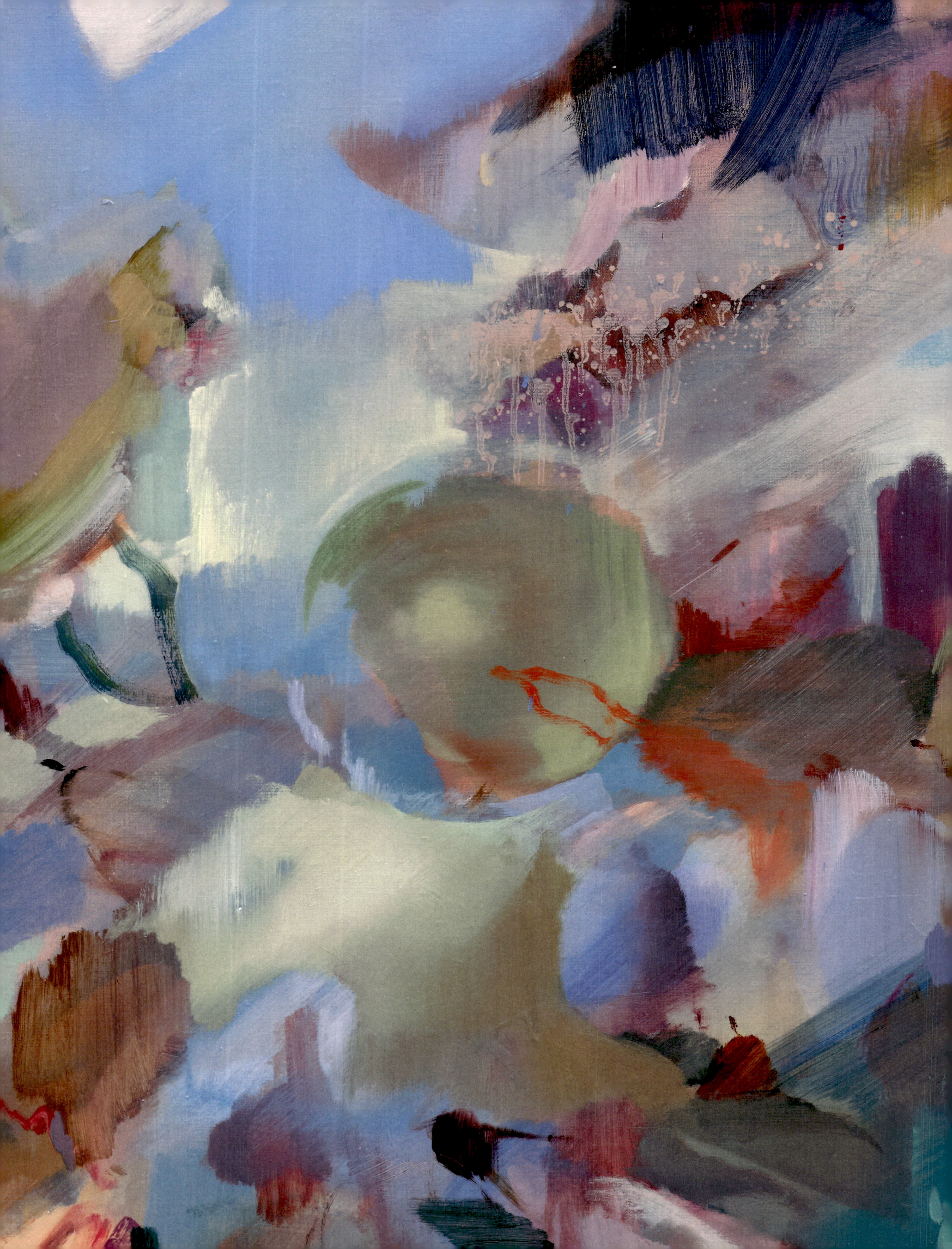

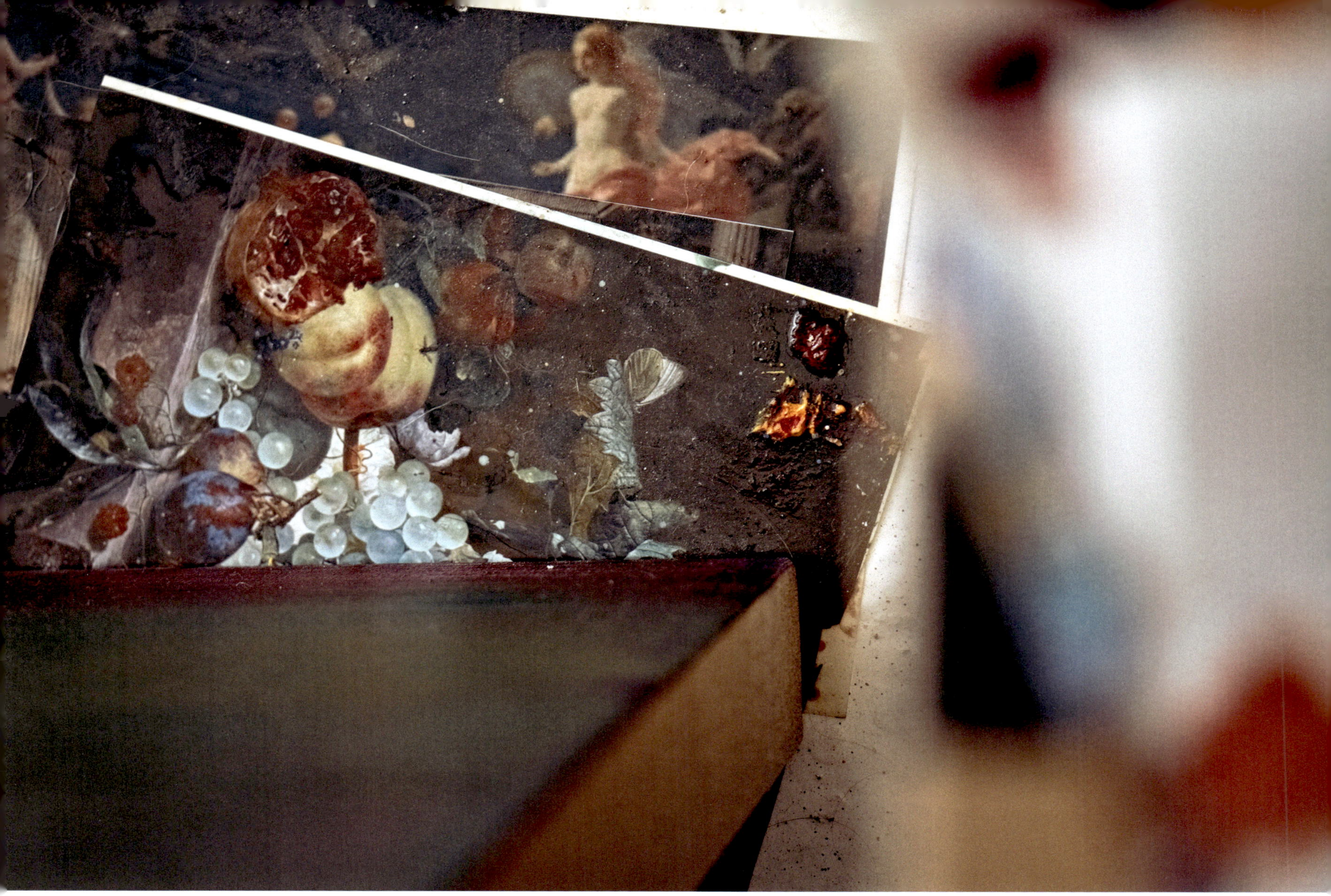

Once I begin, the paintings start to inform the research. A moment in the painting might bring to mind another idea that was not intentional but resonates with the conceptual realm I am exploring. It cracks open another avenue of research for me. In that way, I feel like I gain a lot from making each painting, I learn from it.

I considered how the columns in the gallery space might feed into the work. I was contemplating how to give a rhythmic logic to the painting so the chaos can read in the exhibition space. I love Peter Paul Rubens, who always has a very rigorous underlying structural scaffolding. I think it gives you a solid footing so you can follow the wobble in the curves without getting lost. Columns are a quite a good way of doing this whilst also speaking to Roman architecture—its denotation of power and its fall.

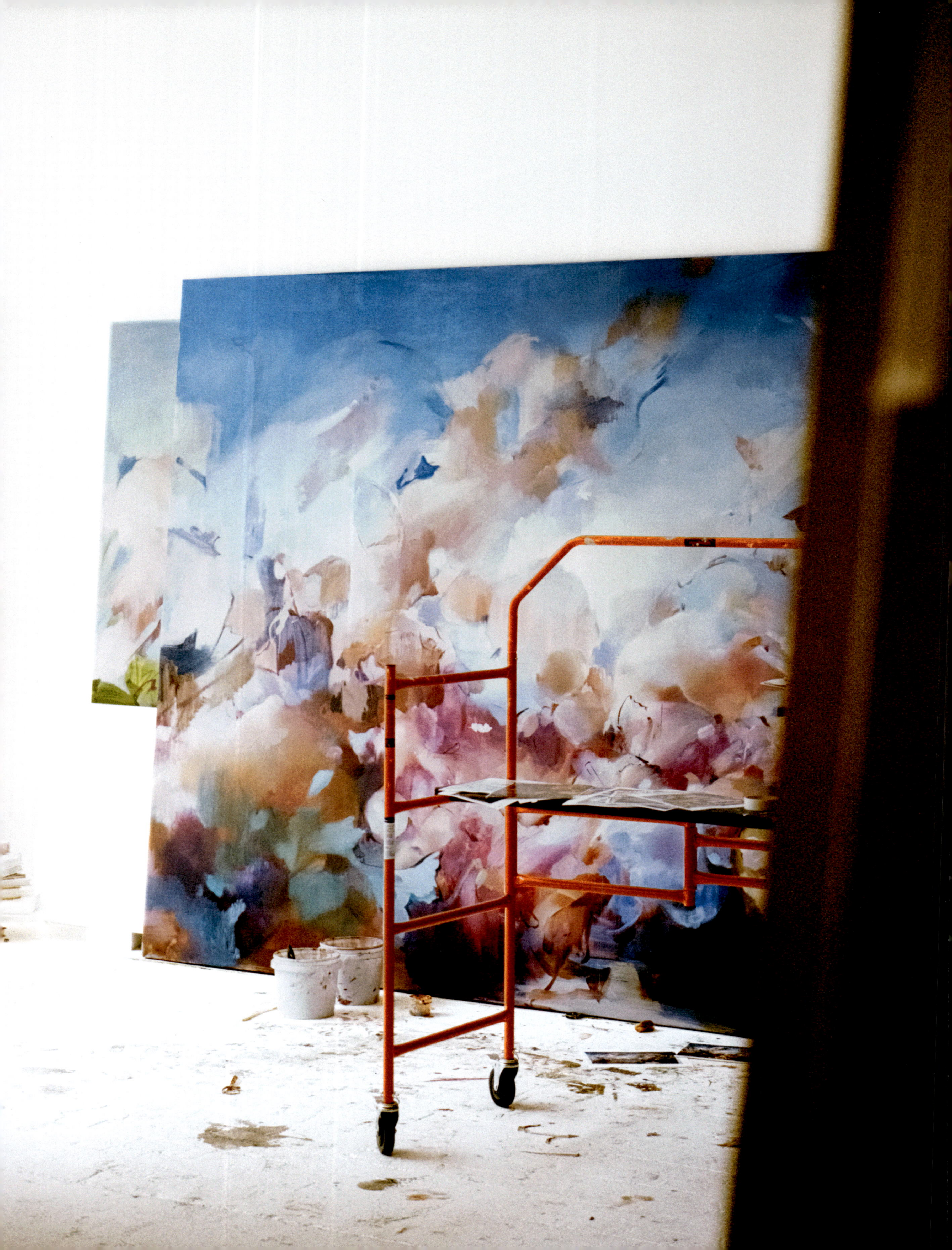

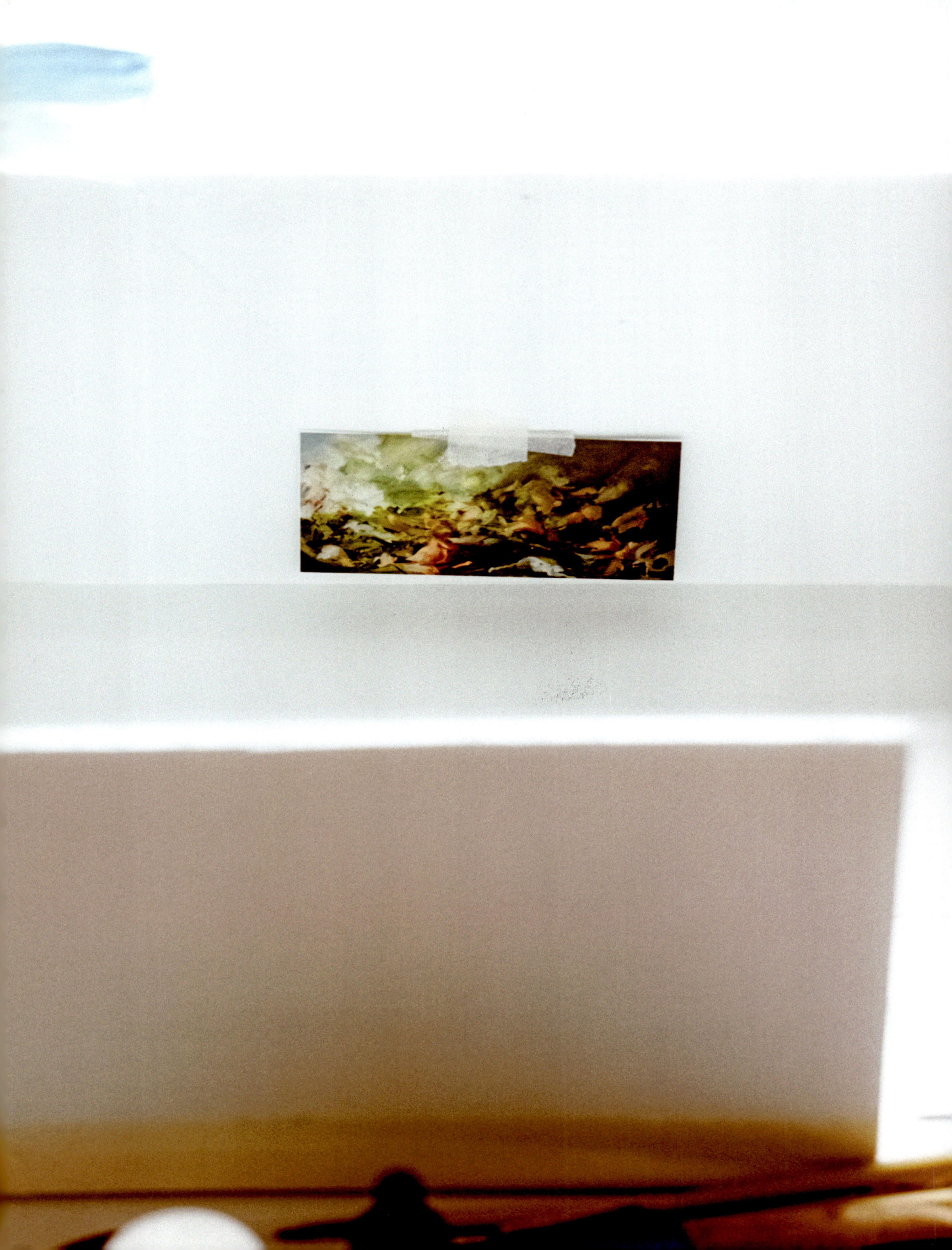

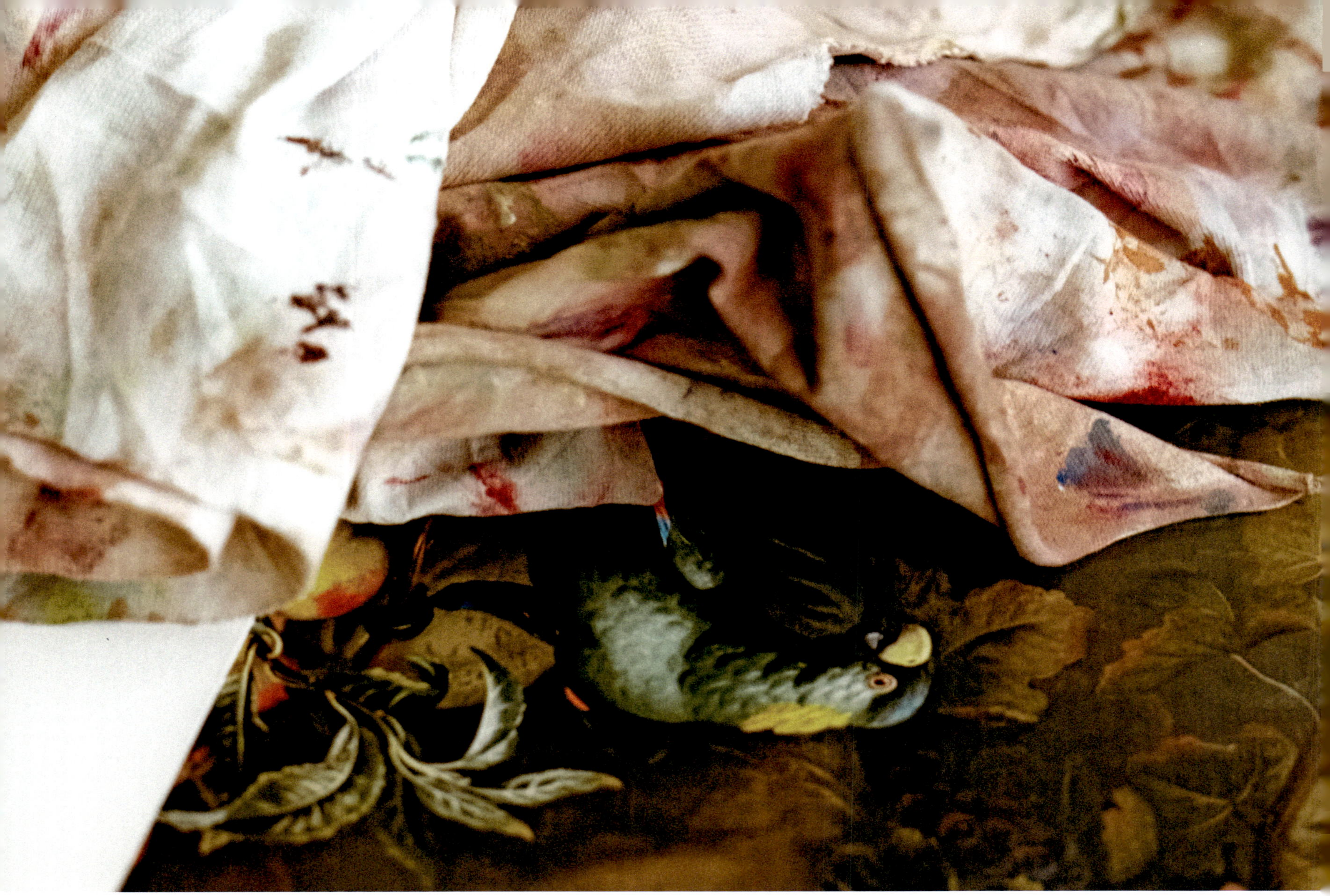

It is said that Elagabalus was a young Roman emperor who drowned his guests in petals—there were so many that the guests quite literally suffocated. He killed his guests with decadence. When Lawrence Alma-Tadema painted *The Roses of Heliogabalus* (1888), he had thousands of roses shipped to him from France. The production of the work, itself, became an act of excess and decadence, too.

Alexandre François Desportes painted these huge Louis XIV-esque table scapes like *Still Life with Silver* (ca. 1720s). I loved the precariousness of it, which really speaks to that time in France, the excess that ends up toppling the Ancien Régime, something that is piled so high it might fall or that is so ripe it might burst. And there is a relish in the painting of each of these items—the painting process becomes another facet of the excessive pleasure.

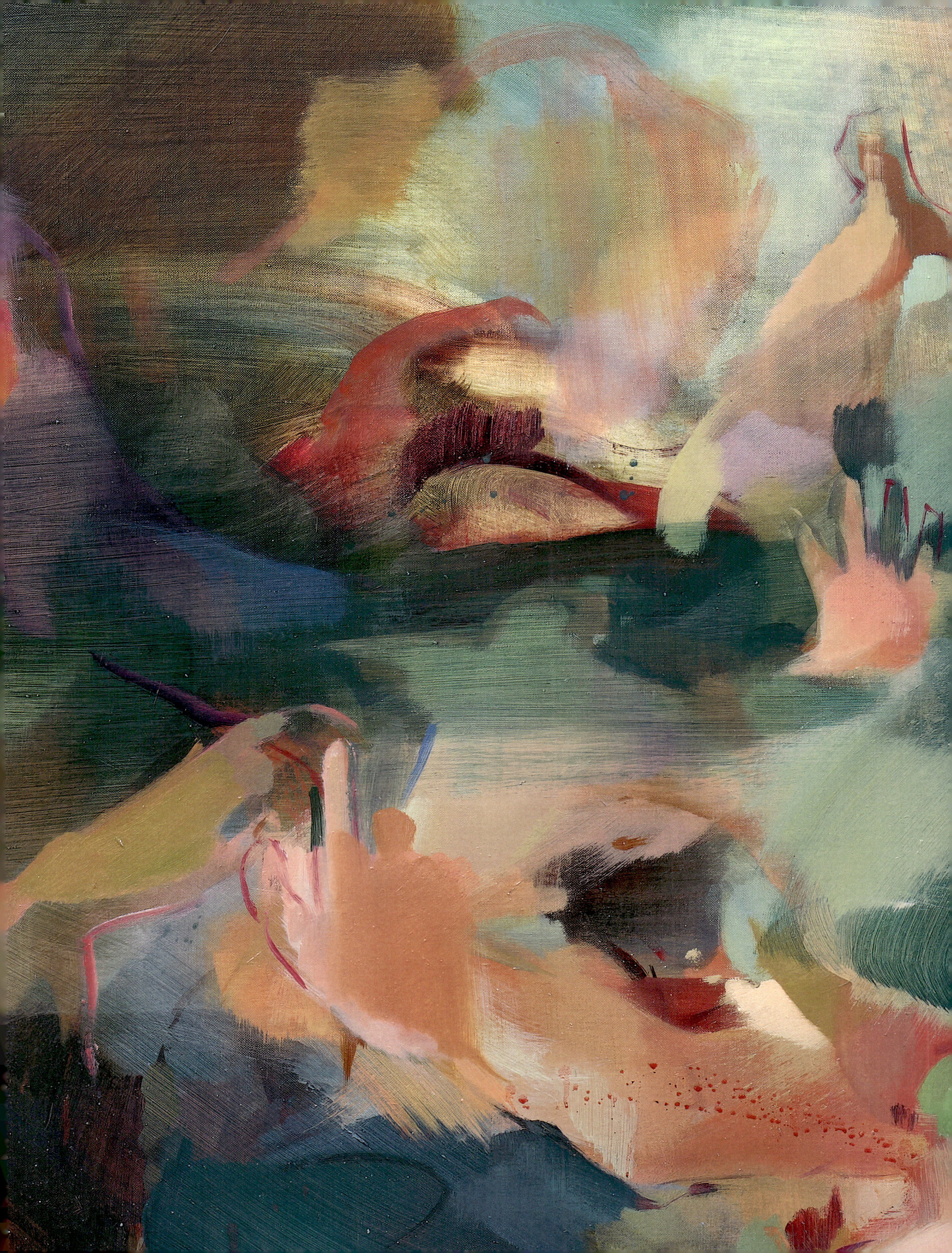

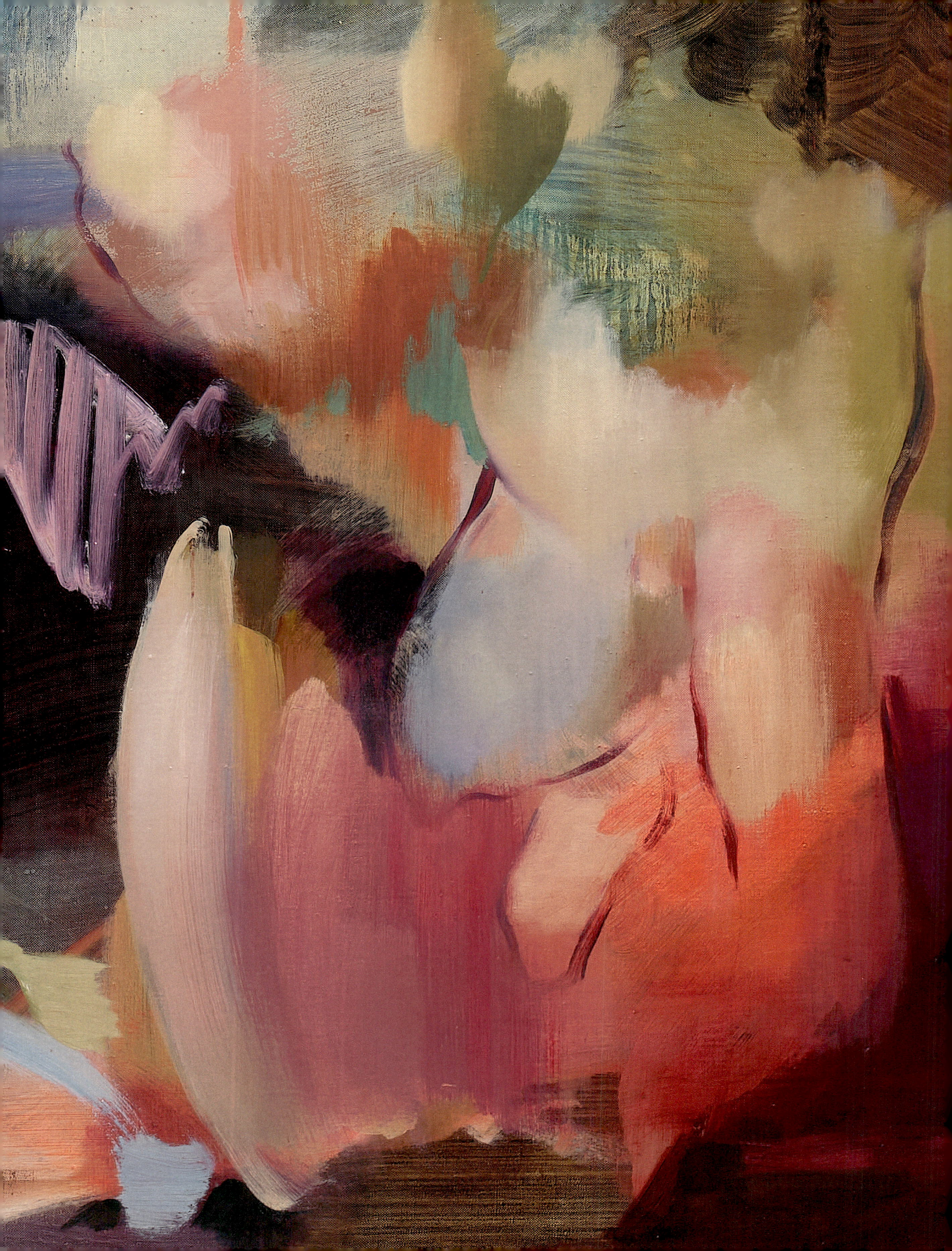

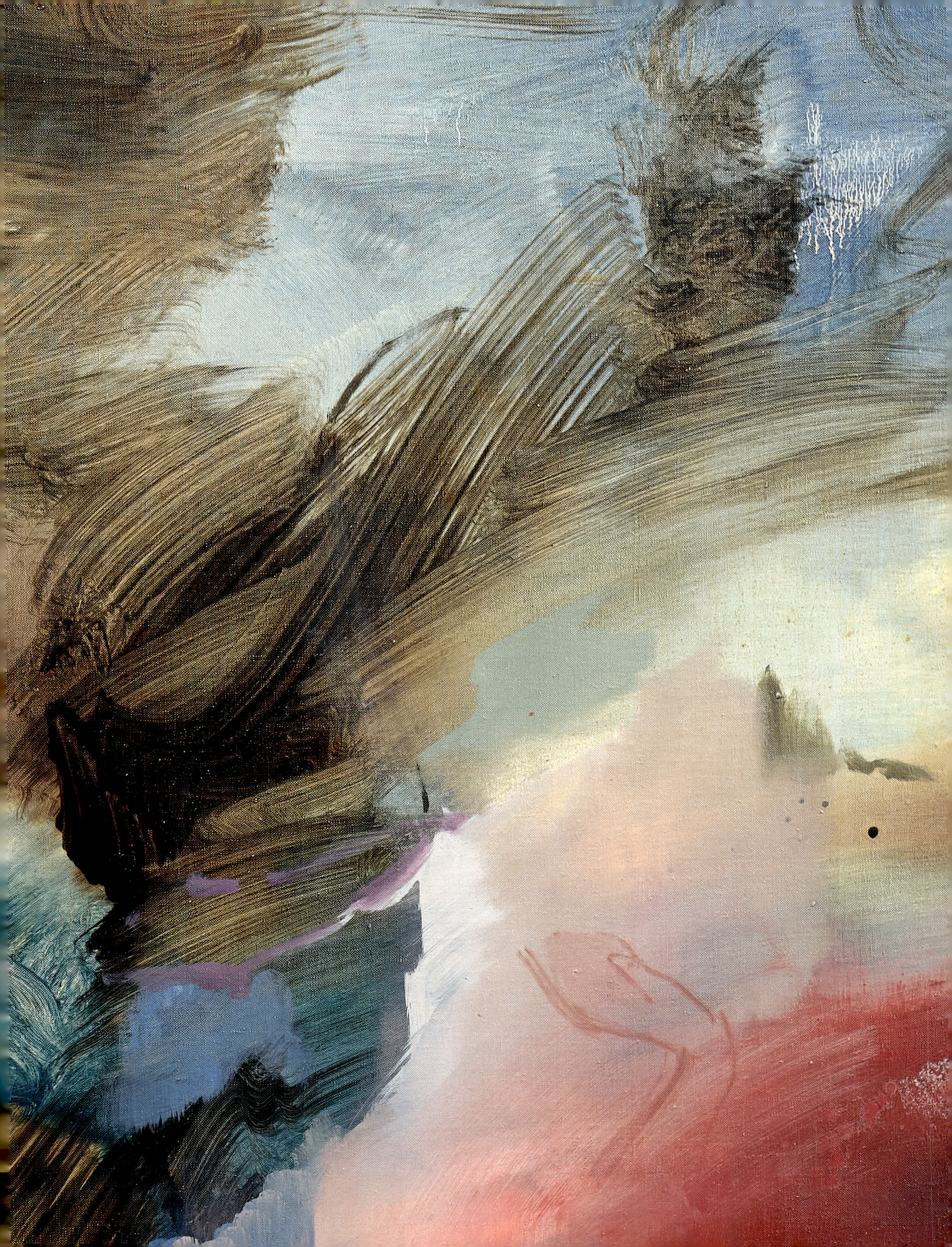

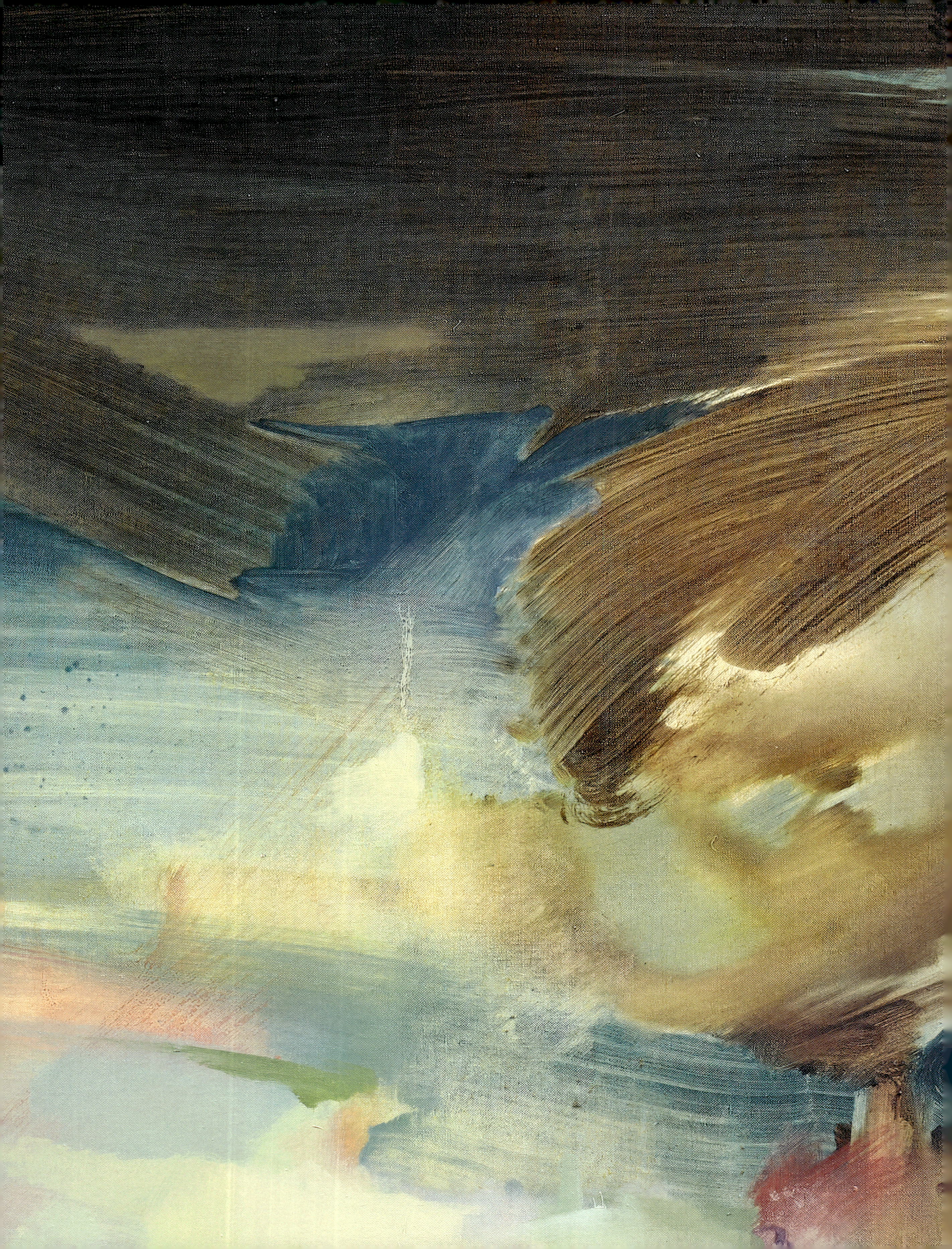

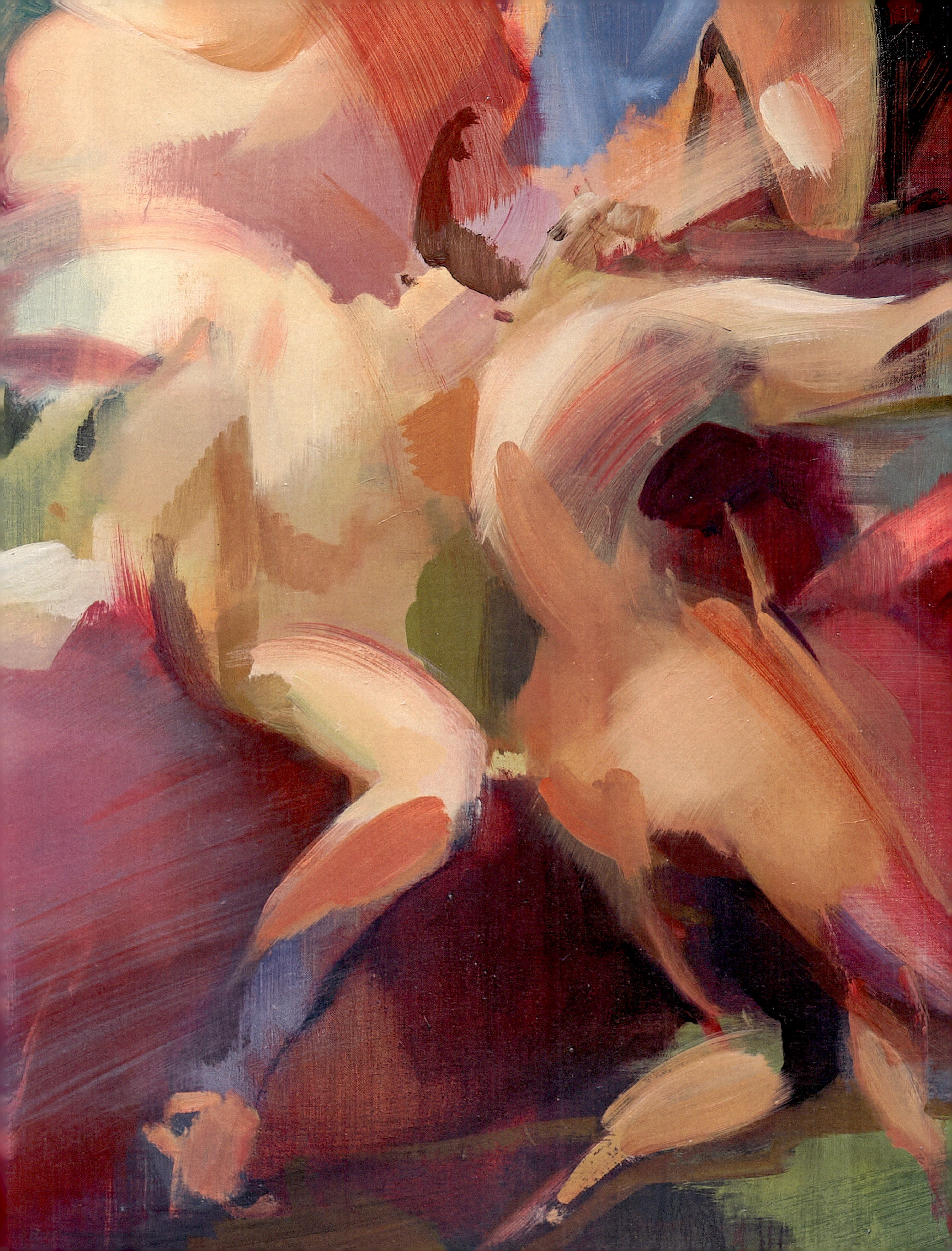

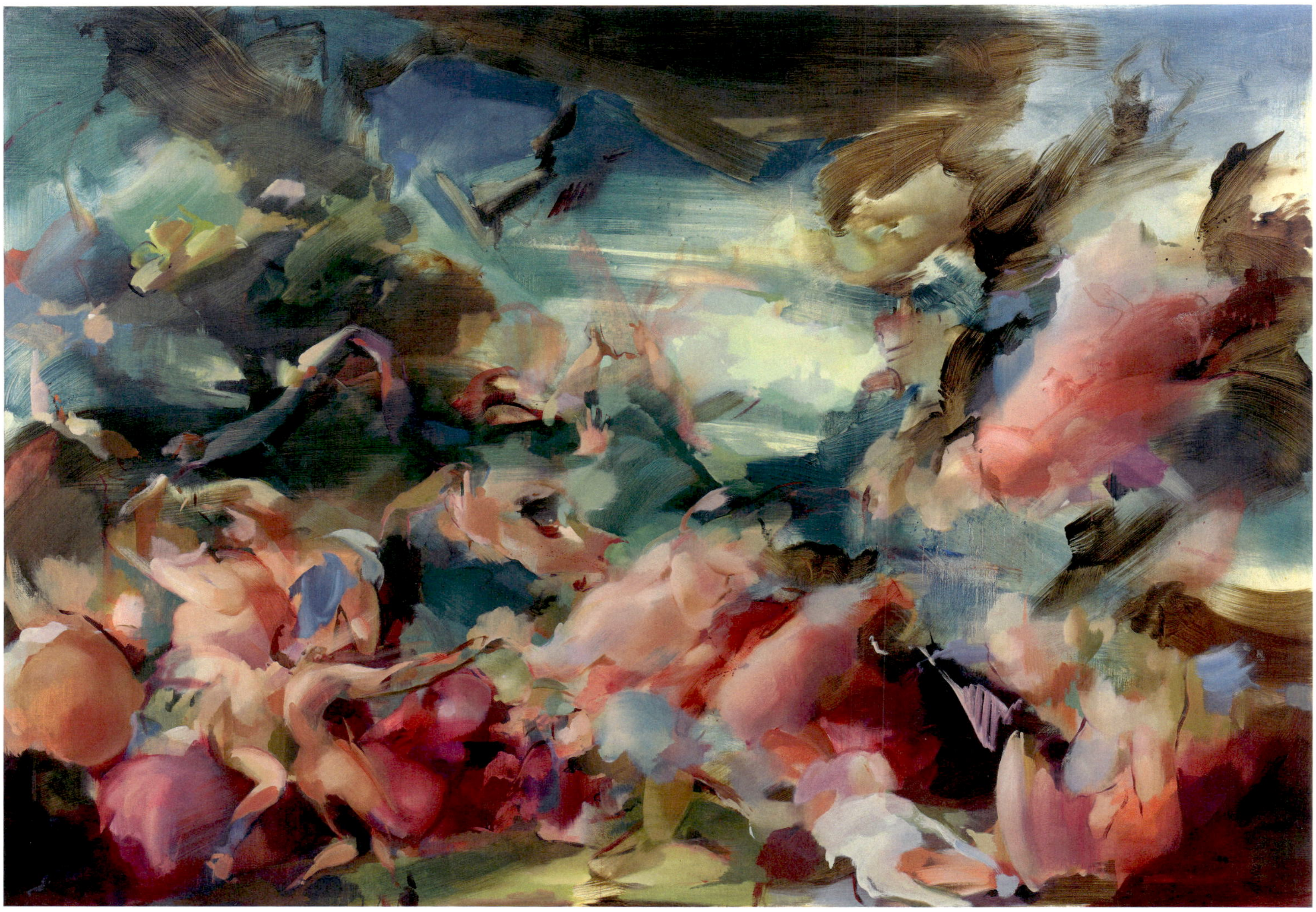

TARANTELLA
2025. Oil on linen, 78¾ × 110¼ in. (200 × 280 cm)

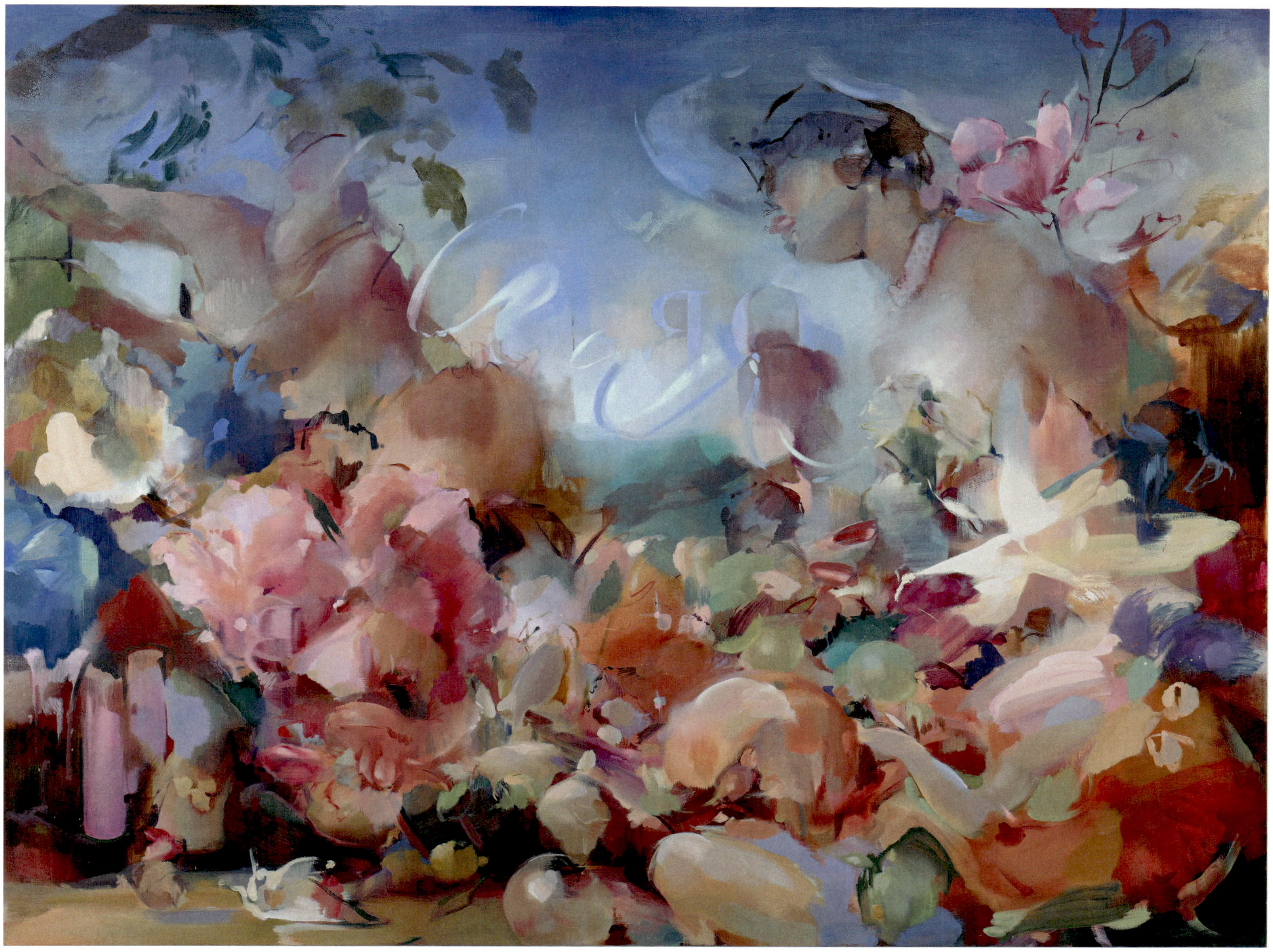

LUNCHEON
2025. Oil on linen, 78½ × 102 in. (199.4 × 259.1 cm)

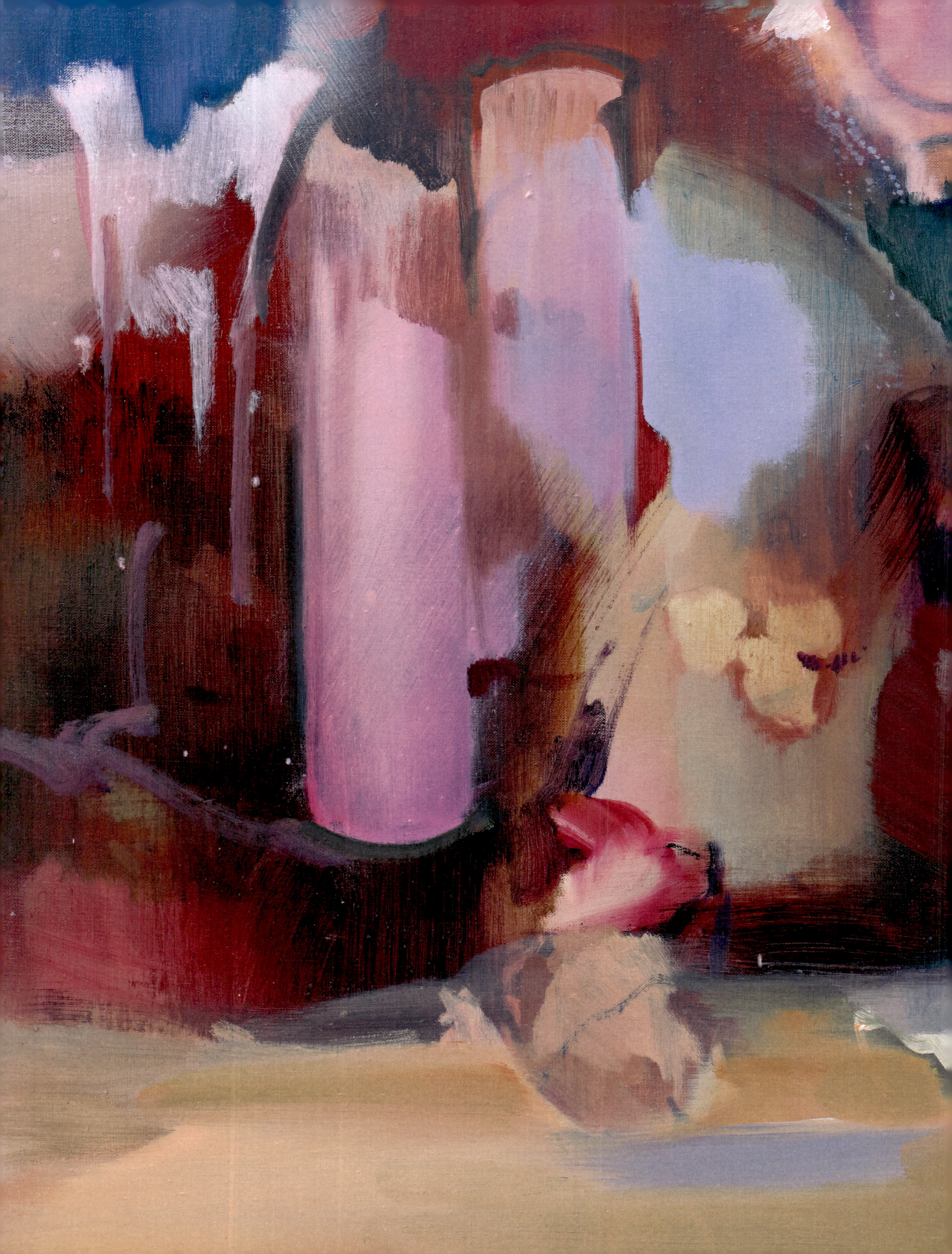

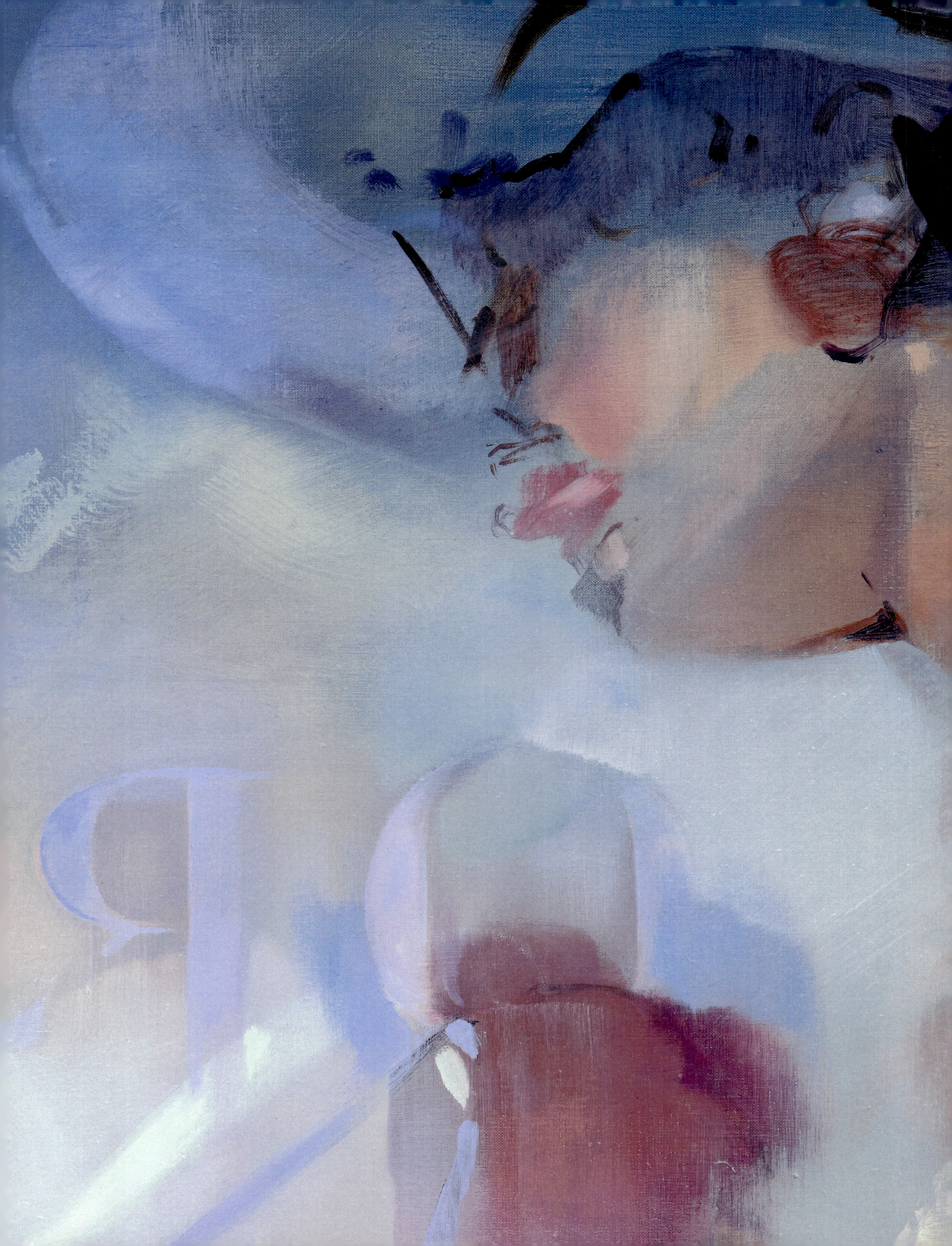

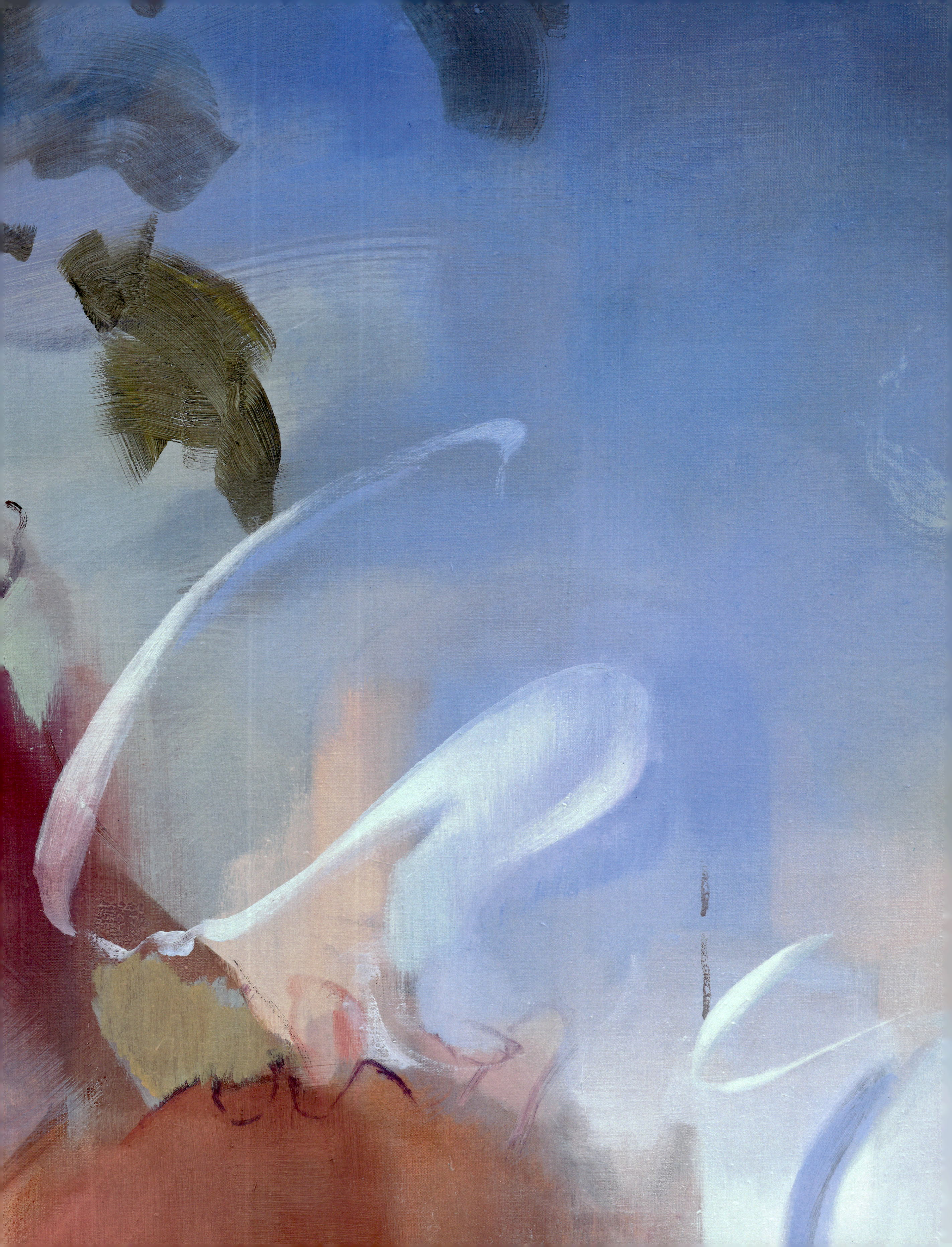

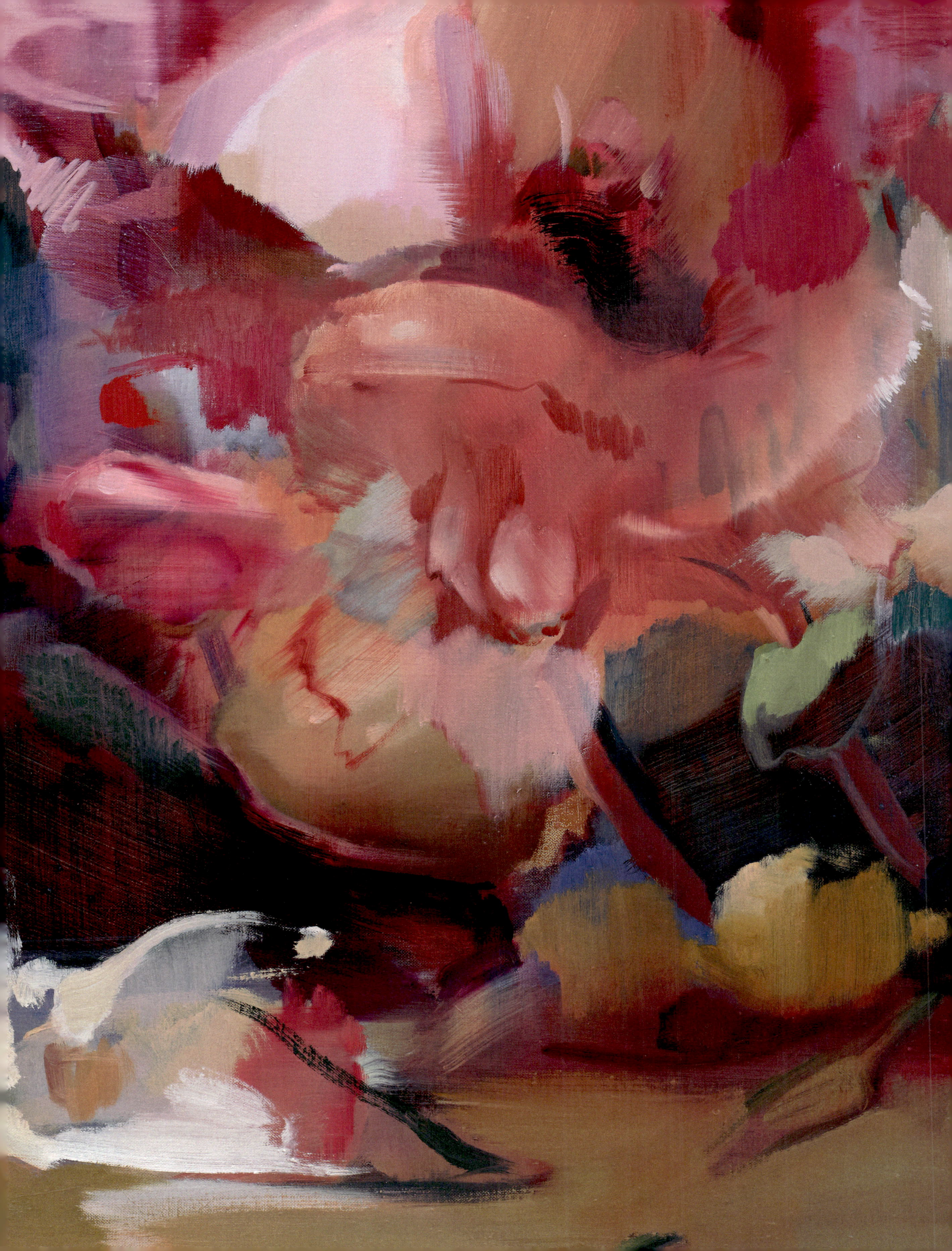

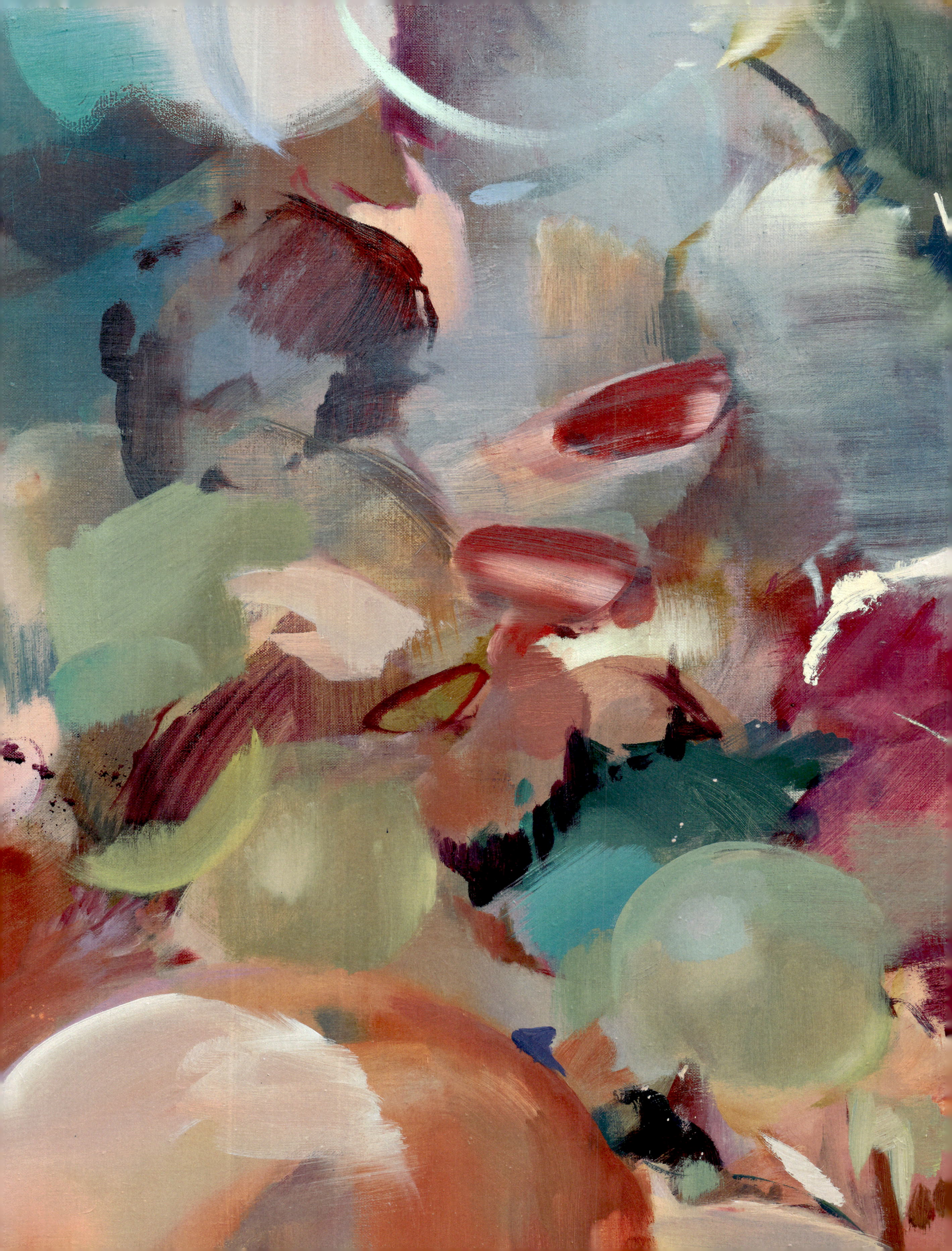

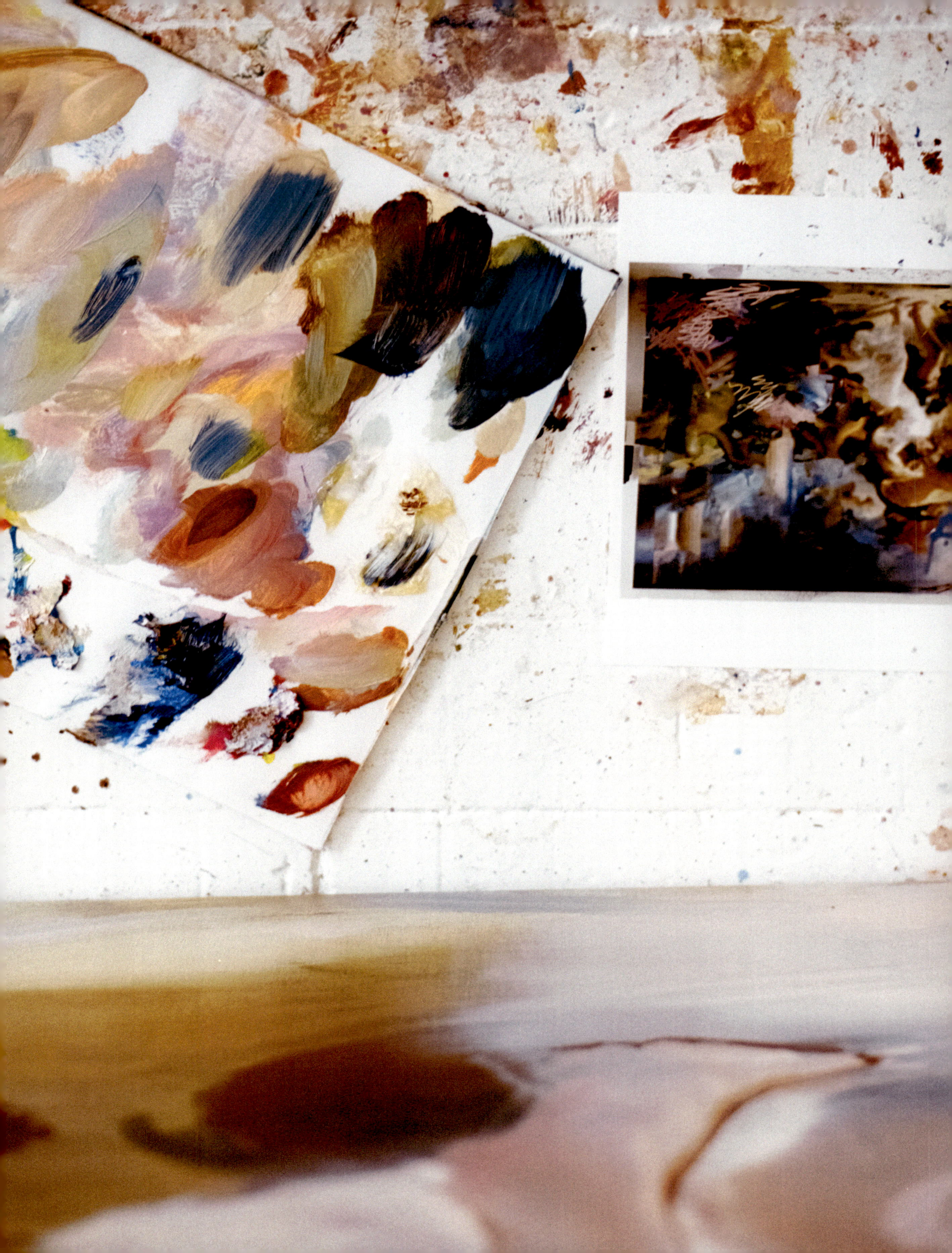

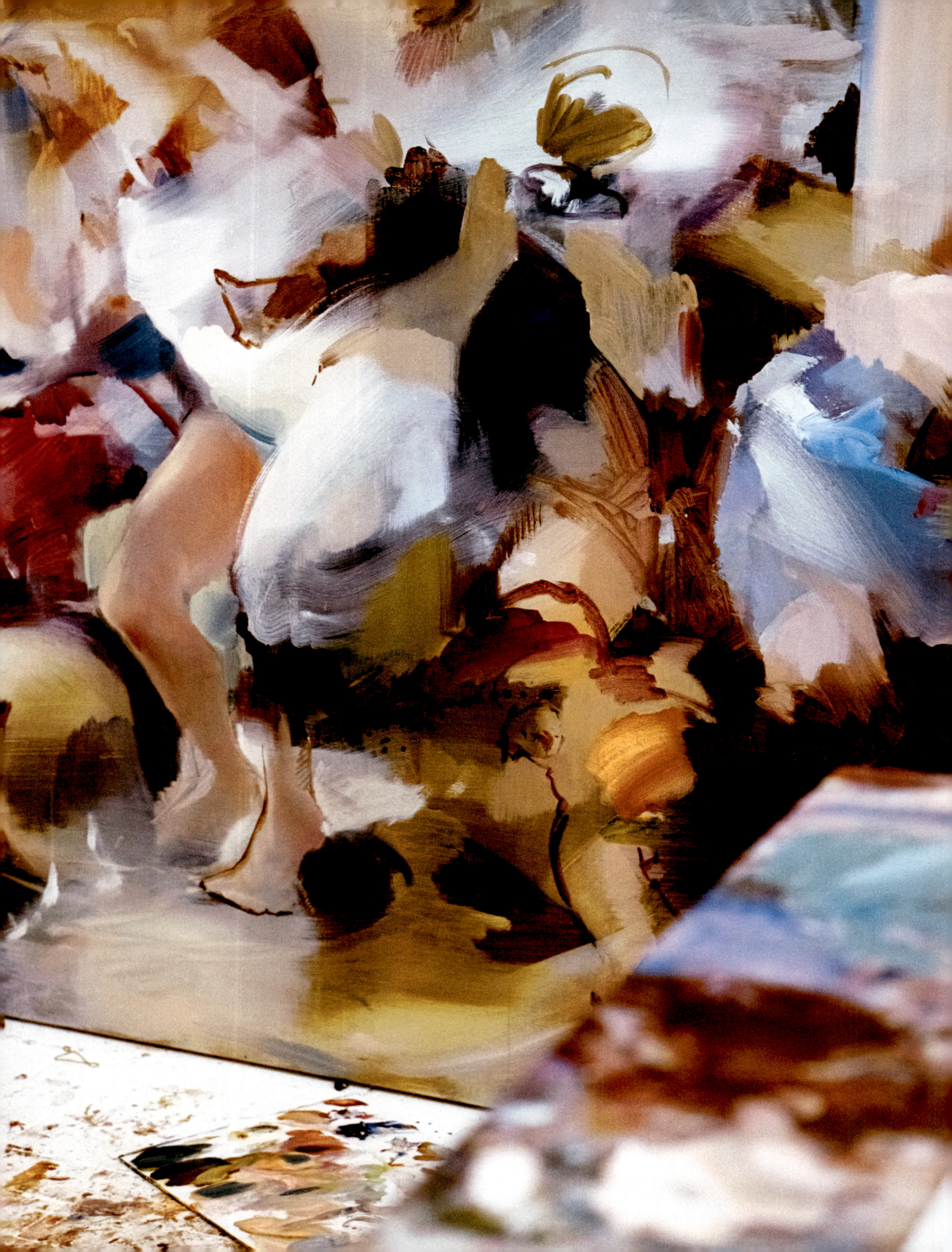

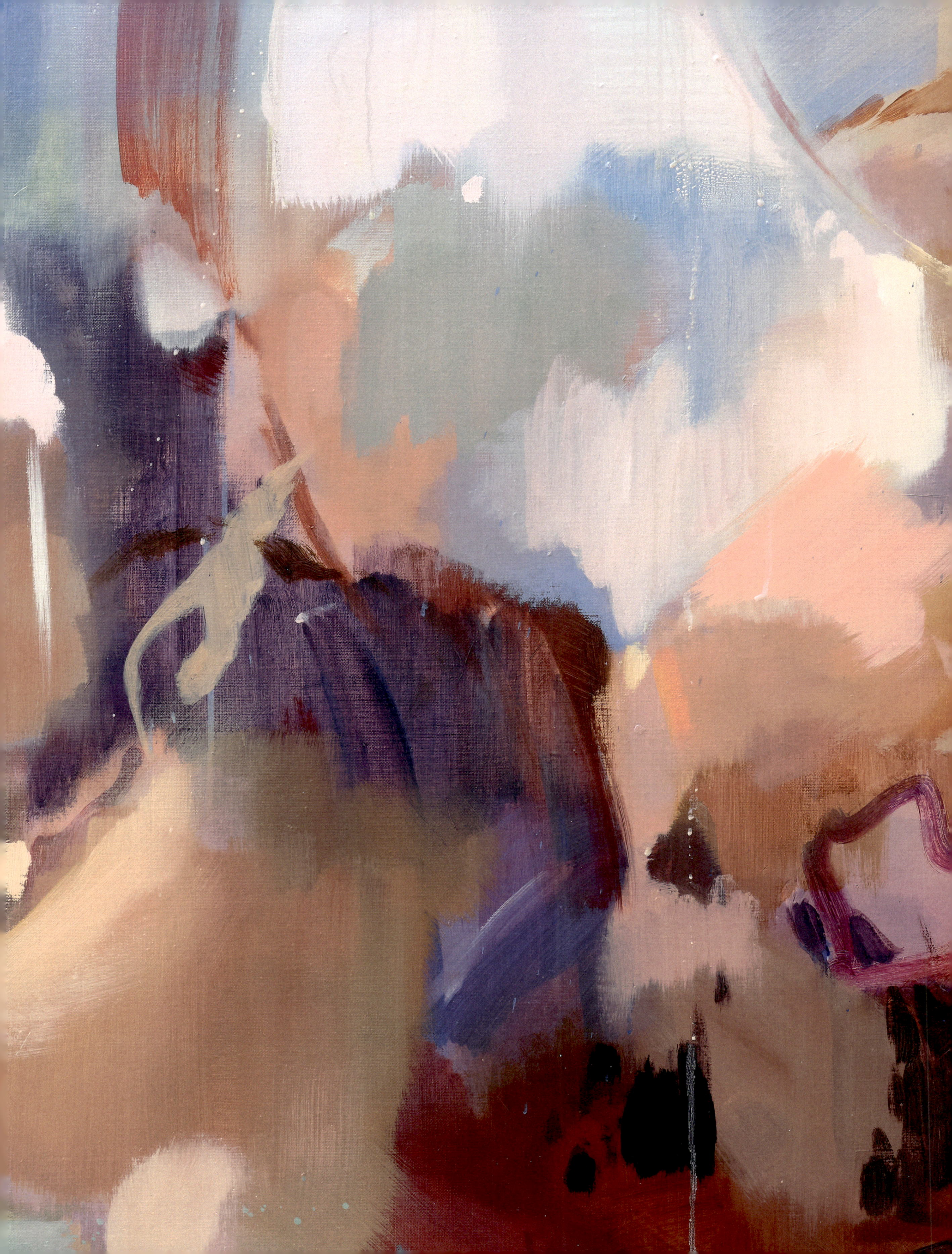

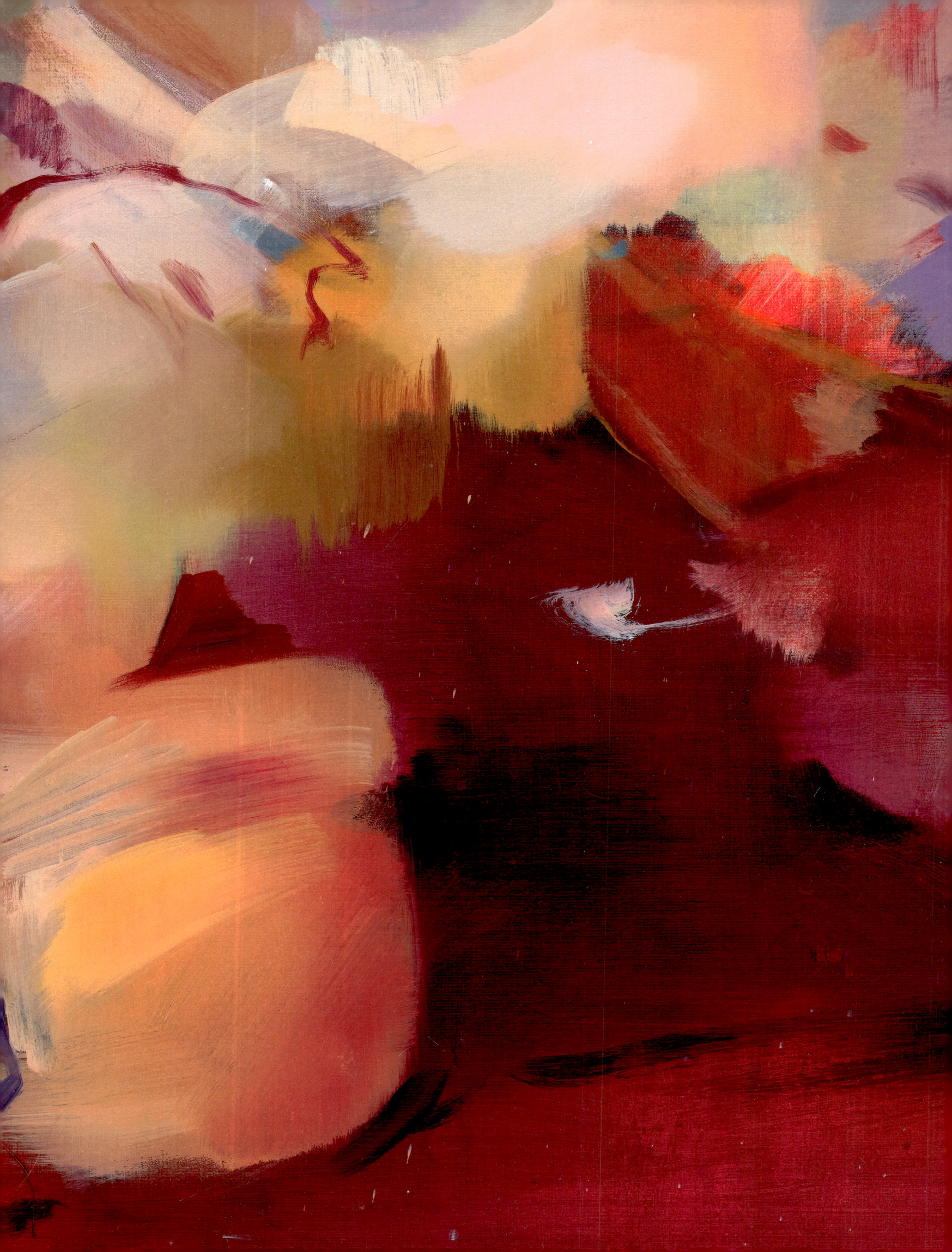

This book is published on
the occasion of the exhibition
Flora Yukhnovich: Bacchanalia,
at Hauser & Wirth Downtown
Los Angeles, on view from
October 30, 2025–January 25,
2026, which included all
works from 2025 reproduced here.

Flora Yukhnovich's art explores materiality and process as vehicles for meaning, with cascading and swirling forms evoking rhythm and energy that blurs the boundaries between representation and abstraction. Her immersive paintings splice glimpses of art historical styles—from French Rococo and Italian Baroque to Abstract Expressionism—together with references drawn from contemporary films, music, literature, and consumer culture. In her work, Yukhnovich addresses the dynamics of power inherent in received readings of art historical subjects and their associated hierarchies, in particular by questioning notions of femininity and gender that are hardwired into the aesthetic language of color and form. Born in Norwich, United Kingdom, in 1990, Yukhnovich completed her MA in Fine Art at City & Guilds of London Art School in 2017.

Eleanor Nairne is the Keith L. and Katherine Sachs Curator of Modern and Contemporary Art and Head of Department at the Philadelphia Museum of Art, a position she has held since 2024. Previously she was Senior Curator at Barbican Art Gallery, London, where she organized exhibitions on Jean-Michel Basquiat, Lee Krasner, and Alice Neel, among others. A regular contributor to catalogues, Nairne's writing has been published in the *New York Times*, the *London Review of Books*, and *frieze*.

Publisher
Michaela Unterdörfer
Managing editor
Jake Brodsky
Assistant editor
Susannah Faber
Editorial support
Kean Hughes, Zoe Sperling, Stefan Zebrowski-Rubin

Book design and typography
Damien Saatdjian
Artwork photography
Elisabeth Bernstein (unless otherwise noted)
Jack Hems (Bacchanalia; Fast and Loose)
Sarah Muehlbauer (Tarantella)
Studio photography
Dan McMahon
Prepress
prints professional, Berlin
Production coordination
Christine Stricker
Printing and binding
DZA Druckerei zu Altenburg

Cover
Magno Satin, 135g
Endpaper
Surbalin Lagune, 115g
Paper
Magno Volume, 150g; IBO One
Typeface
GT Super and RL Zeta

Cover Art
Luncheon (detail), 2025

Flora Yukhnovich: Bacchanalia

www.hauserwirth.com

Distribution:

North and South America
ARTBOOK | D.A.P.
75 Broad Street, Suite 630
New York, NY 10004
artbook.com

All other territories
Thames & Hudson Ltd.
181A High Holborn
London WC1V 7QX
thamesandhudson.com

ISBN: 978-3-907493-21-2
Library of Congress Control Number: 2025945555

Printed and bound in Germany

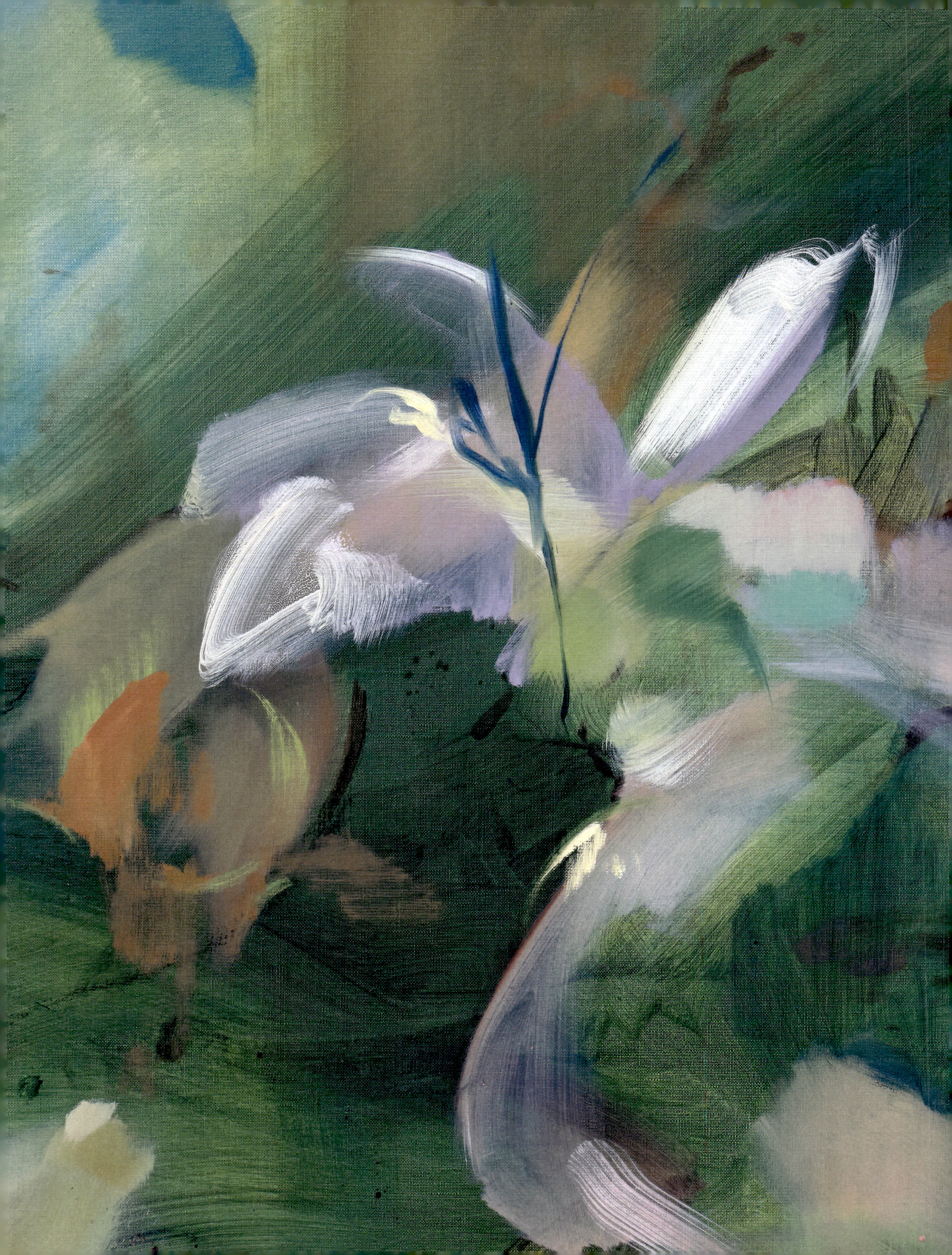

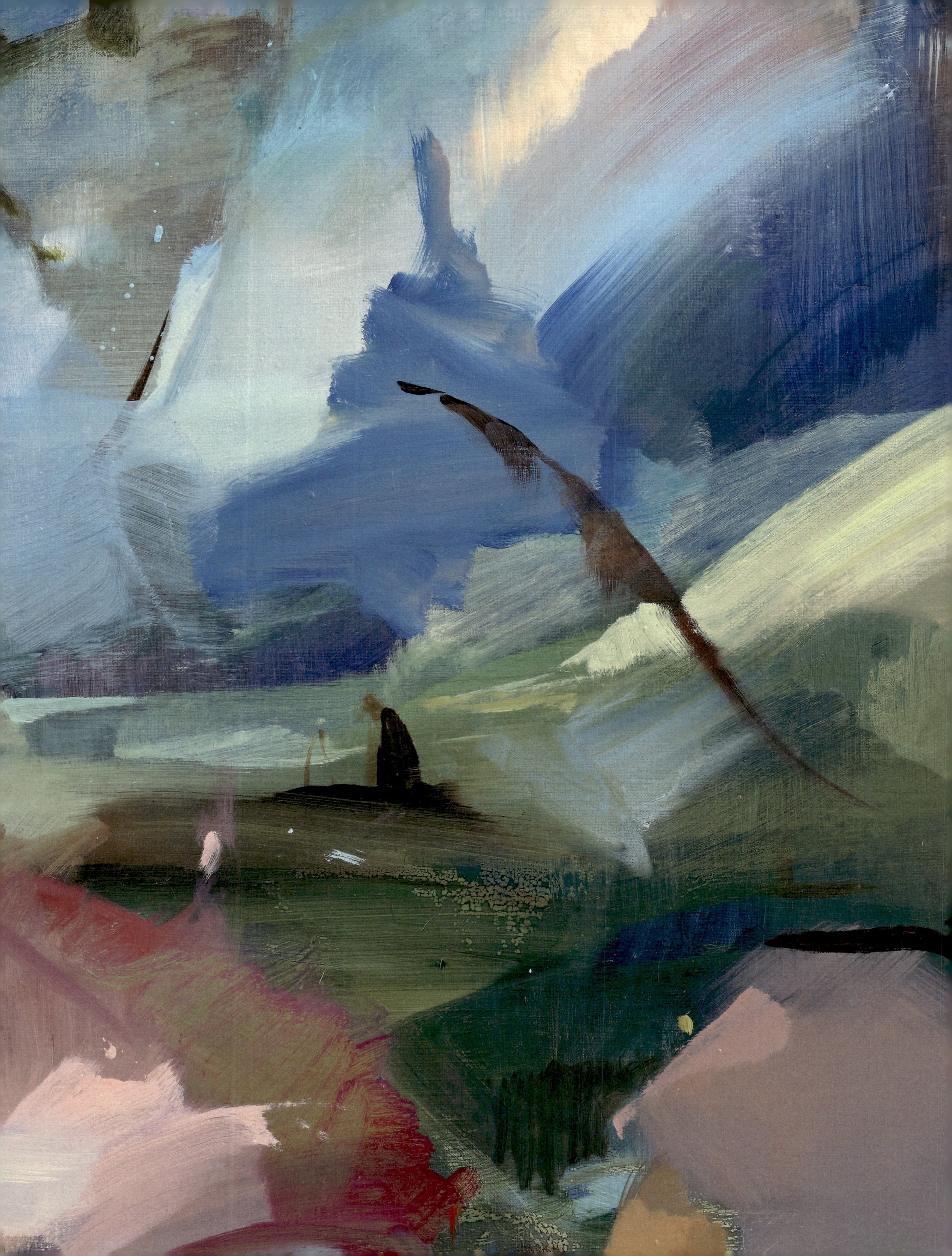

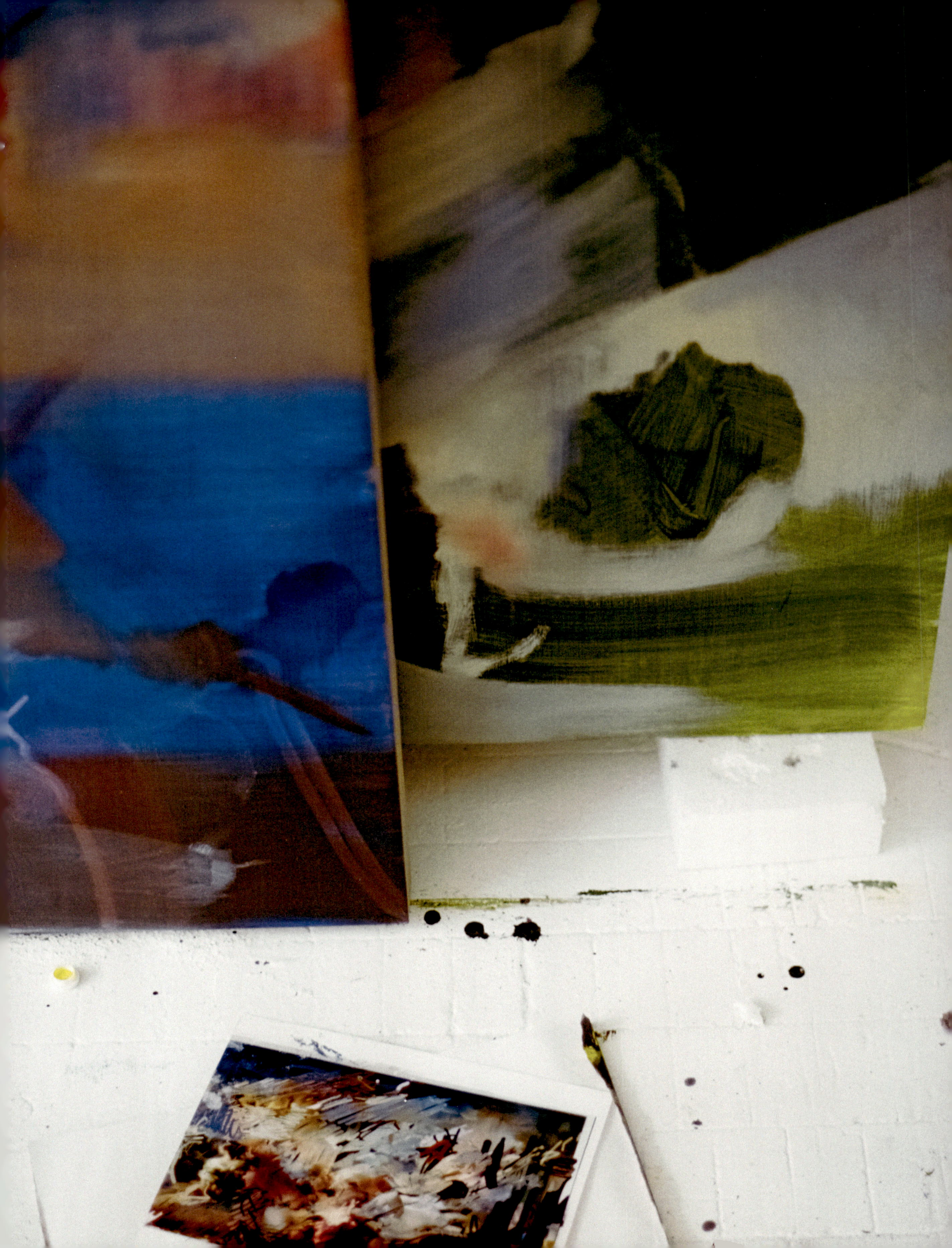

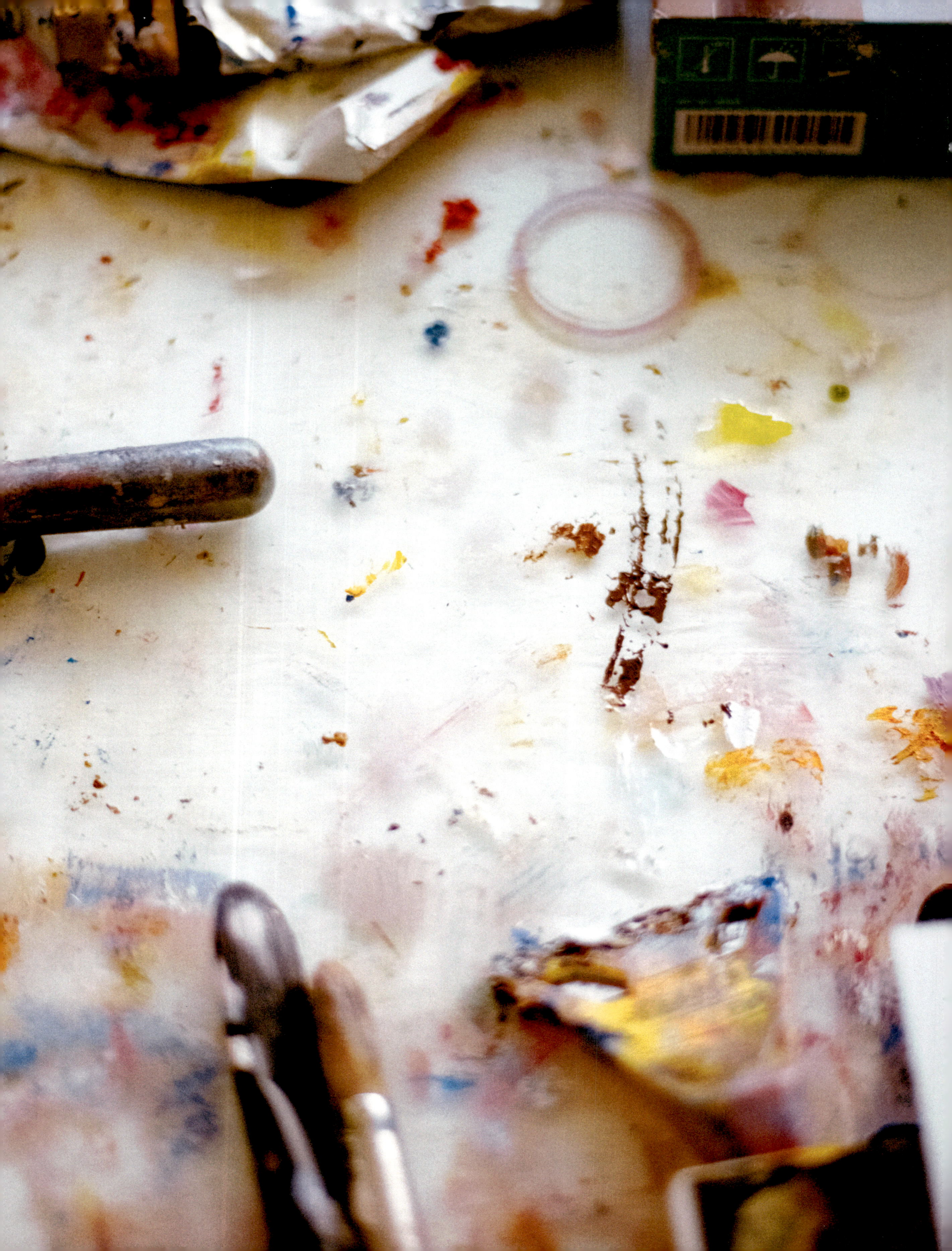

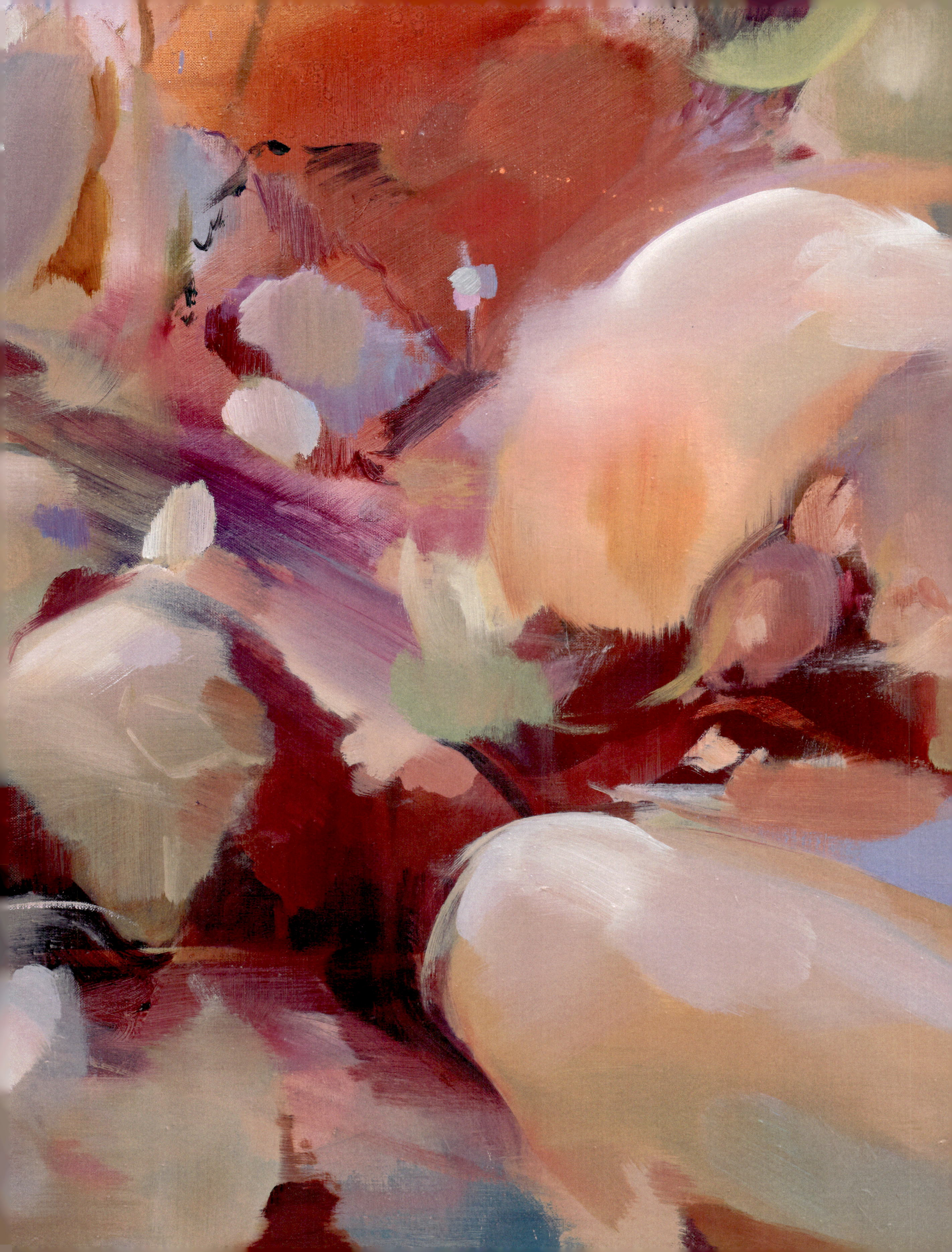

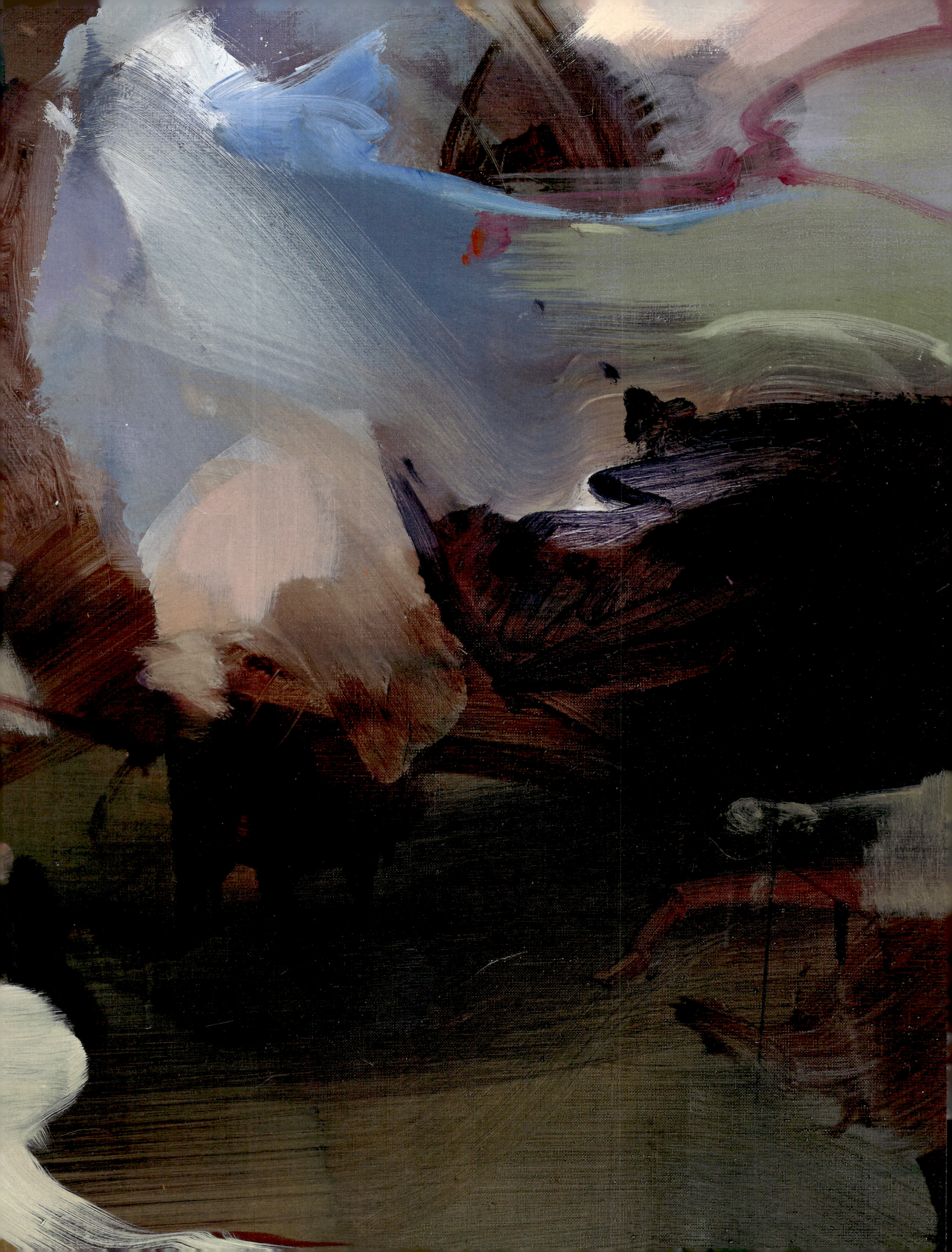

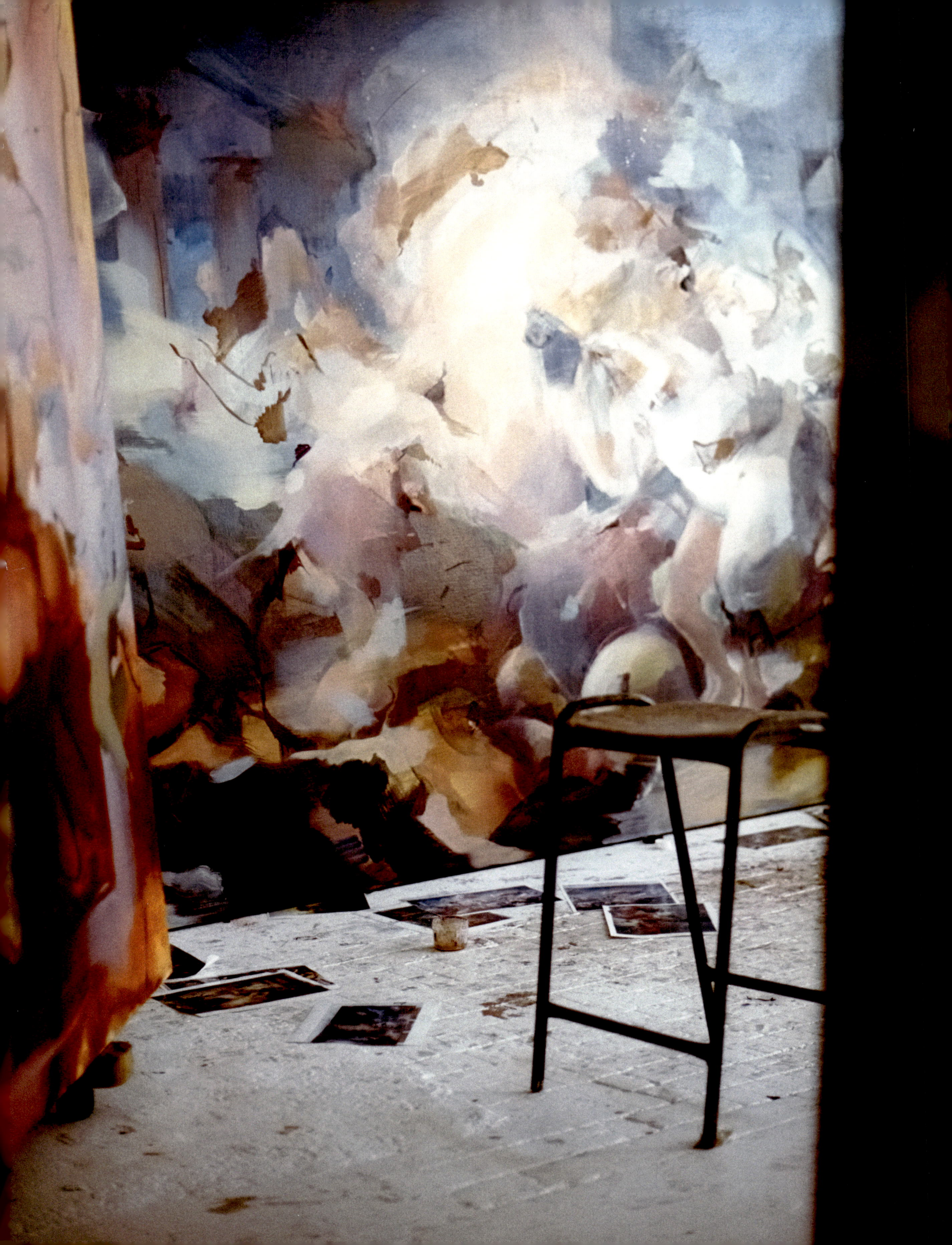

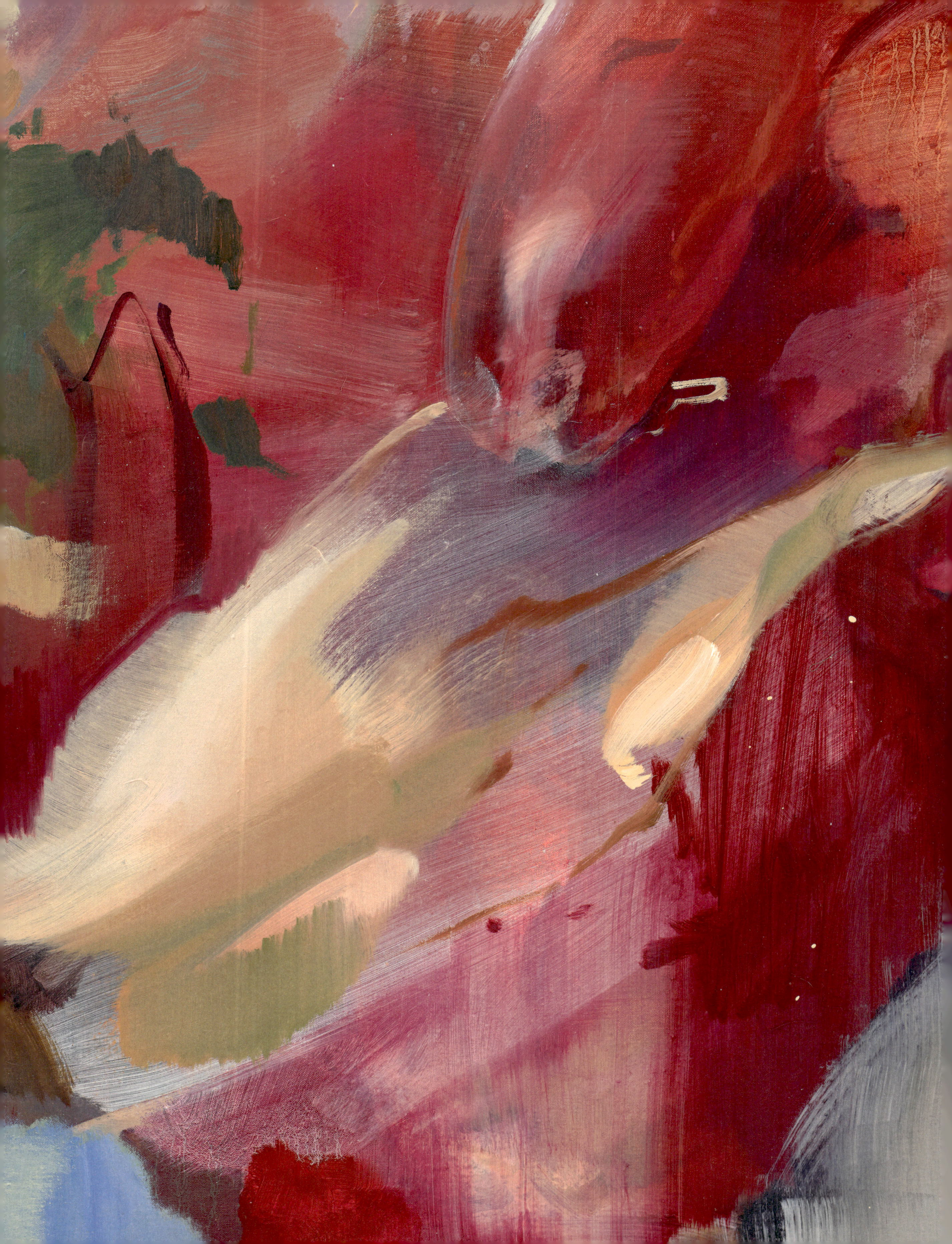